DAVE MACINTYRE

D1352598

Scottish White Water

The SCA guide

2nd edition

Pesda Press

www.pesdapress.com

Proceeds from this guidebook will go to

The Access Trust

which is being set up to:

- Promote and protect access and egress for canoeing and kayaking to all Scottish inland and coastal waters.
- Promote education and understanding of responsible access.
- Conserve and protect Scottish inland and coastal waters for their own sake and for the inspiration and sustenance they give to humanity.

For further details, membership, etc., please send an S.A.E. to:

> The Scottish Canoe Association,
> Caledonia House,
> South Gyle,
> Edinburgh,
> EH12 9DG.

Or contact: www.scot-canoe.org
              Tel. 0131-317-7314

Front cover - Allt Mheuran - Bridget Thomas
Back cover - Morriston - Pete Kyriakoudis
              Etive - Dallness Falls - Ryan Clement
              Garry - www.breadandbutter.me.uk

First published in Great Britain 2001 by Pesda Press
2nd edition 2004
'Elidir', Ffordd Llanllechid
Rachub, Bangor
Gwynedd
LL57 3EE

Design and artwork HappyBoater@hotmail.com
Printed by Cambrian Printers - Wales
Copyright © 2001 Scottish Canoe Association

ISBN 0-9547061-1-0

Scottish White Water

Foreword

Welcome to the wonderful world of Scottish white water, and the 2nd edition of the white water guide. One of the most notable achievements of the first edition is that it inspired many people to get out there, get off the beaten track and paddle something new. In an age where park and play is becoming ever more popular, it's been great to see paddlers once again seeking out the wilderness experience that for me is such an important part of what makes paddling special.

Published in 2001, we had no idea that the 1st edition would sell out so quickly. So many thanks to everyone who bought a copy and helped raise money for the access fund, and also to everyone who wrote in with corrections, comments, suggestions and new descriptions for the 2nd edition. Once again, all proceeds from this guide will go towards the SCA access fund, and if you bought direct from the SCA, even more of your money will go towards promoting and improving access in Scotland.

In this edition, we have tried to give more information on all those tantalising runs just mentioned last time round. We have also included 2 completely new sections and a total of 42 new rivers. So why not push the boundaries, go somewhere new and discover what those less well-known runs have to offer. For those who like the unknown, there's still more out there waiting to be explored, so it's not too late to make your mark and see your name in print next time around!

The 2nd edition has also given us a chance to update paddlers on the access legislation that came into force in Scotland in the autumn of 2004, to tell you more about the threat that our wonderful rivers face from new hydro-electric developments and to let you know about the Water Levels Website developed by the SCA to help paddlers find out which rivers are at a good level.

I hope you enjoy this guidebook and that, like its predecessor, it will inspire you to try new things, go new places and come back full of the wonder of Scottish white water.

Bridget Thomas
Guidebook Editor

Go with the Flow

Northern Exposure

Torridon & Wester Ross

Easter Ross

The Rivers of Loch Ness

Strathspey

Skye's the Limit

Up fae Dundee

Glen Spean

Fort William Area

Tay & Tribs

Glen Etive & Glen Coe

Loch Lomond & Argyll

Central

Urban Delights

The Borders

Burns Country

Contents

The North

Go with the Flow

Northern Exposure

Torridon & Wester Ross

Easter Ross

The Rivers of Loch Ness

Skye's the Limit

The West

Fort William Area

Contents

Important Notice

Paddlers should need no reminding that white water paddling is an adventure sport involving an element of uncertainty and risk taking. Guidebooks give an idea of where to access a river, where to egress, the level of difficulty and the nature of the hazards likely to be encountered.

Conditions vary considerably with changing water levels. Erosion can block a river with fallen trees or change a rapid by moving boulders and even collapsing bedrock.

This guidebook is no substitute for inspection, personal risk assessment and good judgement. The decision on whether to paddle or not, and any consequences arising from that decision, remain yours and yours alone.

Access

Canoeists in Scotland have traditionally enjoyed a freedom of access to Scotland's rivers and lochs. The Land Reform (Scotland) Act 2003, now provides a statutory right of access to most land and inland water. This right of access must be used responsibly and a code, the Scottish Outdoor Access Code, explains how you can do this.

Scotland now has a framework for access which is amongst the best in Europe. The Act means that it's important for everyone to understand their rights and responsibilities. This section of the book sets out the responsibilities for canoeists and explains how you can best enjoy the right of access by paddling responsibly.

Key Principles

Your main responsibilities are to:
* care for the environment
* take responsibility for your own actions
* respect the interests of other people

These key principles apply equally to canoeists, anglers, other water users and land managers, in fact everyone who either works or takes recreation in the outdoors should follow them. If you follow these key principles and apply a healthy dose of common sense then you won't go far wrong.

Enjoying Responsible Access on Land

Many of the access disputes involving paddlers actually relate to our activities on land rather than water. A little forethought can ensure that you can get to and from the water without compromising the interests of others.

* **Respect people's privacy** by staying away from houses and private gardens - access rights don't apply in places like these. It's also important to take care and try to be discreet when changing or going to the toilet. If you are wild camping choose a spot well away from roads and buildings and be sure to remove all trace of your camp.

* **Drive and park carefully** particularly in rural areas. Remember that the boats on your roof let everyone know that you are paddlers and it is easy for the actions of a few to give everyone a

bad name. Access rights only apply to non-motorised activities so don't drive on private roads without permission.

- **Help landowners and farmers** to work safely and effectively by taking care when crossing land. Leave any gates as you find them and be careful not to damage fences or walls. Check for alternatives before entering fields with animals, and in fields with crops avoid causing damage by sticking to the edge of the field or following paths or tracks. Watch for signs highlighting hazards and follow any reasonable guidance given.

Enjoying Responsible Access on the Water

Access rights apply to inland water such as rivers, lochs, canals and reservoirs. It is important to take care and respect others' interests when paddling. Friendly communication can go a long way to understanding each others' position and avoiding problems developing.

- **Respect the needs of anglers** by avoiding nets and other tackle. When close to anglers keep noise and other disturbance to a minimum.

- **Care for the environment** and be sure not to damage or disturb wildlife, plants, or your surroundings, especially in sensitive places or during sensitive times of year. Don't pollute the water. You can help care for the environment by leaving the outdoors cleaner than when you found it and reporting any pollution or suspicious activity to the relevant authorities.

Rivers

On rivers, keep an eye out for anglers. If you see someone fishing, try and stop upstream and attract the angler's attention before passing. If they have a line in the water, wait for a signal to proceed and then follow any route indicated if safe and practicable to do so.

Lochs

If anglers are present, keep a safe distance to avoid interfering with their activity. If the water forms part of an intensively used commercial fishery always speak to the land manager before going on the water.

Canals

In canals be aware of other traffic and give way to motorised craft. Remember access rights do not apply to passage through locks and lifts. On some canals, access is managed and you may be required to register your activity with the operator. Follow any regulations or local guidance.

Reservoirs and Hydro schemes

For your own safety, avoid going close to water intake points, spillways or other hydro infrastructure. 'Stay clear, stay safe'. Remember that water levels can change quickly and without warning.

Sea

Our coastline provides valuable habitat for nesting birds and other wildlife. Take extra care to avoid causing damage or disturbance.

Land Managers' Responsibilities

Land managers must respect access rights in their day-to-day work. Sometimes for Health & Safety or animal welfare reasons they may have to lock gates or suggest alternative routes around areas of work. Co-operating with such situations helps land managers to work safely. Anglers are asked to respect access rights and to allow canoes to pass at the earliest opportunities.

Local Authorities / National Park Authorities' Responsibilities

Local/National Park Authorities have a responsibility to uphold access rights. If you feel you are challenged unreasonably, or otherwise prevented or discouraged from enjoying your access rights you should report it to the relevant Access Officer.

Andy Jackson
SCA Access and
Environment Officer
October 2004

Sharing the Water

Please follow the advice in the Scottish Outdoor Access Code and remember the key points of respecting the interests of other people, caring for the environment and taking responsibility for your own actions and those of others in your group. These access arrangements should allow you to safely enjoy the fantastic opportunities offered by Scotland's waters. Happy Paddling!

Getting Help and Information

You can find more information on the Land Reform Act and the Scottish Outdoor Access Code, as well as contact details for Access Officers, at www.outdooraccess-scotland.com. Further advice and information is also available from the SCA website www.scot-canoe.org. The Association of Salmon Fisheries Board website contains details on fishing seasons along with Board contact details www.asfb.org.uk.

River Advisers

About a quarter of the rivers in this guidebook have river advisers. They are happy to be contacted for information about likely flows, any current access difficulties or considerations, or new hazards. You can help a river adviser by reporting any new hazards or incidents after your trip on the river. Please remember that it is a voluntary service and that river advisers have other jobs – be sensitive about the times you contact them. You are under no obligation to contact a river adviser, but if you are planning a trip with a large group or are uncertain about detail of access to a particular river or stretch of water then it would be best to seek advice. There is a list of river advisers on the SCA website www.scot-canoe.org.

SCA Access Committee

The Access Committee looks after all aspects of access in canoeing. We work to an Environmental Policy, which seeks to preserve and enhance waterways of all kinds. We promote the concept that canoeing is an environmentally sound and healthy activity as valid as any other outdoor recreation, and that the sport has a long history of access to water in Scotland.

The overarching belief of the SCA is that as paddlers, we have a freedom to travel over water, akin to the walkers' freedom to roam over land. Our policy is to promote shared use of water resources but not to enter into agreements that are formal, legal or binding in their intent. The Access Charter expresses this right which comes with responsibility.

The Access Committee seeks to educate all paddlers to exercise this right with responsibility and adhere to the Access Code.

Hydro Campaign

You can't read this guidebook without failing to be impressed by the sheer range and quality of white water that Scotland has to offer. From small mountain creeks to big volume play runs, it's got it all. A real paddler's playground!

Sadly, many of the fantastic rivers featured in this guide are now threatened by the development of new hydro schemes. The government has set a target for 40% of Scotland's power to be supplied from renewable sources by the year 2020. Although the remaining hydro potential in Scotland's rivers is tiny compared to the other types of renewable energy available, there has been a flood of applications to build small scale hydro projects.

Where these schemes are built on rivers used for canoeing they can have a devastating impact. The main problem is that as water is diverted from the river there will be less good spates to support paddling. This means less days available for canoeing and less days when the river reaches a good challenging level. The construction of associated dams, power houses and pipelines can also spoil the river environment and destroy rapids valued by paddlers. Canoeing is a positive, healthy activity enjoyed by many. The related tourism spend from those on paddling trips also provides a valuable income for rural communities. It is vital that any new hydro projects are sensitively sited and designed in order to protect the rivers we value and the resource that supports our sport.

The Braan, one of the rivers threatened by proposed hydro schemes.

The SCA is working hard to highlight the threat to canoeing activity and to make the case that any impact on canoe recreation should be fully considered in the assessment of new hydro schemes. We recognise the importance of renewable energy, but feel it is essential that the potential benefit of individual schemes is weighed against any social and economic impacts.

We need the involvement of paddlers to help make the case to protect the rivers we all enjoy. A dedicated campaign website has been established which includes an interactive database of all the schemes proposed.

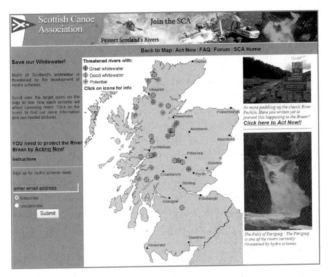

www.scot-canoe.org/access/hydro

Please visit the site and find out how you can help. If paddlers don't protect these rivers who will?

We have used this symbol in the book to highlight rivers which are currently affected by proposed hydro schemes. New schemes are being added all the time so please visit the website for the most up to date information.

Water Levels

Working in partnership with the Scottish Environmental Protection Agency (SEPA) and Visit Scotland, the SCA has established an online water levels service. The aim of the service is to showcase the wealth of white water available in Scotland and to help paddlers choose the best river to paddle at the right water level. Many of the most popular runs are covered by the service and it is hoped that we will be able to add new rivers as the service develops.

Wherever you see this icon in the guidebook you can go online and check the latest recorded water level. Just visit www.scot-canoe.org and follow the link to Scottish White Water. The service provides a fantastic 'at a glance' view of water levels across the country along with other useful information on access issues or known hazards. Levels are shown on a scale of 'Empty' to 'Huge' along with an actual reading in metres. A link to the SEPA site also provides a graph showing the water level over the last few days. Remember that on many rivers levels change quickly, and to make best use of the information you need to check the time given for the last reading, and factor in whether the river is currently rising or falling. Used in conjunction with a weather forecast and with a little trial and error, the service will help you get the best out of your paddling.

Don't forget to use the feedback form on the site to help us fine tune the water level categories. Take a minute after your trip to compare the level shown on the site with your experiences of the river and let us know how the system is working.

Special thanks to SEPA and Visit Scotland for their funding and support in making the water levels service possible. Thanks also to Kenny Biggin of Deanton who gave birth to the site and is responsible for the web design.

www.scot-canoe.org

Grading

Rivers and rapids in this guide are graded under the international grading system. This rates white water on a scale of 1 to 6, taking into account both technical difficulty and seriousness. Although a far from perfect system we feel it does give the paddler enough of a 'steer' to help them decide if the run in question is for them. A river runner's perception of the difficulty of a river will depend on their level of experience, the water level they find and their personal fear factor!

The river grades in this book have been arrived at by a consensus of the paddlers who know these rivers well. Taken together they give a good picture of the rivers available in their varying moods. If you are new to the runs in this book it would be wise to start off on a trip which you are confident is well within your abilities. If you know a few of the runs well check how the given grades match with what you have experienced. That way you can 'find yourself' a comfortable level within the grading system and not have any nasty surprises. Whenever you paddle in a new area you should spend time becoming familiar with the local interpretation of the grading system.

The 1 to 6 system does tend to lead to large variations in the difficulty of runs even within a given grade. As the standard of paddling has gone up, rapids have tended to become squeezed into the upper grades. We have tried to address this by applying the grading system across the whole range of runs. As a result some trips have found themselves down graded to give a better feel for how they relate to harder runs. As well as the plus or minus sub division paddlers should read the grade in the context of what is described in the rest of the text. Words such as 'continuous', 'steep' and 'committing' can help the reader see what they are getting themselves into.

By its very nature grading rivers is a far from precise business. We hope that as well as many happy days on the river, this guide will bring many happy hours arguing over the grades in the pub afterwards.

Some of the runs in this book have been written as a result of perhaps only one or two descents and contributors have had to hypothesise to some extent as to what effect more or less water would have on the difficulty of the run. The best advice is to go to a river with open eyes and an open mind, proceed with caution, take nothing for granted and make your own mind up.

Andy Jackson

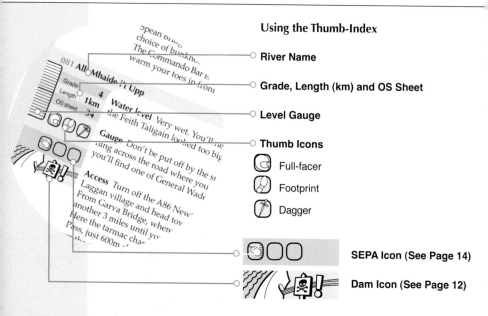

Using the Thumb-Index

○ **River Name**

○ **Grade, Length (km) and OS Sheet**

○ **Level Gauge**

○ **Thumb Icons**

Full-facer

Footprint

Dagger

○ **SEPA Icon (See Page 14)**

○ **Dam Icon (See Page 12)**

Grade Ranging from 1 to 6, allowing for +/- grades.

- 4/5 indicates that the run has rapids of both grades shown. For example, the Lower Brann has been graded 4/5.

- 4 + or – indicates that the author feels the run is at the harder or easier end of the grade.

- If a river contains one or two rapids which are harder than the rest of the run, but the trip could feasibly be tackled by someone intending to portage the harder sections, this is shown by using brackets. For example the Middle Orchy becomes 3/4 (5).

Level Gauge The majority of Scottish rivers will vary greatly in their severity at differing water levels, many are only runnable after heavy rainfall. The white area in the gauge gives a rough indicaton of suitable water levels. The top of the scale denotes flood or sustained heavy rainfall, the bottom, drought. *Attention must be paid to actual and forecast weather affecting the watershed.*

Thumb Icons Full-facer, this is a short boat run of a rocky or precarious nature, best to come equipped with full-on gear; Footprint, the approach to this run requires a significant walk-in; Dagger, this section is not a tried and tested milk-run, the authors may have only run it once or twice, or the rapids may be subject to periodic change, proceed with due caution.

The guide breaks down into 4 geographical areas North, South, East and West with each of these chapters being further divided into sections grouping rivers of the same locality. Generally these sections are based around the river basins of the larger rivers but we have made exceptions to this in an effort to ensure that the rivers appear in the book in the most useful order to the reader 'on the ground'.

A lot of attention has been paid to giving useful and accurate descriptions of the best places to access a given run. Put-ins and take-outs are given for each trip along with the relevant directions for finding them by road and by foot. In some cases an access point may be described which, although not necessarily the shortest or easiest way to or from the river, avoids conflict with landowners or local people.

To make life simple, distances are generally given in miles when travelling by car and in km's when on foot or afloat. Most of the time a road atlas will suffice for finding your way to the river but having the relevant OS map to hand will often make the task much easier. Six figure grid references are often given with a location.

Directions on the river are always given from the paddler's point of view. So river left is always that seen when on the river and looking downstream. Sizes of drops and falls are given in metres and you should be aware that these are also very much from the paddler's point of view. Generally speaking the more often a drop has been run the smaller it gets and those which get portaged tend to somehow grow!

Using the Maps

Symbols and Icons

River (numbered beneath)	⓴
Road identifier	A27
Significant Town	Glenfinnan ●
Significant Peak	▲ Mountain
Chair lift	Chair Lift
Hospital	Ⓗ

Flipstrip© courtesy of **another KOGG day**

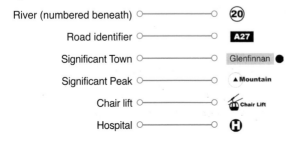

Do you enjoy paddling on Scotland's rivers, lochs and sea?

Join the SCA
And support our work on access

New access rights
New facilities
Water releases
Free flowing rivers

The SCA is working hard to protect and enhance access to Scotland's fantastic water resource. By joining you will be supporting this work and adding your voice to those who share a passion for canoeing in Scotland.

Recreational membership is available for only £15 and includes:

- **Scottish Paddler magazine**
- **Civil liability insurance**
- **Selected discounts on tours, events, services**
- **Cheap camping at Grandtully and many other benefits.....**

To Join today log onto:

www.scot-canoe.org
or call
0131 317 7314

and help stop this...

Even if you live outside Scotland, for only £10 you can join as a supporter and help contribute to our access campaign.

The North

Contents

Go with the Flow

Northern Exposure

Torridon & Wester Ross

Easter Ross

The Rivers of Loch Ness

Skye's the Limit

⫽⊒ Scottish Hydro Electric

Enjoy the whitewater

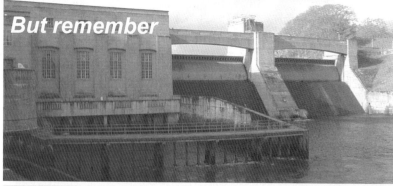

But remember

Stay clear

Stay safe

For your own safety -
- Avoid going close to water intake points or spillways.
- Remember that water levels can change quickly and without warning.

Go With the Flow

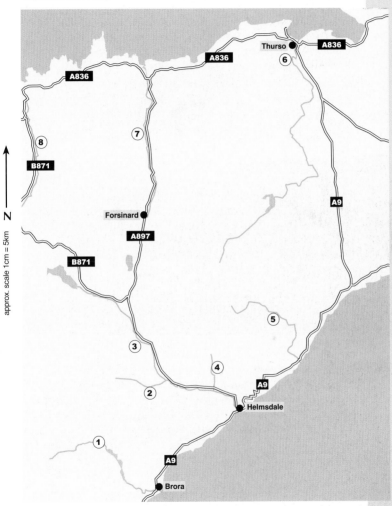

approx. scale 1cm = 5km

N

Go with the Flow

This area provides good entertainment for both white water fans and those looking for touring trips in a remote area. The addition of some of these rivers on the SEPA gauge system means it should be possible to visit when they are at a reasonable level.

It is worth noting that most of the rivers in the area are very popular salmon fishing rivers. There has been little conflict over access in the past, so please follow the access code and good relationships should remain.

001 Brora (Upper)

Grade	**2**
Length	**9km**
OS sheet	**16**

Introduction The Brora flows from its headwaters in central Sutherland to the east coast at Brora. The 5km long Loch Brora divides the upper and lower rivers.

Water Level Wet/Very wet. The upper river requires considerable rainfall.

Access The Upper Brora can be accessed via Craggie, taking care to close the gate, at Braegrudie near the end of the road in Strath Brora (718 098).

Contributors:
John Ross
and Gary Smith

Description The upper put-in is reached by walking up 500m from the end of the road to above a short grade 2 gorge, which then leads through a tree-lined valley to the road bridge at Dalreavoch where a stopper forms at a stone weir. The river then continues at a steady grade 1/2 for 5km before coming back close to the road where it is possible to get out.

001 Brora (Lower)

Grade	**2**
Length	**5km**
OS sheet	**17**

Water Level Moderately wet/Wet. The lower river can be run at a range of levels as it is regulated by the outflow from the loch.

Gauge The lower river is passable at a range of levels from 0.9 on the SEPA gauge up to 2.2 when the main rapids become washed out.

Access The lower river is accessed by paddling 500m of flat water to the end of the loch. Take out at the harbour slipway in Brora.

Description The river starts with a couple of playwaves. Grade 2 water leads to a ford and footbridge where there is another playwave. Shortly after, the river splits around an island before another stone weir leads to a fast continuous wave train. A couple more islands lead to the Rock Pool where a playwave and a large eddy form. The river then gradually narrows and deepens until the take-out is reached after the railway bridge.

Contributors:
John Ross
and Gary Smith

Craggie Water 002

Introduction The Craggie Water is a small rocky tributary of the Helmsdale and provides some entertaining kayaking at medium flows.

Grade	3/4
Length	2km
OS sheet	17

Water Level Wet. The burn is only runnable after considerable rain.

Gauge As a guide if the Helmsdale is reading at least 1.2 on the SEPA gauge, the Craggie Water should be worth checking out.

Access The burn can be inspected where the Glen Loth road crosses it a couple of miles from Kildonan Station. Carry up from this bridge about 500m to the start of the gorge.

Description At the put-in there are two consecutive grade 3 drops into deep pools. This is followed by a very tight, rock-filled, sheer-sided gorge section which then runs straight and fast to the road bridge. From here a series of tricky grade 4 drops and tight turns lead to a large pool. The next 500m are grade 3 with a couple of deceptively tricky drops with large stoppers before the burn levels out and passes under the railway before the confluence with the Helmsdale, where a flat paddle of approximately 1km leads to the take-out.

Contributors:
John Ross
and Gary Smith

003 Helmsdale / Abhainn Illidh

Gd. **3/4(4+)**
Length **7km**
OS sheet **17**

Introduction The Helmsdale, a major salmon fishing river, flows from Loch Badanloch in central Sutherland to the east coast at Helmsdale. The river winds its way through the Strath of Kildonan, scene of one of the most notorious of the Highland Clearances and also famous for its Klondike gold rush in the 1870s. It is still possible to get a permit, hire a gold pan and take your chance of finding a nugget in the Kildonan Burn at Baile an Òr (912 214) if there is insufficient water for canoeing. For most of its length the river is featureless, but for a couple of miles near Kildonan Station it offers quite challenging boating.

Water level Moderately wet/Very wet. The river can be paddled at a range of levels with the river being regulated by the outflow from the weir at Badanloch. At higher levels the section above and below the bridge at Kildonan Station becomes more powerful.

Gauge The main white water sections require a level of at least 0.9 on the SEPA gauge.

Access The river can be inspected from the A897 at Kildonan and can be accessed from the road about 1km above Upper Suisgill, where a small cottage can be seen on the far side of the river. It is possible to take out by Kildonan Station where vehicles can be left at the old school yard. However, to catch the last main rapid, take out anywhere along the next section beyond the farmhouse where the river meanders close to the road.

Description From the put-in, around 1km of grade 2 water leads to a footbridge and a series of grade 3 steps. As the river moves away from the road, there is a series of narrow rocky channels and small drops. Just upstream of Kildonan Station, the river takes a turn to the left and is split by a central rock. The left-hand channel is blocked by rocks whilst the right takes you through a pour-over; this grade 4 rapid warrants inspection. At low/medium levels an undercut on the right-hand side of the boulder can become a hazard. The small vicious eddy that forms to the right of the slot can have a tendency to slow you down enough to feed you back into the stopper and thus the undercut. Next, a long pleasant grade 3+ on river right leads down to the bridge by the station, and the upper take-out. A series of grade

2/3 ledges lead, after 500m, to a two tier drop (Gd 4+). There is pinning potential at low/medium water levels as the bottom of the second slot is shallow and an undercut ridge of bedrock runs parallel to the run-off from the slot. After this, the river levels out and continues at grade 2-. There is little to interest the white water boater downstream, but for touring paddlers the river continues in a broad open strath in a series of meanders for a further 10km to the sea. There is a big concrete weir that can be seen on this section in the distance from the road, which may not be runnable.

Contributors:
John Ross
Gary Smith
Colin Matheson
and Ron Cameron

Kilphedir Burn 004

Introduction Kilphedir Burn is a small, steep tributary of the Helmsdale River. It is a short run of small drops and big rock slides.

Grade	**4(5)**
Length	**1km**
OS sheet	**17**

Water level Wet. This run is at its best following heavy rain and drops off very quickly.

Gauge If there is no bedrock showing in the rock slide under the road bridge (989 187) the burn may be too high! In high water this run would be continuous grade 5+ and most mortals, excepting the intellectually challenged, would probably decide to leave it for another day.

Access From the south take a left-hand turn onto the A897 in Helmsdale signposted for Melvich. Follow the single track road for about 4 miles, until some sheep pens are passed on the left-hand side. Kilphedir Burn flows under a small arched road bridge with a gravel car park immediately to the right. The short steep gorge can be inspected during the walk-in on river right. The put-in is above a 3m rock slide that is reached after about 20-30 minutes walking. Above this point the burn appears to flatten out. Take out after the large rock slide under the road bridge.

Description The run is made up of vertical drops of approximately 2-3m and rock slides with small pools in between. Trees on both sides of the burn may become potential hazards at certain levels.

Contributor:
Colin Matheson

Other important points I have witnessed the burn in full spate and it is a fearful sight! If, however, the burn is in good condition, why not climb back up to the top for another adrenaline fix! If it is too high to run, the Helmsdale may be a good alternative.

005 Berriedale Water

Gd. **2/3(4+)**
Length **12km**
OS sheet **17**

Introduction The Berriedale Water is the main river draining the flow country of central Caithness and the hills of Morven, Maiden Pap and Scaraben. The river reaches the sea through a deeply incised valley at the notorious Berriedale Braes. This river is a long paddle through a remote and spectacular Highland glen. Sadly estate staff have been very 'anti' in the past.

Water Level Very wet. The river is only runnable during or after considerable rain or snow melt.

Gauge The level can be checked at the A9 road bridge at the bottom of the braes. A reading of around 2 feet 3 inches on the gauge on the upstream bridge abutment will give an excellent trip.

Access The take-out is at the A9 road bridge, but an 11 mile detour is necessary to get to the put-in. From the A9 at Dunbeath it is necessary to take the minor road to Braemore. The put-in is at the bridge by the phone box at the end of this road.

Description From the put-in the river is grade 2. Watch out for a deer fence after about 1km. The river then enters the glen and becomes narrower with continuous grade 2. Another 2km leads to a small gorge with a footbridge above it. This hides a grade 3 drop over a 2m fall, followed by a couple of tricky rapids. The valley sides become more imposing as the river continues at grade 2 and 3 down the glen before a gradual narrowing leads to a series of grade 4 drops. These can only be inspected from the metal footbridge high above the gorge. A further series of grade 2 drops, and a low level bridge which could be hazardous at high flows, lead after a water gate to the narrower tree-lined continuous grade 3 section. Take out by the twin bridges at the A9, or alternatively at the harbour, which will mean a short carry back up to the road.

Contributors:
John Ross
Gary Smith
and Colin Matheson

Other important points Under the A9 road bridge there is a confluence with Langwell Water. The lower part looks very good, however, you would need access up the locked private estate road to get on the river. Estate staff have declined access in the past.

Thurso (Dirlot Gorge) 006

Introduction The River Thurso flows through Loch More and then on to the sea near Thurso over a distance of some 30km. Dirlot Gorge (Gd 2-3) is on the lower section. If you happen to have travelled up north for the surf breaks around the north coast, and find the surf isn't running, this river may offer at least a little bit of consolation… It is, however, not the place to be with the wind howling around your ears due to the extremely exposed location!

Grade	**2/3**
Length	**5km**
OS sheet	**12**

Water level Very wet/Wet. The more water the better!

Gauge This section is best paddled with at least 24 inches on the gauge found under the bridge in the village of Halkirk. At higher levels, 36 - 48 inches or more, the short gorge is continuous grade 3 and a really good paddle for intermediates. There are large pools below most rapids to collect any swimmers, making it a fairly safe paddle for beginners at lower levels, less than 24 inches.

Access From Thurso take the B874 to Halkirk. Drive through Halkirk (checking the gauge if necessary) and continue for a couple of miles until you reach a T-junction. Turn right at this junction, after about half a mile you cross over a bridge at an old water mill, Westerdale Mill (131 518). Although there is a good grade 3 rapid downstream of the bridge, there are miles and miles of flat water above and below it. If the bedrock on river left below the bridge is covered, the river is up! Drive on down the single track road for about 3 miles until you next see the river below to the left on a right-hand bend. There is a small gravel car park just round the bend and also a lay-by after another 50m. To access the take-out, drive back down the single track road and take the first turning you come across to the right. This road leads you through a disused quarry. Keep on going on the gravel

road, through a number of gates until you reach a fishing hut on the right.

Description From the put-in the river starts off with a series of small man-made weirs (Gd 2) interspersed with flat sections. Some of the weirs can provide good playwaves at higher levels. After about 2km the start of the gorge is obvious, inspect from river right if required. The gorge itself is a fairly continuous series of small ledges and bedrock rapids, some of which create sizable stoppers at high flows. There is an excellent surf wave in the middle of the gorge at high levels. The exit rapid below the old cemetery may warrant inspection. It has a big boulder in the middle of the river, behind which a large pour-over forms at high flows. Most of the excitement is now behind you with some wave trains and about 1km of flat water until you reach the take-out at the hut on river left.

Contributor:
Colin Matheson

Other important points If the level on the gauge at Halkirk is above 36 inches, a good grade 2(3) section, from the railway bridge upstream of the village to a big house (Braal Castle) just east of the village, comes into condition. Fairly fast and continuous wave trains make up most of this run which is good for beginners.

007 **Halladale**

Grade   **2/3**
Length   **6km**
OS sheet **11**

Introduction The Halladale is one of the main rivers draining the flow country of central Sutherland. It meets the sea at the spectacular beaches of the north coast and is mostly in a wide open strath.

Water Level Wet/Very wet. The river requires a fair amount of rain to bring it into condition.

Gauge As the river is parallel to the road, inspection is easy from the car.

Access Travelling north along the A897 from the station and RSPB bird reserve at Forsinard, the river starts as a mere trickle but gradually increases in size until it is worth paddling. With a good deal of rain, it should be possible to enter the river about 2km past Forsinard. The take-out is where the forestry road bridge crosses the river at Dyke.

Description The run starts with continuous grade 2 water with some slightly more difficult drops. As the river leads towards the road bridge crossing, it enters a small rocky gorge where there are a series of grade 3 drops before the river opens out again into the wider strath. In high flows it is possible to carry on further downstream, and although there is nothing of note for the white water paddler, this section may be of interest to touring canoeists.

Contributors:
John Ross
and Gary Smith

Naver 008

Introduction The Naver drains a large catchment of central Sutherland through Loch Naver along a wide open strath for 25km before reaching the sea at Bettyhill. Strathnaver was emptied of many of its inhabitants during the clearances to make way for sheep. There are several reminders on the Strathnaver trail of the many pre-clearance villagers that once populated this Highland glen.

Grade **2**
Length **25km**
OS sheet **10**

Water Level Wet/Very wet. The river requires a fair amount of rain to bring it into condition.

Gauge A minimum level to make the Naver navigable is 0.7 on the SEPA gauge.

Access Access can be made from Loch Naver and as the river is never far from the road it is possible to get on or off at many points along most of the river's length.

Description The Naver offers little sport for the white water enthusiast, but nevertheless can at high water levels be a good beginners' trip, or alternatively a very pleasant touring river, with the opportunity to study the abundant wildlife of the strath.

Contributors:
John Ross
and Gary Smith

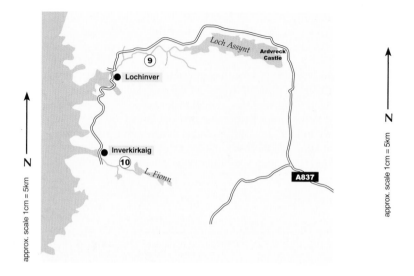

Etive - Glen Etive and Glen Coe - Neil Farmer

Northern Exposure

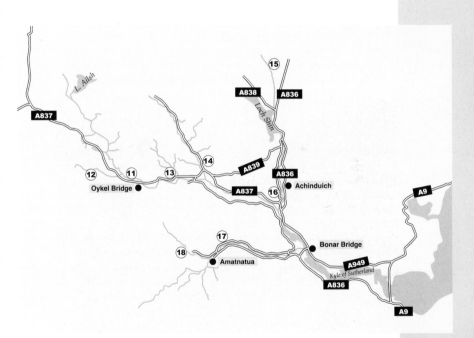

Northern Exposure

For most paddlers it's a long drive to the rivers in this, the farthest
flung corner of Scotland. Those who make the effort will be
rewarded with uncrowded rivers set amidst spectacular scenery.
The Carron and the Inver are the classics of the area with large
catchment areas providing generally predictable flows. You have
to reckon that there is a great deal of potential left untapped in
this vast area. Many good-sized rivers look to provide generally
straightforward runs and there is a seemingly endless supply of
steep burns just waiting to be explored. Hopefully the runs featured
will give you a taste of the area and feed your desire for more.

009 Inver / Abhainn Inbhir

Grade	**4**
Length	**5km**
OS sheet	**15**

Introduction The river flows out of Loch Assynt, in north-west
Sutherland, and enters the sea at Lochinver village. A small dam
controls the volume of water leaving the loch. Initially the river is
wide, meandering, shallow and best avoided. About 5km from
Lochinver it enters a rock gorge that is short but worth a paddle.
Below this the river reverts to something like its original character
for a couple of kilometres. As it nears Lochinver it enters a rocky,
wooded gorge which provides spectacular and exciting paddling.

Water Level Wet. Considerable rainfall is needed as the bedrock
of the river is inclined to be of the sharp, plastic ripping variety. In
big spate the final section would be a very serious undertaking
and a visit to Ullapool, a few miles to the south, may be the most
sensible option for most.

Gauge The final gorge is quite constricted. When viewed from
the bridge at the take-out, the river should be flowing well, but
not look too full-on. If in doubt it would be wise to wander up the
path river left to check out the gorge and decide for yourself. It's a
1km walk from here to the top of the gorge.

Access A car or bike can be left where the A837 crosses the river,
as it enters the village of Lochinver (096 231). To find the put-in,
go back up the A837, and follow the signposts for Bracklock
(123 237). Cars can be parked in the lay-by beside a locked gate
and boats carried across rough grazings to reach the river. This

Oykel - Northern Exposure - John Ross

Craggie Water - Go with the Flow - John Ross

Meig - Tea Cup Falls - Easter Ross - Chris Dickinson

Meig Gorge - Easter Ross - Andy Jackson

Abhainn Coire Mhic Nobuil -Torridon and Wester Ross - The Brighton St. Posse

gives a short paddle with all the best rapids. Alternatively continue up the road for the full 3 miles and park on a bit of old road where the river is close to the road (135 246). Jump on.

Description A few hundred yards of rock gorge with a couple of playspots (Gd 3) follow the higher put-in. The river then goes quiet for a couple of kilometres, but is navigable after rain. After Bracklock the river enters attractive forest and another nice grade 3 gorge. A weir with nasty wire baskets (portage recommended) leads to the final gorge. In good flows, the paddling from here will be both heavy and technical. A few playspots exist that may tempt advanced paddlers. Lesser mortals will be grateful just to keep going. There are a couple of nice drops and plenty of solid geology. Just above Lochinver is The Cave. This looks intimidating but is easier than it first appears. However, all but the totally deranged will inspect. Water pours into a narrow passage behind a big block on river right. Anyone who goes in there isn't coming out to play tomorrow. There is no need for such fears however; for if you stick to river left the flow will carry you away from the cave down a steep narrow chute. Roped protection is probably a sensible precaution. A few more drops, stoppers and pour-overs lead under the bridge and into the briny.

Contributor:
Ron Cameron

Other important points I once saw the Inver in huge spate and fled in terror. When it is really big, it gets pretty scary!

Kirkaig 010

Grade	**3/4**
Length	**3½km**
OS sheet	**15**

Introduction The River Kirkaig drains the large loch complex lying to the south of the dramatic Suilven mountain. The river plunges impressively over the 18m Kirkaig Falls, which are well worth a visit. At high flows putting in below these falls gives 3-4km of bouncy paddling with plenty of surf waves.

Water Level Wet/Very wet. The Kirkaig drains a couple of large lochs so it will keep its level quite well. If the River Inver is at a reasonable level, and you don't mind carrying your boat, it's worth popping down to the Kirkaig.

Gauge You can get a good feel for the level at the take-out.

Access To get to the take-out, head south on the minor road out of Lochinver. South of Inverkirkaig, there is a car park on the right just before the road crosses over the river (085 193). From here carry your boat up the path on the north side of the river for as far as you can be bothered. Kirkaig Falls can be found at (111 178).

Description The excuse we had for paddling this river was to go and see the falls. It seemed sensible to carry our boats up and paddle out afterwards, if possible. It turned out 3km was a long way to carry a canoe. Still the falls were certainly worth looking at. We could see most of the river on the walk in, and it all looked deceptively easy from the path high up on the valley side. Optimistically, we assumed we'd be able to stop and check the sections we hadn't seen! It had been raining very heavily for a couple of days before our visit so the river was (to use a technical phrase) humping. Maybe 500m below the falls, we came across a slightly ominous looking stopper and decided to ditch our boats there. Off for a quick look at the falls and back for some fun. On a fine day it would be worth strolling that little bit further for the view of Suilven over Fionn Loch. The river itself was an excellent paddle, basically just big, bouncy waves at that sort of level. We did however get the feeling that whatever rock formations were under the waves might still be worth a look in lower water.

Contributor:
David Matthews

Other important points I would seriously recommend putting on below the falls. This is apparently a very good salmon river.

011 Oykel / Abhainn Oiceil

Grade **3(6)**
Length **12km**
OS sht.**15/16**

Introduction The River Oykel flows east into the Kyle of Sutherland and the Dornoch Firth. The white water section is just above and just below Oykel Bridge Hotel (385 009, OS Sheet 16). This is a short stretch of river where gravel bedded pools rapidly give way to channels running between bands of exposed bedrock. It flows in a wide glen covered with plantation forestry. Several options exist for extending the trip if the rivers are high.

Water Level Moderately wet/Very wet.

Gauge Check the flow at Bridge of Oykel. It will be obvious from these rapids what mood the river is in.

Access The Oykel can be reached by the A837 from Bonar Bridge in the east, or by the A835 and A837 from Ullapool in the west. Put in where theA837 crosses the Allt Eileag, (309 072, OS Sheet 15), about 8 miles north of Oykel Bridge. Alternatively if the river is low, park in a lay-by near a field and gate where the river runs away from the road ½ mile upstream of Oykel Bridge (377 013, OS Sheet 16). Unless you intend continuing to Bonar Bridge, egress can be taken on river right below Oykel Bridge, just above the confluence with the River Einig. Parking should present no problems.

Description The Allt Eileag provides some steepish grade 3 water, with a short gorge in the middle, which may reach grade 4 at high flows. It has some interesting holes and ends in a ramp leading to a tight drop. After the confluence, the Oykel provides a largely straightforward run, flat to grade 3. The main white water on the Oykel is contained in the elbow where the river turns away from the road. The only hazard to note are the Falls of Oykel marked on the map at (383 012, OS Sheet 16). It may be prudent to walk up the north bank, river left, from Oykel Bridge, and note their position before running the river. A portage is recommended. He who fights and runs away, lives to run away another day. Get out well in advance, and walk down either bank. Getting back on the river is quite a pantomime, and a rope for lowering boats is useful. Continue down good white water until you reach the take-out. Beyond the usual take-out the river becomes placid and largely featureless for approximately 30km before entering the sea. This placid stretch might be attractive to touring canoeists.

Contributors:
Ron Cameron
and Kingsley Ash

Other important points This river can be combined with a paddle on the Inver, Shin or Carron.

Allt Coire Chonachair 012

Water Level Wet / Very wet. This run needs water, but comes up very quickly after heavy rain.

Grade	4
Length	1km
OS sheet	15

Access Park at Lubcroy, 2½ miles upstream of Oykel Bridge, and carry up river left for a little under a kilometre.

Description A tributary of the River Oykel, the Allt Coire Chonachair offers a short section of grade 4 paddling in a small gorge.

Contributor:
Andy Jackson

It is possible to continue on beyond the confluence and paddle the main white water section on the Oykel.

013 Tuiteam Burn

Grade **5(5+)**
Length **2km**
OS sheet **16**

Introduction The Tuiteam Burn is a tiny tributary of the Oykel and is below the usual take-out for this larger river. The barren hillside opposite the wee hamlet of Doune has just the right gradient to lure the lusty waterfall seeker out of their van and into their boating apparel. This tributary has the feel of being as way out there as Mars. From the top of the first fall you can't see the bottom pool where you will end up in a very short period of time. Once over this, the rest of the river is a bit of an anticlimax, although it does still have some interesting falls. Contained within a small gorge, the rest of the river doesn't give the exposure of the main event.

Water Level Wet/Very wet. Best when lots of rain has fallen over the last couple of days but there has been nothing for 24hrs.

Gauge The fall upstream of the bridge has to look 'comfortable'.

Access Park at the road bridge approximately 3 miles from Oykel Bridge, halfway to Invercassley (437 015). From here you can see the falls at the take-out. Head up the sheep track on river left. The walk to the top fall takes about 1 hour.

Description This burn is what some people might refer to as a 'rocky ditch' or a stunt. First is a series of drops that total 35m in height. It is possible to eddy out in a micro-eddy after the first 9m, but the consequences of blowing this move are horrific as the rest of the fall is continuous ending in 9m of freefall, which misses the cliff by a hair! You will be interested to know that this pool is nice and deep. If your bottle has gone, or you need a hospital, it is possible with some considerable effort to get out of this pool on the right side. Otherwise it's straight into the second fall, a drop of a mere 12m bouncing off a wall halfway down. The next four drops are a bit of an anti-climax now - the one with a kidney shaped pool at the bottom of it is shallow. The last two drops down to the road bridge are the most conventional and give a fine end to a short but action packed run.

Contributors:
Alastair Collis and
Mark Sherrif

Other important points The last fall on its own would make a quick addition to the Oykel or Shin if you've still got your kit on.

Cassley 014

Grade	**2 (4/5)**
Length	**1km**
OS sheet	**16**

○○○

Introduction A tributary of the River Oykel, the Cassley drains a long glen running to the west of Loch Shin. It is one of four major rivers draining into the Dornoch Firth at Bonar Bridge. Most of the river is grade 1/2, with the exception of two short sections of falls, one just above the confluence with the Abhainn Gleann na Muic and the other just above the A837 road bridge at Invercassley.

Water level The whole river is runnable at medium levels. The two sections of falls may well be feasible at lower and higher flows. A hydro dam at the head of the glen has an adverse effect on the flow, but the river is a reasonable size and is not normally dry.

Gauge There are gauges painted on the downstream side of the A837 road bridge, which give roughly the same reading. A medium flow would be about 2-3 on the gauge.

Access A single-track road up the glen provides easy access to the run. Turn off the A837 at Rosehall. You can put on at the head of the glen and run the whole river, but most white water drifters will want to skip between the 2 sections by car. Passing places provide the only parking close to the river at the beginning of both sections; hence there is not enough room for large groups. The first set of falls are at the top of a small gorge which is fairly obvious about 9 miles up the glen. For the second set of falls, park a short way up the glen road where the river comes close for the first time.

Description From Duchally Lodge, the Cassley is grade 1, until it drops over two falls (Gd 4/5) into a small gorge after about 3½km. From here it is grade 1 and then grade 2 until about 1km above Invercassley. The river then drops over a series of three consecutively more difficult falls/rapids including Achness Falls, which can be inspected easily and paddled/portaged as desired. Nice drops in a nice setting.

Other important points The Cassley is used by anglers. I first discovered this run on a chance glance at the front cover of a fishing magazine!

Contributor:
Ben Hughes

015 Tirry

Grade	**2(3)**
Length	**6km**
OS sheet	**16**

Introduction The Tirry is a central Sutherland river feeding into Loch Shin, one of Scotland's largest lochs and part of a hydro-electric scheme catchment, with the headwaters of the Brora being diverted into the Tirry.

Water Level Wet/Very wet. The river requires a fair amount of rain to bring it into condition.

Gauge The river level may be inspected from the A836 road which is adjacent to the river.

Access Travelling north from Lairg, access can be taken at the road bridge at Rhian.

Contributors:
John Ross and
Garry Smith

Description With a good deal of rain it is possible to enter the river at Rhian where a short series of grade 3 steps lead down the Abhainn Sgeamhaidh to the main river. This is unfortunately followed by about 4km of grade 1 water before the river picks up at Dalmichy to a steady grade 2 adjacent to the road. Another couple of grade 3 drops followed by a further 1km of continuous grade 2 leads down to the take-out at the bridge on the A838 at the edge of Loch Shin.

016 Shin / Abhainn Sinn

Grade	**3(4)**
Length	**2km**
OS sheet	**16**

Introduction The Shin is found in south-east Sutherland, between Lairg and the Kyle of Sutherland. The river flows out of Loch Shin, which is really just a huge hydro dam. It runs down a wide wooded glen. Initially the channel is wide, shallow and gravelly with a few rock bars. In its lower half the river has created a deeply incised, rocky sided gorge, which is the focus of the available fun. This really is a one hit wonder.

Water Level The whole river can only really be run when the dam is releasing or after prolonged rain when it is spilling (I don't know if the dam releases on a regular basis, but I suspect it may happen on Sundays in summer).

Gauge If the volume of water pouring over the Falls of Shin looks dangerous or intimidating, go elsewhere.

Access It is possible to get on near the lower dam at Lairg on the west side of the river (580 058). Parking isn't a problem but the river has little to commend it at this stage and most adrenaline junkies will prefer to park some 4 miles farther south down the B864 at the Falls of Shin Cafe car park, where there is ample parking space and good facilities. A path leads down to the river to enable bus loads of visitors to view the falls that you are intent on paddling; the posers dream come true! Either follow this path down and climb over the barriers and barbed wire entanglements at the bottom to gain access to the river, or get in from a lay-by just upstream. For those who continue down the river after the falls, egress can be taken from the river at Invershin Power Station at the junction of the A837 and B864 (575 975).

Description The Falls themselves are the obvious attraction. They have in the past been vastly overgraded, in terms of technical difficulty, at grade 5. Good solid grade 3 paddlers can manage them at a reasonable flow. The river turns left and then right before rushing down a ramp. Watch out for a couple of half-submerged rocks on the left and the big black kettle hole, which could trip up the unwary. Breaking out in the black hole is a cool move that sets you up well for the subsequent charge down the ramp and horrifies the other visitors to the spot. The line down the ramp is to the left of centre. The current river adviser does not know of anybody who has done this in big spate and there is no information on what happens to people who capsize on the ramp. Both of these activities could be extremely hazardous. After the fall there are a couple of other nice rapids (Gd 3) with play possibilities when the river is running well. The egress is about 2km below the falls.

Contributor:
Ron Cameron

Other important points This distraction can be combined with a trip on part of the Carron or Inver, but nobody can ever be bothered going after a trip to another river.

017 Carron / Abhainn Carrunn (Upper)

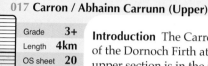

Grade	**3+**
Length	**4km**
OS sheet	**20**

Introduction The Carron is a major river flowing into the head of the Dornoch Firth at Bonar Bridge. The main interest on this upper section is in the initial gorge, which has some powerful stoppers at high flows (Gd 3-4). After this the river becomes easier and 'scrapey' in low water.

Water Level Wet. This section can rarely be paddled in its entirety, although the initial gorge is usually possible.

Gauge The upper stretch is best run when gauge on Gledfield Bridge near Ardgay (585 910, OS sheet 21) reads 2 feet or more.

Access At Ardgay leave the old A9 and drive up either side of the River Carron to a new concrete bridge at East Amat (487 915). Continue up the public road on the north side of the glen for one mile, then turn left at a telephone box, reaching Glen Calvie Lodge after a further 2 miles. Park in the lay-by at end of public road. Put in just downstream of the bridge near a sign saying 'No access to Glen Calvie Falls'. The section ends at East Amat Bridge (487 915), just above 'Granny's Hole'. Suitable parking is available on the north side of the bridge.

Contributor:
Ron Cameron

Description The Upper Carron has no portages and no serious hazards. The gorge is a fine feature and this section is a useful alternative if the middle section is very high and paddlers don't want to tackle it.

017 Carron / Abhainn Carrunn (Middle)

Grade	**4**
Length	**4km**
OS sheet	**20**

Introduction The Middle Carron flows over a series of rocky rapids and waterfalls in a broad wooded glen which contains two impressive rocky gorges.

Water Level This section can be paddled at any level, even after prolonged drought, when it is tight and technical although a bit 'scrapey' between the rapids. In full spate it is awesomely powerful with major stoppers and should only be attempted by very strong and confident paddlers.

Gauge On the downstream southern side of Gledfield Bridge (585 910, OS Sheet 21) there is a flood gauge. If this reads below 0 the middle section is low. At 1 foot on this gauge the river will be at a good flow and the middle sections will have plenty of power. At 2 feet the run will be demanding, and at 3 feet or more the river will be in no mind to take prisoners.

Access From Ardgay, drive to Gledfield Bridge and look at the flood gauge. Continue up the road on the north side of glen to reach a new concrete bridge at East Amat (487 915). There is convenient parking in a bay at the north end of this bridge. This is the get-in point. To reach the take-out by car, drive down the road on the south side of the glen past an old school on the right. Leave a vehicle in the lay-by just before the next house on the left, a new bungalow about 1 mile beyond the school (517 925). The last fall is about 500m downstream of here and you have to walk back up the bank to return to your car. Take care to close the gates.

Description Put in above the rapid upstream of the bridge if there seems to be enough water to paddle it, otherwise scramble down beside the bridge. The big rapid below the bridge is generally run down the right. 'Granny's Hole', the fall on the left, has been paddled after periods of prolonged drought when it is very low. After a further grade 4 rapid, Am Bo Bhan (The White Cow), the river becomes easier until the Green Bridge Gorge is reached. Inspection of this impressive feature is recommended, if only to check for trees wedged in its narrower sections. Half a mile beyond this gorge, the river runs over a series of shelves in a second wider gorge. There are four falls or rapids of about grade 4, with ample opportunity for pinning and generally getting trashed. Inspection is recommended when you can't see where you're going. Beware of the first narrow channel on the left below a cliff. It's going nowhere. This section ends with a drop, turn and drop sequence or a nice little fall on the left. Get out on the right and walk back up the bank to the lay-by.

Contributor:
Ron Cameron

Other important points I've paddled this river on innumerable occasions since 1985 at all levels up to about 3 feet, the level at which it destroyed my shoulder. Beyond this I flee in terror or paddle the upper or lower section. Two strange paddlers from Dundee told me they ran the section in a Topo Duo at 7 feet and it was easy. I don't know if they went over or round the houses.

017 Carron / Abhainn Carrunn (Lower)

Grade	**2(3-)**
Length	**3km**
OS sheet	**21**

Introduction In this section, the Carron flows through a wide glen with crofts on either bank. There are two or three rocky sections but mostly it has a gravelly bed. With adequate water, it is an ideal teaching stretch suitable for paddlers with limited river experience.

Water Level Sustained rainfall is needed to get this section flowing.

Gauge Should the gauge on the southern, downstream side of Gledfield Bridge (585 910) read less than 0 it will be horribly 'scrapey' and frustrating. 2 feet is a good level for even fairly novice paddlers. Above this level it starts to get powerful. At about 3½ feet the river starts to flow over a large rock below Little Falls and forms an impressive stopper. At 4ft good intermediate paddlers can have a meaningful experience.

Access From the A9, drive up the A836 to Ardgay. Turn off here and continue up Glen Carron to Gledfield Bridge, where there is a gauge. This is the take-out, and vehicles can be left parked on the roadside to the north of the bridge. To reach the put-in, continue up the north side of the glen to where there is a lay-by close to the river at Culeave (550 910). It is possible to park in a number of large lay-bys nearby.

Contributor:
Ron Cameron

Description An interesting introductory play stopper is found below a small weir, overlooked by a holiday cottage, at the end of a deep gorge. Little Falls (Gd 3-) is found about 1km after this. Easily portaged on the left, it is tricky for beginners when low, and pleasant at about 2ft.

018 Blackwater

Grade	**4**
Length	**½km**
OS sheet	**20**

Access To reach the put-in, drive up the north (river left) side of the Carron until the road end, just past Croick Church. A 5 minute walk around the side of a house and over a footbridge, brings you to the white water.

Contributor:
Kenny Biggin

Description The Blackwater is a tributary of the Upper Carron which makes a fun short trip if there is plenty of water around. There is a reasonable 2-tier waterfall and a nice 'toy' gorge. A great setting and a nice short 'bimble' and photo call.

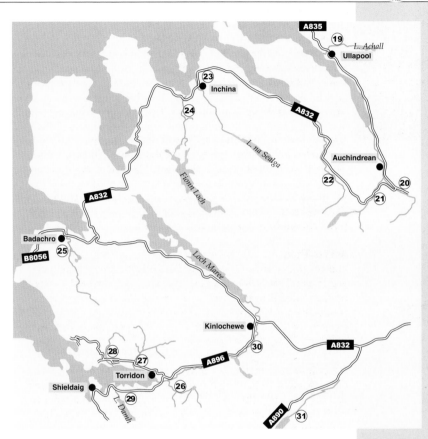

N

approx. scale 1cm = 5km

Torridon & Wester Ross

Torridon & Wester Ross

A fantastic area for paddling, both Torridon and Wester Ross have some excellent rivers tucked away amongst impressive mountains. Paddlers looking for harder runs will find they are spoilt for choice, but there are one or two less demanding options. In Torridon recent exploration has uncovered some great steep and technical grade 5 runs, which come into their own when there is some water around. The two burns coming from Ben Alligan are both worth doing and, if it is really wet try the Abhainn Thrail, which lies across the valley and needs loads of water. The Balgy and Gruinard are both reasonable sized rivers fed by large lochs so, if you miss the rain by a day or two, they should still have enough water to be worth doing. At Kinlochewe you will find a bunkhouse and pub as well as free wild camping, ask at the Beinn Eighe Visitor Centre. There are also Youth Hostels at Torridon, Gairloch and Ullapool. A generally unspoilt and sparsely populated area, this is a great place to escape to, and options for walking, climbing and general exploring abound.

019 Ullapool / Abhainn Ullapul

Grade **3+**
Length **4km**
OS sh. **19/20**

Introduction The river flows from Loch Achall to the east of Ullapool in Wester Ross to enter Loch Broom just north of the town. A steep river dropping an average of almost 70m/km, its boulder-strewn channel follows a narrow wooded glen.

Water Level Wet/Very wet. Prolonged heavy rain will probably be needed to get this run going. The Ullapool can be paddled as an alternative to the Inver if the latter is too big for comfort.

Gauge The best place to judge the flow is at the bridge by the take-out.

Access Follow the A835 north out of Ullapool. Turn right up the hill just before a bridge over the river (129 949 OS Sheet 19). Follow this road past a gravel pit until accosted by a private road sign. Park and carry down to the river or carry along the road and put in where the road crosses the river (155 954 OS Sheet 20). The get-out point is at a low foot bridge, 500m downstream of the main A835 road bridge just outside Ullapool.

Description The river begins with a few pleasant drops and grade 3 rapids. Soon a narrow gorge with very steep rock walls is encountered. At low flows the gorge ends in a nasty looking fall. At higher flows, this fall looks OK, but a river-wide hole forms near the start of the gorge. The fall can be inspected from river left, but deer fences on this bank mean that it's best to make the portage on river right. Putting in below the fall, 2-3km of pleasant grade 3 water leads down to the town.

Contributors:
Ron Cameron and
Kingsley Ash

Broom 020

Access Driving south from Ullapool on the A835, the forestry car park at Auchindrean gives good access to the River Broom. To find the take-out drive north alongside the river, and select your spot.

Grade	2/3
Length	4km
OS sheet	20

Description If all the rivers in the area are huge and scary, the River Broom should provide a grade 2/3 blast over the boulders.

Contributor:
Andy Dytch

Cuileig (Upper) 021

Introduction The Cuileig is a tributary of the Abhainn Droma, which flows through the Corrieshalloch Gorge. A true adventure, this is gorge boating at its deepest. The whole river is enclosed in a deep canyon which means that escape is almost impossible. The intimidating setting gives the rapids a much harder feel than if they were out in the open. Be warned there is one killer fall just below the take-out for the upper section that could 'sucker' the unsuspecting into its inescapable run in.

Grade	4/5
Length	1km
OS sheet	20

Water Level Wet/Very wet. As a large chunk of water is now lost to the new hydro scheme, larger spates will be required to bring the river into condition. The intake point is above the main road, so the flow you see under the bridge is an accurate measure of the current conditions.

Gauge This river doesn't need to be running too high. Take a look at the first rapid at the top of the gorge: if it looks out of control it may be wise to go elsewhere.

Access The top section follows the A832. Access is from the pull-in next to the road bridge, approximately 2½ miles from the junction with the A835, Garve to Ullapool road. Climb down the right-hand side of the unrunnable fall just downstream of the road bridge. To find the take-out, drive north-east along the A832 for a little under a mile. At the point where the river drops deeper into the gorge and further away from the road, you will find the falls that separate the upper and lower sections. Cut down through the forest next to a fence and locate the falls and footbridge. Make sure you identify the final eddy and a route of escape up out of the gorge before getting on!

Description If you aren't put off by the climb down into the gorge just next to the falls, then get ready to rock. The first two rapids at grade 5 are the hardest on this section. Walking these is an option, but after this there is no option to walk. The next fall has a formidable horizon line, but once you go over the edge (try near the far left) the pool is big and deep. From here the technical grade of the rapids never exceeds grade 3+ (maybe 4- in higher flows); however the uncertainty factor is grade 5. The ability to read and run is a must. The take-out is a small eddy on river right on a left-hand bend, at the point where the river disappears away in to a tight defile. Make sure that you have marked the take-out before you start and be confident you will be able to make the eddy. Do not get on if you feel this eddy is too small.

Contributors:
Alastair Collis
and Andy Jackson

Other important points I have run this section a couple of times and have had a ball each time. Water levels are rather critical and flood boating is definitely not an option.

021 Cuileig (Lower)

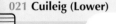

Grade   5
Length **2½km**
OS sheet   **20**

Introduction The run starts below a portage that separates the upper and lower sections. This part of the Cuileig has no real scenery due to the depth of the gorge; in fact it has little sunlight either. Down in the gorge, no one can hear you scream! Take some supplies as help, if you need it, will be a long time coming. This is definitely for those who have a sense of humour and the nerve to match. Scouting the section is the first challenge, reserved for those who dare to risk crossing the iron bridge built in the 1800's by Sir John Fowler. Now closed to public access, it looks as if this bridge has never been replanked. The river at this point is way down below you and what looks like 1m ledges are in fact over 5m high. Similarly what looks like small playholes are 2m pour-over ledges.

Water Level Wet.

Gauge If you have run the top section, then this is also a good bet.

Access The access to the top of this run will eventually kill someone, as the footbridge mentioned above is the shortest route to the put-in, and the planks can't last forever. The alternative is to walk in from the top or bottom, or find a take-out for the upper run on river left. Once on the left bank next to the bridge, follow the path downstream and descend the second gully you come to. The first gully looks an easier way down to the river, but brings you out above a very serious looking rapid. A classic abseil from a tree at the head of the gully (10m) will establish you in the snot ridden gully bed. From here 5 rappels of 10m each, on loose boulders and tree debris, will see you at a small slippery rock from which you can seal launch. Take out just below the junction of the Cuileig with the Abhainn Droma, which flows through the Corrieshalloch Gorge. A five-minute walk along a very faint farm track on river right will bring you back to the A835 at Braemore Square farm buildings.

Description Descending the second gully leaves you in a small eddy up against the cliff wall. A stiff ferry glide away from the undercut left wall will see you into a nice eddy and a prime seat to strain your neck looking up at the top of the gorge. Not to spoil a top day out, I will spare the details but say that the river here starts with some tough grade 4 action that leads to a big horizon line. This is a nasty class 5. The first half can be portaged but the later half of the rapid can not be portaged and can only be protected with difficulty. Boyakasha must be run after only distant viewing from river right. From here on there is stiff grade 4+ boating, with only small eddies to boat scout from. In a couple of places, river-wide holes provide a good challenge. Just as the gorge is becoming worryingly narrow the river spits you out and the bank falls away. It's a nice feeling to leave the gorge and even

better to know that some of the best white water is still ahead. A 10-minute float brings you to the first of the lower falls. Every river should finish this way as these four falls, each around 3m in height, are sculptured bedrock with clean pools. The top fall is an obvious horseshoe shape, hidden on a left-hand bend (Gd 5). The following three rapids Moss Falls, Bridge Flats and the Twins are more of the same grade 5 calibre.

Other important points Escape from the hardest rapid, Boyaka-sha, is feasible but a climbing rope would be useful, as it looks decidedly dodgy ground. This section is definitely not recommended for larger groups due to the lack of space in any of the eddies, two boats were more than enough to be coping with in the upper stretch of this section. It is possible to walk up the river to run only the lower 4 falls, walking time 30 mins. Good luck and bon voyage.

Contributors:
Alastair Collis and
Andy Jackson

022 Dundonnell

Grade **4/5**
Length **2½km**
OS sheet **19**

Introduction The Dundonnell drains into Little Loch Broom. This steep and exciting river runs next to the road, making portaging easy.

Water Level Medium wet/Wet.

Gauge From the road, you can see many of the rapids and get an idea of the level.

Access Driving from Inverness to Ullapool, turn left at Braemore junction onto the A832 to Dundonnell. After about 5 miles, the road starts to run parallel to the river. Continue until the road crosses the river, and park at a lay-by on the right after a further ½ mile. From here you can look upstream into a gorge with three big waterfalls. Get in below these. To find the take-out, drive downstream for less than two miles to where a footbridge crosses the river. Make sure you don't miss this take-out.

Description Getting in below the obvious three waterfalls, the run starts with a nice rock-slide rapid. Below this, a big 2-tier fall can be portaged on the right. This fall, which consists of a 3½m straight drop followed by a slightly higher twisting drop, has been run in high water. It provides an exhilarating horizon line as you approach the lip - elbow pads come well recommended. At good flows it is continuous grade 4+ from here with one or two harder falls near the bottom. These get very hard with lots of water (Gd 5). Make sure you take out above the footbridge, as the gorge below is narrow, ugly and not a good place for a kayak.

Contributors:
Neil Farmer and
Kingsley Ash

Gruinard 023

Grade	4
Length	1km
OS sheet	19

Introduction The river flows out of Loch na Sealga in the Fisherfield Forest and runs for approximately 10km north-west until it meets the Atlantic, near Gruinard Island. This run is a blast, albeit a short one. The white water section of the Gruinard is often run in conjunction with other rivers in the area. When paddled at its best, it is a compact and fast flowing roller-coaster ride with large waves and stoppers.

Water level Wet / Very wet.

Gauge Take a look over the road bridge, and get on if it looks fast and fun.

Access The put-in is on river left, just above the road bridge on the A832 Dundonnell to Poolewe road (962 910). The egress is river right, just before the water turns salty. Cars can be parked river right very close to the egress (960 919).

Description The put-in above the bridge is easily accessible after a very short carry. However it offers little in the way of a warm-up before the main rapids begin. The fun starts with a bouldery rapid beneath the road bridge. From here the run remains continuous until the take-out is reached. There is one slightly bigger rapid about halfway down, which hides some large holes in high flows.

Other important points If you decide to take a swim on the way down ensure the tide at Gruinard Bay is on the way in, or Gruinard Island is likely to be where you would end up. Gruinard Island known locally as 'Anthrax Island', was a government testing site used in biological warfare research. Although the island has recently been given the all-clear, I believe it has yet to appear as a stop-over venue on the SCA's touring calendar!

Contributor:
Pete Gwatkin

024 Little Gruinard

Grade	**4/5**
Length	**4km**
OS sheet	**19**

Introduction The Little Gruinard flows north from Fionn Loch, and boasts some of the finest scenery in Britain. The unexpected grandeur, an idyllic setting and its very isolation add an extra ingredient to this excellent paddle. There are several nice drops and continuous boulder sections, leading to a rather nasty sabre tooth fall upstream of the road bridge, followed by continuous exciting rapids to the sea.

Water Level Wet. Loch fed and with a reasonably large catchment, the Little Gruinard flows fairly regularly after a good day's rain.

Gauge To gauge the flow, look downstream from where the A832 crosses the river. This should look worth paddling for the trip to be on. As a rough guide, if the Gruinard is running, this one should be as well.

Access Follow the A832 from either Poolewe or Dundonnell. Parking is limited around the bridge. If the water level is right, follow the footpath alongside the river for 2½ hours. The path goes away from the river for a while before dropping back down to the put-in.

Contributor:
Chris Forrest

Description The action soon starts with a series of drops. All very enjoyable, but watch out for one technical drop with a rooster tail (Gd 5). The river then opens out to give bouldery rapids. These eventually lead to a section of small ledges, indicating the approach of Sabre Tooth Fall. Get out in plenty of time. Continue from just above the bridge, down the steep technical boulder field to the sea.

Other important points Don't underestimate the rapids below the road bridge.

025 Badachro

Grade	**4(5)**
Length	**4½km**
OS sheet	**19**

Introduction Draining the northern slopes of Beinn Alligin and Beinn Bhreac, the Badachro flows through a system of lochs, entering the sea in a quiet bay south of Gairloch. This is a gem of a run, providing steep paddling in a beautiful setting, with 2 possible sections.

Water Level Wet/Very wet.

Gauge Look over the bridge on the B8056 just before the village of Badachro. The river can be seen flowing out of Loch Bad a Chrotha over a long weir. There should be a reasonable flow at this point.

Access Turn off the A832, about 3 miles south of Gairloch, onto the B8056. Follow the road to the bridge mentioned above and check the flow. This is the put-in.To find the take-out, continue on and take the first right into the village of Badachro. Park near the jetty. To reach the upper put-in, drive back towards the A832. About 2 miles after the bridge, a track leads away past a farm on the right-hand side. Park and walk up this track for just under 2km, until you reach a small lochan. Paddle across this to a tiny outlet on the far side. This leads to a larger loch, which in another 200m brings you to the river.

Description The lower section starts with small bouldery rapids, gradually building to a powerful twisting double drop, followed by a short pool and a choice of routes - boof left. A series of fun rapids then leads you out to the harbour at Badachro, where a small playhole and a pub provide a choice of entertainment to suit most tastes.

Other important points If you are seeking wilderness and adventure, it's worth considering the upper stretch. There are a couple of hard rapids and a probable portage, but it makes an interesting day out if you don't mind carrying your boat and enjoy paddling grade 5. A small loch links the 2 sections.

In 2004 the welcome news was received that the Scottish Executive have turned down the application to build a hydro scheme at Shieldaig. The threat has now been lifted on the Badachro and Horrisdale rivers and one of the finest and most remote tracts of wild land in the whole of the country. The SCA welcomes this decision and hopes that it signals a fuller assessment of the impact of planned hydro-electric schemes and a greater consideration of the range of renewable energy sources available. You can find out more about the SCA hydro campaign and how you can help to save other Scottish rivers at www.scot-canoe.org/access/hydro.htm.

Contributors:
Bridget Thomas and
Kingsley Ash

026 Abhainn Thrail

Grade   **5**
Length   **2km**
OS sheet   **25**

Introduction From the stunning mountain setting of Torridon village you can see this burn cascading down the hillside to the south. The Abhainn Thrail is a mixed bag of tricks, a steep continuous boulder run with a cool waterfall.

Water Level Loads and loads, in fact the more the better. One to save for a very wet day.

Gauge Looking up the river from the roadside, you want to see plenty of white!

Access Driving south from Torridon village on the A896, cross the bridge over the River Torridon and turn immediately left up a small track. Park at the end of the track and follow the path up river left for about 2km, getting excited about the river as you go. Carry on as far as the 6m fall tucked away at the top of a narrow gorge, (918 539).

Description The first fall and narrow gorge get the trip off to a cracking start. The 6m ledge offers that fleeting chance of freefall. Next some grade 3+ water leads to the top of the rather large slab 'that you may have noticed' on the walk in. This looks pretty immense and may or may not go. For those lacking in moral fibre portaging on river right and getting on for the 2nd half of the slab works well. The best of the river is now before you. Concentrate hard as the multitude of shoots, boulders, holes and eddies could leave you dazed and confused. This section is quite intense and great fun, grade 5. As the action switches to bedrock slabs, the obvious horizon line is Boof or Die (Gd 4+). It's easy water from here to the car.

Contributors:
Andy Jackson
and Alastair Collis

Other important points A very rocky trip, you really get to know the Torridonian sandstone.

Abhainn Coire Mhic Nobuil 027

Grade	**4/5**
Length	**1km**
OS sheet	**25**

Introduction This burn is about 2 miles west of Torridon on the north shore of Upper Loch Torridon. A mental kilometre of continuous grade 4/5 water in a sheer sided gorge with two large waterfalls, this run is well worth the short walk. From the road bridge looking up, all you see is a 10m fall into a sheer sided gorge. Upstream of the fall is a run that is guaranteed to have turned you into a gibbering fool by the time you've climbed up through the cave at the take-out.

Water Level Wet. It does need water, but could be very dangerous at high levels. Like many mountain streams it rises and falls incredibly quickly, so keep an eye on the weather as you walk up.

Gauge This is the kind of run which deserves a thorough 'reccy' before getting on. As a rough guide, the lip of the big fall should be covered all the way across but with plenty of rocks showing on the run in. The big drop is best seen from river left but the rest of the river is more clearly assessed from river right. Take a run up before getting the boats off the roof and be sure to find an eddy above the two main falls.

Access Approaching Torridon from the east, turn right along the north shore of the loch and drive about 2 miles until you pass over the gorge immediately before a forestry commission car park. Park here and walk up the path on river left until you want to get on. The best of the white water is in the last 1km, accessed by lowering the boats into the gorge below a big unrunnable (?) waterfall at the start of the gorge.

Description From start to finish this river goes off. Continuous hard water in a committing gorge that you'll want to inspect before you get on. Once you're on the water, getting out isn't easy and in many places impossible. About halfway down the run is a 7m fall in a narrow slot, which is portageable with care. Seal launch down the slab next to the fall on river right. You will want to boof the river-wide hole just downstream of here. A long section of grade 4 leads to a narrow passage on river left through which the river flows. Overhung by rhododendron bushes this spooky tunnel contains no nasty surprises. Above the big fall you see from the car park, the river left wall opens out a bit allowing you to get out and

inspect/run away bravely from some serious freefall action. It goes hard river left, and is a long way down if you feel like checking the gravity theory. Once in the gorge below, the only way out involves some serious climbing or a scramble up through the cave on river right just downstream of the bridge. It is probably best to find the egress beforehand, as below here the river drops into another rapid that has a nasty sump in it. After that, all you'll manage to do is float around the car park in a daze, gibbering uncontrollably.

Contributor:
James Brocklehurst

Other important points This run is serious stuff. Make sure you inspect it carefully, marking the take-out and the two falls. In high water it would probably be impossible to egress under the bridge as there would be no eddies. If you aren't happy with it don't get on, as it's flat out all the way, even if you don't run the big fall. Getting out anywhere else may require wings.

028 Abhainn Alligin

Grade   **4/5**
Length   **1km**
OS sheet   **25**

Introduction This burn runs into the north shore of Upper Loch Torridon at Inveralligin, approximately 4 miles west of Torridon village. The Abhainn Alligin is what could be classed 'a rocky ditch'. It's a narrow low volume boulder bash in a gorge that is so steep sided and 'chasm like' that walking along the top, you can only sometimes see the river below. Not everyone's idea of fun, but if you are into tight technical positions, then this will definitely leave you with a satisfied grin under your full-face helmet.

Water Level Wet. It'll run if there has been a bit of rain around that day. Loads of rain and you may require the rapid evolution of gills and a thick armour plate.

Gauge Check the flow over the boulders at the take-out. If you think you can float a boat down this and have fun, then it's running. If there aren't any rocks showing here, then see above for physiological requirements.

Access Approaching Torridon from the east, turn right into Torridon village and follow the road for approximately 4 miles. Pass the road to Inveralligin, and cross over the burn immediately before a 90° right-hand bend; put in here. The take-out is down the road to Inveralligin, where the burn comes out of the gorge.

Description This burn is Topo territory, so unless you've got a short fat round boat, it won't be any fun. Equally, if you like the way you look even just a little bit, then a full-face helmet might be handy. Keep a look out for trees and sheep that might be stuck down in the gorge. A description of any detail is impossible. From the word go, it's just one long boulder bash, that you paddle until you think it might be a good idea to get out and have a better look. The only major feature worth mentioning is a 4m waterfall that you come to about a third of the way down. A pretty straight forward 'weeee … splash' kind of drop, although when you look at it you probably won't think so. You know you've got to the end of the run when you come out of the gorge and start to find bashing off rocks becoming less exciting, either that or you have reached the sea and all the rocks have gone.

Contributor:
James Brocklehurst

Other important points It is possible to camp at the take-out, donations to the local crofters should be left in the box provided.

Balgy 029

Introduction The River Balgy drains Loch Damh and runs north into Loch Torridon. This is a short fun river with one notable gnarly drop.

Grade **3/4(4+)**
Length **1km**
OS sheet **24**

Water Level Moderately wet / Very wet. The river is fed by a large loch and holds its water well.

Gauge If in doubt, nip up and check the level at the Falls of Balgy. If you are a little concerned about the hole at the bottom of these falls the river is probably up. If you are very concerned, it is definitely running.

Access From Torridon, drive west along the A896 towards Shieldaig, and park near the bridge over the river. Go through the gate and follow the path up river right. It is a 20-minute walk up to the put-in at Loch Damh. Have a peek into the mini-gorge as you walk up to wet your appetite.

Description Good 'grade 3 and a bit' action starts from the word go. Generally, it's all good clean fun with a powerful feel at a

Contributors:
Andy Burton
and Andy Dytch

high flow. At the end of the mini-gorge, there is one tight drop with a bit of a hole and some undercut rock. Immediately below this lie the Falls of Balgy, the main event on the river. There are a couple of different lines down this slightly rocky 3m fall. All of them however go through the worrying last hole. Flat water leads to the bridge, but it's worth carrying on further for a short section of grade 3 before the sea. It's a short walk back up the river-right bank to the car.

030 A'Ghairbhe

Grade **2/3**
Length **5km**
OS sht.**19/25**

Introduction Running through Kinlochewe and into Loch Maree, the A'Ghairbhe provides a mixture of boulders and bedrock ledges through the spectacular countryside of the Beinn Eighe National Nature Reserve.

Water Level Wet. At a medium level this run gives fairly continuous grade 2 rapids, with some grade 3, but the whole run is probably more fun, if a little harder, with more water.

Gauge The A'Ghairbhe runs beside the A896 and for much of the length can be seen from the road.

Access You could get in or out almost anywhere from Loch Clair down. The usual take-out is under the road bridge in Kinlochewe. There is a concrete platform river right with steps leading to a gate beside the bridge.

Contributor:
Stuart Ball

Description The main feature is a small gorge about 2km below Loch Clair around the bridge on a forestry track at (019 592). Here the river is narrower and goes over a series of bedrock ledges, formed from ancient metamorphic rock, at about 45° to the river's course. This makes for a series of falls and sudden changes of direction. At the bottom end of this stretch, the whole river falls into a narrow slot which could be nasty in high flows, and may be worth inspecting before you get on.

Other important points It is possible to continue down to the confluence with the Kinlochewe River and then into Loch Maree (about another 4km). This section is flat, though swift flowing.

Carron 031

Introduction The Carron runs through a series of lochs to meet the salt water on the west coast at Loch Carron.

Grade **3/4+**
Length **10km**
OS sheet **25**

Water Level Wet.

Gauge The river runs alongside the A890 making it easy to check the level.

Access Put in at Loch Sgamhain or where the A890 crosses the Allt Coire Crubaldh (087 530). Take out at Loch Dughaill.

Description The river starts slowly, picking up pace until an unexpected grade 4 fall is encountered under the second footbridge. This is followed by 2km of continuous grade 3 with enough corners to keep you on your toes. Watch out for, and portage a messy tree-filled boulder choke on a right-hand bend. More swift grade 3 leads to two gorge sections that need to be portaged. Both gorges are completely blocked by trees and are difficult to inspect, but may (or may not) contain some nice boating. From where you can get back in, the river is grade 3 to a forestry bridge at (049 494). From here a major tributary adds to the flow and 4km of grade 2/3 water bring you out to Loch Dughaill.

Contributor:
Mike Hayward

Other important points Without the tree blockages and if the first gorge has no nasty surprises, this could be a classic grade 3/4 trip - always keeping you on your toes and guessing what is around the next corner... anyone got a chain-saw?

Drive carefully on country roads!

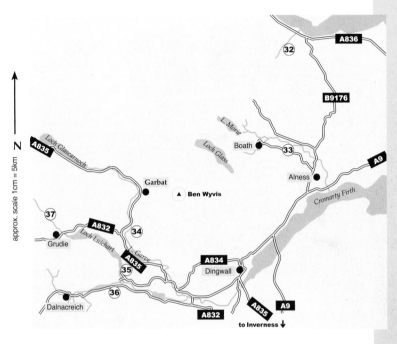

Easter Ross

Easter Ross

All but one of the rivers featured in this section are heavily affected by hydro schemes and their associated dams. That said, there is some fantastic paddling to be had when the rivers are running high, or there is the occasional elusive release by the hydro companies. Best keep your ear to the ground to track these down. When it rains the Blackwater is probably the most popular run in the area as it comes into condition fairly regularly. Its nearby neighbour, the Grudie, is less well known but contains a short, classy section. Solid intermediate paddlers will get a lot from the journey down the Averon of Alness. If the rivers are really low then perhaps it will still be possible to scrape down the Lower Meig, you'll be surprised at how much fun you'll have.

032 Wester Fearn Burn

Grade	4
Length	1km
OS sheet	21

Introduction Just west of Tain by the Dornoch Firth, the hike and hurl of the Wester Fearn Burn gives an hour's high entertainment. The run is a low volume steep ditch consisting of 4 or 5 notable drops, and is well worth the walk.

Water level Very wet.

Gauge The burn should be running brown with enough water to float a boat under the A836 road bridge.

Access Driving north of Tain on the A9(T), follow signs for Bonar Bridge and the Dornoch Firth Bridge roundabout. After about 8 miles, you will cross the burn. Drive another 100 yards to a pull off on the left-hand side. Park up here and walk back along the main road to the bridge. To get to the put-in, hike your boat through the private driveway at the bridge, to a path that leads up on river right through the forest. After 10 minutes or so the glen opens up and this wee ditch levels off. Put in here.

Description With little or no warm up, you're skeltering down a lead-in channel of 15m to a sharp right hander and off the lip of the first drop into a large pool. The river then drops into a small canyon with a couple of steep angled ramps. After this the river widens before the last shallow angled, narrow drop. This is the least impressive with the highest spankability – watch out for the undercut on the left-hand wall. The entire run can easily be inspected on the walk in – worthwhile as I've only done it once and have only vague recollections!

Other important points Access to the path is unknown but definitely gives the feel of walking through someone's garden. Parking is also dubious as it is a fish farm's road access. Use the utmost discretion.
It may also be worth checking out the Easter Fearn down the road.

Contributor:
Colin Aitken

Averon of Alness / Abhainn Abharan 033

Introduction The river flows from Loch Morie in Easter Ross through Alness to enter the sea on the north side of the Cromarty Firth. The watercourse follows a well-wooded glen that provides protection from even the wildest of winds. The upper part of the run consists of an endless series of boulder weirs that have been added to enhance the fishing. In its lower section, below Newbridge on the old A9, the river becomes rockier in character and flows through a deeply incised valley.

Grade **3/4+**
Length **10km**
OS sheet **25**

Water Level Wet/Very wet. Rarely navigable in summer, this river requires a couple of days of good rainfall to get it going.

Gauge There is a gauge on the downstream side of the road-bridge in Alness. 1½ feet is the absolute minimum for the section below Newbridge, 2 feet for the whole river. 4 feet gives a very stimulating paddle.

Access From Alness, cross the B817. Follow a single-track road up the south-west side of the river, signposted Boath, to a car park, gate and private road sign. Park the car and carry your boat down the road for 5 minutes to reach the river. Put in opposite another flood gauge (568 747). Take out at the Averon Centre in Alness, on the north bank of river, just upstream of the bridge. The Averon Centre will allow use of its showers and changing facilities for a small fee.

Description The river is changed every summer by the fish people who build new weirs and change others, so you never know

what you will encounter. Over the years they have also added a variety of hazards to paddlers, the current ones being two steel footbridges close to river level between Ardross Castle and Newbridge. These are dangerous in mid-flow but you can paddle over them at very high flows (above 4ft). When in spate, the river develops a number of strong stoppers, most of which can be seen from a distance and outflanked. There are plenty of fun play-spots, but perhaps no real classics. There is one rapid significantly larger then the others, which may warrant inspection. It is about ½km downstream of the castle, and comes up very quickly when the river is high. The river turns left, then right, before a big white rock in the river marks the approach of the rapid. Take out on river left. Those wanting a shorter paddle can put in at Newbridge on the B817 (642 715). There is only limited roadside parking. From here it is 2km to Alness, perhaps 40 minutes paddling time.

Contributor:
Ron Cameron

Other important points The flood gauges on the Averon tend to give very consistent readings, probably only varying by a maximum of 6 inches between the top and bottom gauge at any time. They are graded in feet and tenths of feet, (creeping metrication!)

034 Blackwater (Upper)

Grade **3/4**
Length **5km**
OS sheet **20**

Introduction The Blackwater drains away from Ben Wyvis, south-eastwards through Garve and Contin. The river changes character along its length from a steep, rocky, mountain stream to a more mature pool-drop river. The upper section is a continuous bouldery run that needs a lot of water.

Water Level Very wet.

Gauge The run can be inspected from the road, making it easy to gauge the flow. 0.5 on the SEPA gauge should be considered a minimum level.

Access Driving north from Dingwall, take the A835 towards Ullapool, and put on after about 6 miles where the gradient flattens. To find a good take-out, head back south along the main road.

Description The run consists of narrow, twisting, continuous grade 3/4 water with plenty of micro-eddies to catch. There is one notable drop, a little less than 2m, recognisable as a distinct horizon line and best inspected on river left.

Contributor:
Andy Jackson

Other important points This is not a good place for a large or inexperienced group.

Blackwater 034

Introduction The most commonly paddled stretch (described here) is the middle section from below Silver Bridge. A picturesque run, it may be worth running for the first time at more moderate flows.

Grade   **4(5)**
Length   **2km**
OS sheet   **20**

Water Level Medium wet. The main section starting from the picnic area 3 miles north of Garve can be run at modest flows, when it offers tight and technical paddling. When the river is pumping, this section is a much more serious proposition, and should be treated with care. Perhaps the upper river would be a better option?

Gauge Check the level at the Silver Bridge picnic site, where the A835 crosses the river. The rapid immediately above the bridge is generally portaged but you should get a good idea of the flow from here. If no rocks are showing, or just the tops are visible, then this run is a peach. If you are unsure of the level, it is possible to walk the length of the run using the footpath on river right. 0.35 on the SEPA gauge should be considered a minimum level.

Access To reach the put-in at Silver Bridge, follow the A835 north from Garve for a few miles. To find the take-out, go back down the main road towards Garve and turn off left to a very picturesque old bridge and picnic area.

Description This section contains the best bedrock drops the river has to offer and can provide everything from enjoyment to unmitigated fear, depending on the amount of water and your personal fright factor. The rapid immediately above the road-bridge is generally considered nasty, with plenty of potential for a pin or entrapment. You may choose to put in below it! The half dozen rapids on the short section down to the picnic site all run at grade 4, unless the river is particularly high. This section is pool-drop all the way, but some of the falls may form nasty stoppers

Contributor:
Dave Aldritt

when the river is in spate. There are also some good opportunities for playing in this section, and a handy path for those who wish to have their moment of glory captured on film. The last rapid under the bridge has claimed a few victims and those who have had enough fun for one day may be happy to take out above this drop.

034 Blackwater (Lower)

Grade **3/3+**

Length **2km**

OS sheet **26**

Introduction Further down the river below Loch Garve, there is still more action on the lower section.

Water Level Wet / Very wet.

Access Turn off the A835 two miles north of Contin at the well signposted Falls of Rogie car park. Take out in the village of Contin, by Craigdarroch Drive.

Contributors:
Duncan Ostler and
Ian Murray

Description Put in below the Falls of Rogie, which are very shallow and not recommended. The rest of the run provides good entertainment. There is a useful playhole near the end, which can also be reached by walking down from a lay-by on the main road. Medium high flows are required to make the playhole work, although it can be very retentive at high levels.

035 Conon

Grade **4+(5)**

Length **1km**

OS sheet **26**

Introduction Strathconon is a large valley to the west of Dingwall. The white water stretch of the River Conon flows from the dam holding Loch Luichart. Sadly this awesome dam-released river rarely runs. At high flows, it is a real big volume trip with a few hard rapids and not much flat. It is probably worth inspecting the whole run from the bank before getting on.

Water Level Extremely wet. Water is only rarely released from the dam and there needs to be a lot of water coming over the top to make the trip worthwhile.

Gauge The rapid upstream of the bridge at the take-out needs to look quite full-on for the river to be working.

Moriston - Rivers of Loch Ness - Pete Kyriakoudis

Moriston - Rivers of Loch Ness - Pete Kyriakoudis

Garry - Rivers of L. Ness - www.breadandbutter.me.uk

Moriston - Rivers of L. Ness - Andy Jackson

Fechlin - Before work on the new hydro scheme...

The same rapid Summer 2004

Access From Inverness take the road heading to Ullapool. Shortly after the village of Contin, turn left opposite the Achilty Hotel and follow the single track road until you come to Luichart Power Station. This is the take-out. To get to the put-in, take the next road off to the right and drive up towards the dam. A gate before the dam is open during the day and there should be no problem driving on up the track to the dam. Put in here, or further downstream if you don't fancy the first couple of rapids.

Description The first rapid is within sight of the dam. It has been run via the narrow undercut fish ladder on the left which leads directly to a 3m drop, two very meaty holes and another undercut rock (Gd 5). A short pool leads to Viagra Falls, best portaged on river right. Below the falls lies Terminator (Gd 5). This long rapid consists of drops and large stoppers and makes for very technical boating. It is best inspected from river left. There are several possible lines, but none are straightforward and all have severe consequences. From this point the river eases slightly. Pinball Wizard comes next. Here the river charges through a mini-gorge, giving some 400m of good technical grade 4/4+ paddling through drops, stoppers and crashing waves. It looks very intimidating, but is not mega demanding. Saying that, a solid roll is required as a swim would be nasty! At the end of this rapid there is a great playhole, which is meaty but safe. The next ½km of grade 3 has a few good playspots. A small gorge and the final grade 4 rapid, which channels into a great splat rock, bring you to the take-out.

Contributor:
Keith Bremner

Other important points This river very, very rarely runs and is a serious undertaking when it does. Be warned! In several places ugly looking fishladders have been formed from concrete on the river bed and these lurk just below the surface on the steeper rapids.

036 Meig (Upper)

Grade **2/3**
Length **2km**
OS sheet **26**

Introduction The Meig lies in the heart of Strathconon, and is a tributary of the mighty River Conon. The upper run starts at Strathconon village. It can be done at varying levels and is a marvellous introduction to white water. It provides space and opportunities for group play, bridge jumping etc.

Water Level Medium / Very wet. Although this river is best at high to medium flows, it can be run with less water, and comes up very quickly in rainy conditions.

Gauge Check out the level as you cross the bridge, approximately 1½ miles from the end of Loch Meig. If there is gravel visible downstream of the bridge, the river is anything up to medium flows (depending on the amount of gravel showing). If no gravel is visible, the river will be good.

Access From Muir of Ord, drive towards Marybank on the A832. Turn off here and head on up the glen to the Strathconon Hotel. Park in the lay-by, or the hotel car park if you fancy a quick drink after your run. The put-in is above the road-bridge. To get to the take-out, drive back down the glen for about a mile to the swing bridge. There is a small parking place here; please park considerately.

Contributor:
Duncan Ostler

Description Depending on the level, this run can be fast and furious, or friendly and technical. Starting above the bridge in Strathconon, nice bouldery rapids and funnels soon bring you to the biggest drop at grade 3. From here the river continues to provide grade 2 enjoyment with some good scenery until the take-out at the suspension bridge. The run can be extended to include most of the glen, but with little added excitement.

036 Meig (Lower/Gorge)

Grade **4**
Length **2km**
OS sheet **26**

Introduction The Lower Meig starts below the dam that forms Loch Meig. A steep, technical gorge run with little in the way of protection, it doesn't need a lot of water to provide an entertaining run. Even at low flows it's a magical place to be, with great rock features and a natural rock arch that spans the river.

Water Level Dry - Moderately wet. Although the normal dam release is just enough to scrape down this run, it is best to wait until heavy rain swells the flow a little, but not too much!

Gauge On a standard compensation flow from the Meig Dam, a small amount of water runs down the fish ladder and on into the gorge. This meagre flow is enough for a first trip down. On subsequent visits you may want a little more water to keep life exciting. If the rapids below the dam don't look a bit scrapey, the river is probably too high. To make sure you're not letting yourself in for an epic, cross the dam and drive down on river left for about ½ mile. Park up and head down to the river for a peek.

Access From Muir of Ord, take the A832 to Marybank. Turn off here and drive up Strathconon for about 8 miles to the Meig Dam (below Loch Meig). Park in the lay-by next to the forest road and after checking the flow, scramble down the grassy bank to the river. To get to the take-out, drive across the dam and down the track on river left. After about a mile, look for a suitable lay-by.

Description The run starts with a small weir, followed by a succession of technical drops, including a couple of potential portages at some flows. The whole river drops steeply through a narrow gorge with some impressive natural rock features. At anything other than a low flow, powerful river-wide stoppers can form in the gorge and although difficult, detailed inspection is recommended before putting on.

Contributor:
Duncan Ostler

Grudie 037

Grade	**4**
Length	**½km**
OS sheet	**20**

Introduction The Grudie lies tucked away at the head of Loch Luichart on the road from Garve to Achnasheen. This is a 'beautiful wee run', a kind of mini Etive, with several small falls all close together and all more exciting than stressful.

Water Level Very Wet. As most of the water for this trip gets diverted from Loch Fannich, you are relying on the remaining catchment area below the dam. It will need to be very wet to put enough water down the river for a worthwhile run.

Gauge Judge the flow at the bridge on the A832 by the Power Station. If the rapids just upstream look easily floatable you are in for a good time. If it is absolutely raging, this may be a grade 5 trip.

Access Driving from Garve, there is a large lay-by on the left-hand side just before the bridge over the river at Grudie Power Station. On the other side of the road a track leads up the glen, river left. Although the gate at the bottom is normally locked, it's a short walk on a good road and well worth the effort. After approximately ½ km you will notice the river flattening off. Carry down through the trees to put in immediately above a good set of falls.

Contributors:
Bridget Thomas
and Andy Jackson

Description The obvious triple falls at the put-in are the best on the trip. In fact they are so much fun you may be tempted to carry up and try them again. Below these is a series of fun rapids and rock-slides. The falls come in quick succession and you're back at the bridge before you know it. Take care to get out upstream of the bridge to avoid being sieved through the grill at the power station! It may be worth crossing the road for a quick play on the powerful rapid that spews from the power station. Sadly there is no more white water on this river, which always has a good volume.

Other important points You could consider a trip starting further upstream but there is less white water for the walk.

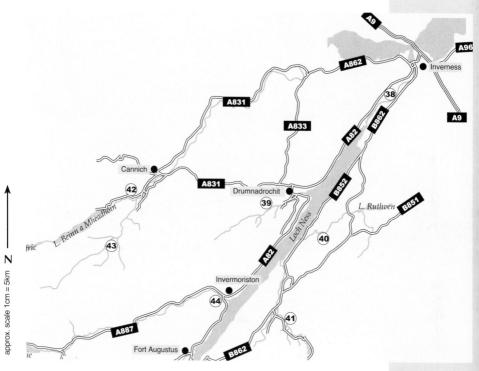

Rivers of Loch Ness

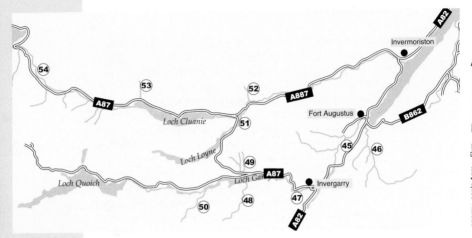

approx. scale 1cm – 5km

Rivers of Loch Ness - continued

The Rivers of Loch Ness

The deep and mysterious waters of Loch Ness are fed by some excellent rivers. Draining from the north, Glen Garry and Glen Moriston contain major rivers who's waters are largely diverted by hydo-electric power schemes. The best chance of catching these runs is to take advantage of the weekly compensation flows released in the summer months. From the south, the rivers Fechlin and Farigaig are classic runs on a wet day. For those who like to explore there are many great adventures to be had on the smaller rivers of the area; the Tarff standing out as a superb journey through an impressive gorge. If you are after an easier trip then the Oich and Ness at opposing ends of the loch provide a tamer alternative. When dry you will find this area rather limiting. It does however come into its own when the rivers are 'maxing out'. The Fechlin can, and has been paddled with almost as much water as you could care to imagine and the Coiltie is another river which must wait for a 'super wet' day.

Ness 038

Grade	**1/2**
Length	**9km**
OS sheet	**26**

Introduction The Ness flows from the north end of Loch Ness, through Inverness and into the Beauly and Moray Firths. It has a series of grade 1/2 rapids with sections of gentle grade 1 between. All the rapids can be portaged, but generally easy routes become evident if scouted. Small surf waves and good eddy lines can be found at different locations depending on river levels and movement of rocks; there is always something to provide some fun.

Water Level This river runs all year round, though it can get a little 'scrapey' here and there.

Gauge The Ness is tidal up as far as Bught Park/Islands, so the best gauge is the Dochfour Weir. If you can see rock all the way along, it's very low; no rock and it's high; partially covered, it's normal flow. If strong westerly winds have been in force for some time it can push water down Loch Ness and into the river, improving conditions.

Access The usual access point is at Dochgarroch (618 404) about 3 miles down the A82, driving from Inverness to Fort William. If the

car park is full, or you fancy a bit of loch paddling first, then you can put on in Lochend, the next village 2 miles upstream. The take-out is in Bught Park, Inverness (664 440), either at the end of the playing fields or by the white suspension bridge at the islands.

Description From Dochgarroch paddle up the canal to where the river starts, either carry over the grass weir bank or continue up to the top weir to begin your trip. The first weir, Dochgarroch Weir, is usually paddled down the main chute. In times of flood, a surf wave appears the full length of the weir. A series of flat sections and short rapids follow. Have a look for playspots on the way down as many of the rapids provide some amusement at the right level. Rapids with good eddy lines for starting those play moves are Fast Eddy (river right of the first mid-river wall) and Dragons Tail (next rapid down, river left). After these entertaining rapids comes another dilapidated weir that gives nice surf waves, then Torvean/Holm Mills Weir with three sluice gates visible (avoid these). Either choose a line down next to them, or paddle to the far end and look at the options. The main chute may have large rocks in it making it unwise to run if there is a possibility of a capsize. These move with time, but inspection before running is recommended. Gentle rapids follow down into Inverness. Kingfishers, ospreys, otters, herons and grebes, amongst others, have all been seen by the river, so keep a good look out as you float along.

Contributor:
Steve Mackinnon

Other important points Weirs are dangerous - although the Ness weirs are regularly run. Rocks, spikes, and debris are common, inspect and choose. The Ness is heavily fished - estate fishing as far as Torvean/Holm Mills Weir, then Local Angling Association down to the sea. Excellent relations are held with the local anglers - please treat their members with the respect they have earned.

039 Coiltie

Grade   **4/5**
Length   **5km**
OS sheet   **26**

Introduction The Coiltie is the smaller of two rivers that flow into Loch Ness at Drumnadrochit. It does however offer far more white water than its close neighbour the Enrick. The Coiltie is a fast and continuous river with rapids that are always pushy, but never desperate. It's a rocky trip with a fair share of trees and other hazards to avoid.

Water Level Very wet. This river requires heaps of water and sadly runs only rarely. It could be a good option if the nearby Affric and Abhainn Deabhag are too high.

Gauge When viewed from the A82 road bridge at Lewiston, the bouldery river bed should be getting on for fully covered for the run to be high enough.

Access Turn off the A82 at Lewiston and drive upstream on the river left bank. Follow the road first right then left to find the small bridge where the public road crosses the river on the way to the Falls of Divach. You can check the level again here. At time of writing there was a tree in the river above the bridge, which needed some thought. To find the road upstream, back-track towards Lewiston and find the forest road that branches off on the river left bank. In a few hundred metres a locked gate is reached and it is on foot from here. Take out in Lewiston on river left, just upstream of the A82 road bridge.

Description It should be possible to run a longer section of river from the head of the glen, starting beyond the edge of the forest. But if like us, your shoulders ache after carrying your boat for 3km you will find a place to bushwhack down to the river some distance before then. From where we put in, the river went straight into the best of the white water in a shallow gorge. It will be worth walking far enough to make sure you find this and it is also a good idea to scout the gorge before entering, as there are a couple of river-wide ledges to jump. After this the river continues in fine form with one more narrow twisting rapid, which approaches grade 5. Now with quite an alpine character, the river opens out and winds its way steeply through the forest as one long boulder rapid with many sharp corners and trees to avoid. After the road bridge the river is considerably easier on the final 2km to Lewiston, but it is still an entertaining and fast grade 3.

Contributor:
Andy Jackson

Other important points There is a fair gradient in the upper river so there must be some good white water above the section described here. Any takers?

040 Farigaig

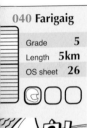

Grade	**5**
Length	**5km**
OS sheet	**26**

Introduction The River Farigaig bursts into the south side of Loch Ness, 12 miles north of Fort Augustus. A single-minded river, the Farigaig is determined to reach Loch Ness by any means possible. In its final few kilometres, it has cut a deep gash through the wooded hillside containing a long series of drops and falls. The journey from open farmland through the narrow canyon and into the wide expanse of Loch Ness feels like a real river journey with a definitive end.

Water Level Wet. Some rain needs to have fallen in the previous week, but it doesn't still need to be raining when you get on.

Gauge At Inverfarigaig the B852 crosses the river, which flows beneath the road via a short tunnel. Looking downstream from here the river should appear navigable with the odd rock showing but definitely not pumping. If you can cleanly float this run out the river has enough or too much water.

Access Coming from Fort Augustus, you take the B862 north-east along the south side of Loch Ness. Follow the signs for Foyers turning onto the B852. You will arrive at the gauge bridge described above. The best take-out is at an old pier on the side of Loch Ness a few hundred metres south of here. Crossing the river continue north on the B852 for 300m to find a road branching right and climbing steeply up the hill. Leave first gear at your peril, and note that to date no successful ascents have been made of this road with a canoe trailer. Follow the aged tarmac for 2½ miles until the electricity pylons join the road. A few hundred yards beyond here park and carry down to the river.

Description From the put-in, 1½km of flat water brings you to an old bridge where your mind should begin to focus on the trip ahead. The river leads you in with some nice read and run water, which has been known to lull paddlers into a false sense of security. A couple of large falls definitely require a scout, including the Falls of Farigaig, which are made more difficult by a tricky step and run in. Even though the successful descent of these falls may be as fresh in your memory as it is in your camera, don't relax too much, the river still has many more tricks to throw. Watch out for Tree Top Falls - a 3m slide that is uglier than it first appears.

The final section of the river is announced with a large bedrock slab. From here there are no more large drops. However, the river doesn't ease quite yet, and the final boulder section gives cause for respect, providing non-stop action at high flows. The hectic confined nature of this section is in complete contrast to the sheer expanse of Loch Ness. Turn left for the pier and the take-out.

Contributor: Dave Waugh

Other important points At flood levels this river would be a severe undertaking even by modern standards.

Fechlin 041

Grade **4(5)**
Length **9km**
OS sheet **34**

Introduction The Fechlin lies to the south of Loch Ness and runs northwards. Pool-drop by nature, all the rapids on the Fechlin are easy to inspect, protect, photograph or portage - better still they are all runnable, and if quality grade 4/5 is your thing, this river should not be missed. Sadly a new dam has been added to the River Fechlin and the river is now a shadow of its former glory! 1km downstream of the put-in, a large intake weir takes the lion's share of the water and it's not returned until the final series of rapids. In really big spates, the run will still be possible but exercise caution at the new intake point and associated pipeline crossings.

A further hydro scheme is planned for the upper catchment of this run and it is envisaged that this will leave the river all but unrunnable. You can find more details on this and other schemes affecting rivers in Scotland at www.scot-canoe.org/access/hydro.htm. Please take a look and find out how you can stop other great Scottish rivers suffering the same fate.

Water Level Wet/Very wet. The Fechlin is fed from Loch Killin and responds well to rain or snowmelt. A lot of its catchment is high in the hills and gets frozen up in winter, so wait for that elusive sudden spell of warm wet weather for big levels! The small loch will help the river to stay up for a short period after the neighbouring burns have dropped. When the river is just high enough it will be a slightly rocky grade 3 trip with a handful of tight grade 4's. At a high flow it will feel more like 3/4 all the way with some of the 4's touching on 5. The Fechlin has been paddled at super high flows and is a good run to head to when the rivers are 'maxing out'. The wide river bed and the general lack of tree problems make it a good choice in such conditions. At full flow it's a fast grade 5 trip with one or two terminal holes to portage.

Gauge Due to the new hydro scheme, the best bet for judging the flow is now a distant viewing from the minor road on the way to the put-in. A good covering of the boulder sections is needed to make the run worthwhile.

Access Put in at Loch Killin. Follow the B862 from Fort Augustus taking the right turn just before White Bridge. Park just before the bridge at the end of the loch. The take-out is at the old dam and hydro works, the road to which you will have passed on the way up the glen. Park at the gate by a hydro-electric sign for the 'Fechlin Out-Take'. This is the best parking spot but keep the gate clear for hydro traffic.

Description The Fechlin starts in an uninspiring fashion, high up on a windswept loch and running through shallow boulder fields for the first couple of kilometres. Don't worry - the action starts soon enough. It would be pointless to describe the rapids in detail, but most of them are tight, twisting and difficult to read well from the river so inspection is recommended - if for nothing else than to check for trees and debris brought in by the rise of the river. You may recognise Multiple Choice (Gd 4/5). At most levels this is the most challenging rapid with several lines possible, criss-crossing from left to right or right to left to finish either side of the final drop. There are about five grade 4 rapids, a couple of grade 5's (but not at the hardest end of that grade) and a sprinkling of grade 3's to keep you entertained. You will need a good few hours to run the river, and even a small, slick group of 4 paddlers will take a couple of hours to reach the take out. A larger, less-experienced group will take all of the available daylight - and why not? It is after all a very photogenic, constantly interesting and difficult river. The Fechlin is not full of interesting playspots but there are some tempting splat-rocks and the occasional hole or pour-over with enough depth to sink an end or two.

Other important points Beware of the deer fence a few hundred metres above the dam. Paddlers from warmer climes (Devon for example) should remember that this river is high up in the hills and both the water and air temperature are usually cold. A swimmer is likely to become a hypothermia casualty, so make sure you are adequately prepared with the right equipment and the right attitude for Scottish winter conditions. Take out above the second hydro dam on river left. It is a short walk back up the track to the car. If enough water is going over the dam you can continue on downstream to White Bridge. Portage round the barrage on river left. Cross the bridge just downstream and follow the track on river right for 50 metres. You can then scramble down a gully to get back on the river just below a nasty cataract. From here at a high flow it is a short bouncy run down to White Bridge.

Contributor:
Dave Alldritt and
Andy Jackson

Affric 042

Grade **4/5 (5+)**
Length **5km**
OS sheet **26**

○○○

Introduction The section described runs down the east end of Glen Affric, a beautiful and sparsely populated area west of Drumnadrochit. This is a classic run that provokes normally sane individuals to rave incoherently for months. A good trip, but with a fair share of portaging.

Water Level The flow is dam controlled, making this a difficult run to catch at the right height. A small amount of water is released at all times, but this is not enough to do the run. Flood conditions are way too high, but provide a good playhole at the put-in. The river is best run as the water drops off after a big spate.

Gauge If the top section, which runs beside the road down to Dog Falls, looks runnable but not huge, the trip is worth considering.

Access From Drumnadrochit, drive up the A831 turning left at Cannich. Follow the road through the forest and into Glen Affric, an inspiring place. The river spends most of its time well hidden from view in a mini gorge. Put in at the Forestry Commission car park, about a mile before the hydro dam that robs the river of its life-force. Take out above Fasnakyle Power Station, at the obvious roadbridge.

Contributors:
Duncan Ostler
and Duncan Fraser

Description The trip starts gently and builds steadily, until you reach Dog Falls. This gnarly looking fall probably still awaits a descent. Portage and inspect on river left. Good rapids follow, until the river runs through a large boulder choke. It goes on the right with care. A left-hand bend follows, then a right-hand

corner, which marks the start of a gorge, and some big rapids. Madness, a large grade 5+ multi-tier fall, contains some meaty water and is usually portaged. Just upstream lies a tempting 3m drop, The Edge of Madness, which is as fun as it looks. It should however be considered very carefully and no bold or rash decisions made without first checking your insurance policy. A flip here could lead to the first descent of Madness whether you want to or not. The next large 2-stage rockslide is fast and fun and probably the best rapid of the trip. After this another large fall presents itself. It is around 10m high and lands on rocks! It is possible to portage it on the left, up a VS 5a. After this everything is a piece of apple pie with custard.

043 Abhainn Deabhag

Grade	**4/5**
Length	**2km**
OS sheet	**25**

Introduction The Abhainn Deabhag starts off as a little burn flowing down from the head of Glen Affric, before cutting its way through a very deep canyon into which cascades the 80m Plodda Falls. This run starts out pretty normal but then drops into two canyons that feel really committing. It is one of the most impressive runs in Scotland, feeling as though it has been stolen from South America. Deep gorges, hard rapids - a definite must for all adventure paddlers.

Water Level Medium Wet/Wet. This is a good one to do at a medium level for your first time. If the river is high you can still have a fast and exciting trip, but you'll need to portage the gorges. At lower flows when the top rapids would be scrapey you can carry up from Plodda Falls and enjoy a short paddle through the lower gorge.

Gauge Walk down to Plodda Falls from the car park and look into the gorge. For the full trip to be on, the gorge will look pretty powerful. At the put-in most of the rocks need to be covered.

Access From Drumnadrochit, drive up the A831 turning left 1 mile before Cannich. Follow the road to the small village of Tomich. Drive through the village turning left onto a rough track signposted Plodda Falls. Keep going for about 1½ miles until you reach the Forestry Commission car park. This is the take-out and

best place to scout the gorge. The put-in lies 1½ miles further up
the track, at a wooden bridge over the river.

Description There is a grade 4 ledge immediately below the put
in followed by a kilometre of pleasant grade 3/4 with the odd
tricky drop. One of these is possibly grade 5 and has a tree across
the river immediately below it. This brings you to the first gorge,
which is scoutable from river right. The 7m drop into the gorge
(Gd 5) is deceptively hard and was full of trees at the last look.
The next rapids are high-speed grade 5, where a mistake will be
very painful. After this the river eases off a little, before the banks
begin to steepen and almost before you know it, the second
gorge appears. This is about ½km long, providing constant grade
4 and 5 paddling (grade 5/6 in high water): well worth scouting
before getting on. The paddling is quite serious with powerful
holes and the odd tree blocking the way. The action peaks at
the S-bends where Plodda Falls tumbles into the river. Here the
drops come quickly one after the other and care is needed. After
the final drop (or just before if you prefer) you are out of the gorge,
egress on the right and walk up to the car park.

Contributors:
Dave Kwant and
Duncan Ostler

Other important points Care should be taken as this burn can
come up very quickly.

Moriston (Upper) 044

Introduction The Moriston drains in an easterly direction from
Loch Cluanie to Loch Ness. This dam-controlled run has some
dramatic rapids in a beautiful setting. It has two very short action
packed sections, both pool-drop in nature, making for an easy
shuttle if you only have one car. Make sure you bring your camera.

Grade **4(4+)**
Length **500m**
OS sheet **34**

Water Level The dam releases once a week throughout the
summer months and occasionally after heavy rain in the winter.
At the time of writing, the summer release was for 24 hours, starting midday Tuesday. Check www.scot-canoe.org for any update.

Gauge To gauge the flow, look over the old bridge in Invermoriston. It will be obvious if the dam is releasing. If the river is wall
to wall at the playhole under the bridge, you have more water
than a standard release. At the usual release, the whole of the

upper run is grade 4. Sometimes, particularly in the winter, a higher volume of water may be spilling. If you get to the put-in and the river looks high and the rapids full-on, you may wish to take a wander down the bank before you decided to get on.

Access To reach the put-in for the upper section, turn off the Fort William to Inverness road at Invermoriston, and follow the A887 towards Kyle of Lochalsh. After about 4 miles you reach a power station. Park at the top of the road leading to the dam and walk down to the river. To find the take-out, drive back down the road for a little under ½ mile and park in a lay-by made by a loop of old road on the right-hand side.

Description The first rapid is just below the put-in and is probably worth inspecting before you get on. Both sides of the island can be run. The left is an intimidating but straightforward drop, which is nicer than it first looks, whilst the right is more technical – watch out for the undercut left wall! The river continues with a couple of rapids and playspots before a narrow drop brings you to a big pool and next horizon line. This photogenic 1m ledge is best inspected from river right. A choice of routes through the next section leads to a river-wide hole, responsible for some impressive unintentional cartwheel sequences. Taken fast, right of centre, it goes OK even in little boats. A good splat spot, and a couple of waves for those brave enough, bring you round the final bend to a shallow playwave, which improves with a little more water. Take out on river left and climb up the handy granite slabs to the road. Turn left and walk the short distance back to the lay-by.

044 Moriston (Lower)

Grade	4/5
Length	500m
OS sheet	34

Introduction The lower section is shorter but more dramatic than the upper, with an awesome slab and a reasonable playhole for those in low volume boats.

Water Level The weekly summer release provides enough water for this section.

Gauge To gauge the flow, look over the old bridge in Invermoriston. This is the hardest rapid, and not everyone's idea of fun, but it should be obvious from this whether the dam is releasing.

Access To reach the put-in for the lower section, stop at the large public car park next to the A82 in Invermoriston. Cross the main road and view the river from the old bridge. A path leads from the take-out back to the car park, and can be used to inspect the run before you get on.

Description Put in either above or below the rapid just upstream of the old bridge. The main line down the left is a two-stage affair with most of the water crashing into the left-hand wall. Don't even think about getting this one wrong. The chicken shoot down the right is a staircase of small falls. The one just above the bridge is very shallow, and a potential pinning spot for the unwary. A playspot forms beneath the bridge, which is fun, but just not quite deep enough. After a short lead-in the river splits around an island. Take the left channel, down a smooth narrow drainpipe. The last main rapid appears quickly, and has a powerful stopper near the end, just above an undercut wall. Just below this is a good but tricky playspot and one last small rapid before the banks begin to flatten. Take out river left immediately after the last rapid and walk back through the woods to the car park at the put-in.

Contributor:
Bridget Thomas

Oich 045

Grade	**1 (2)**
Length	**9km**
OS sheet	**34**

○○○

Introduction Situated in the Great Glen, this river flows north east out of Loch Oich into the south-western end of Loch Ness at Fort Augustus. Beware of Nessie! The Oich flows parallel to the Caledonian Canal for much of its length and offers an alternative for parties touring the Canal from west to east. It is fairly flat with only one or two rapids of any note. There is also a weir at the start of the river, where it flows out of Loch Oich.

Water Level The river is fairly shallow in places and needs a reasonable flow of water to avoid too much of a bump and scrape in the rapids. Water levels will be increased if the River Garry hydro-electric scheme is releasing.

Gauge Look over the A82 road bridge at Bridge of Oich to check the amount of water spilling over the weir out of Loch Oich. If the whole length of the weir is covered with a stopper/wave formed along it, then the river will be at a good level and most of

the rocks in the rapids will be covered. If only a small section of the weir or none of it is covered then the rapids will be bumpy, a consideration for fibreglass touring boats.

Access There is room to park at Bridge of Oich, between the canal and the river (337 036). Access the river either from the field by the car park or by launching into the canal and paddling round into Loch Oich. Egress at Fort Augustus from the river mouth, river right bank, parking between the canal and the river mouth at (382 094). Further parking is available by the petrol station on the main road.

Description This is a pleasant and straightforward run. The weir at the outflow from Loch Oich can be avoided by keeping to the river left. The run has heavily wooded banks in places and occasionally trees get washed downstream. Beware also of overhanging trees and those blocking the eddies at high/flood levels.

Contributor:
Rory Stewart

Other important points There are public toilets, cafes, a petrol station and a pub at Fort Augustus.

046 Tarff

Grade	**5**
Length	**4km**
OS sheet	**34**

Introduction Running from the north side of the Corrieyairack pass, the river Tarff follows the remains of General Wade's road and eventually joins Loch Ness at Fort Augustus. If you're looking for a bit of adventure in your river running, this one could be for you. The Tarff provides loads of tight, rocky and testing rapids, set in a series of deep gorges. Several unrunnable cataracts make for a trip that is hard work, but very rewarding.

Water Level Wet. A moderate amount of rain is needed; if the Nevis is just high enough to run, the Tarff could be on. This is not a river for flood conditions, when things could get a bit out of control!

Gauge The rapids immediately above and below the take-out give the best indication of the river level. They should be floatable with the odd rock showing. There is a gauge by the take-out bridge, which is in two parts. Looking at the lower half of the gauge 0.9 would be a good minimum flow. 1.1 would be ideal and above 1.2 the upper gorge would be hard and continuous.

Access Turn off the A82 one mile south of Fort Augustus, towards Ardachy. After 300 yards, park at the foot of General Wade's road. It's a long slog up the track to the river. Reckon on 1½ hours walk with your boat to the upper put-in. Take out at the bridge at Ardachy which is ¼ mile further along the road (380 075).

Description The river has been paddled from (388 037), around 4km upstream of the road bridge. Cut down to the river from the point where the high voltage electricity line crosses the track for the 3rd time. There is ample scope for walking further up and exploring the upper river, which must have some good white water. Has anyone paddled this bit? From the put-in described, the river flows straight into a tight and committing gorge (Gd 5). You can inspect this before getting in by walking along the path cut into the wooded gorge on river left. Easier water leads to another tight gorge. This is at the point where a fence drops down to the river on the right-hand side. Don't even think about paddling into this gorge; it has a horrible syphon at the entrance. Portage around on river left using the handy path and lower your boats back into the depths of the gorge. Really good water leads to the next even deeper gorge! And yes, you guessed it, the next portage. A steep boulder rapid blocks the entrance, (384 054). The upper part might be runnable, but we didn't try it. Portage at river level, beneath the towering cliffs on river left. A cunning plan is to seal launch back into the river once you are past the worst and then scamper across to river right, from where you can inspect and run the rest of this impressive rapid. The next section is amongst the best on the river and you could consider getting on here if the river is really high. There are a couple more grade 5's and an awkward portage before the river eases to grade 2 for the last kilometre. The last portage involves clinging to a slimy ledge on river left, feeling as though you might at any moment fall into the jaws of death, as the river tumbles below you. Scary stuff!

Contributor:
Andy Jackson

Other important points Not a river to be underestimated; it is best paddled at a moderate flow to make sure you don't get swept into anything nasty. The run would be lunacy in anything but a short creek boat.

047 **Garry (Upper)**

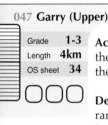

Grade	**1-3**
Length	**4km**
OS sheet	**34**

Contributor:
Bridget Thomas

Access To reach the upper river beyond the Loch Garry, turn off the A87 where the road climbs away from the loch, and follow the minor road towards Kinloch Hourn.

Description This stretch is controlled by a series of dams and rarely has water in it. The river is mainly flat, with several small lochs and some bouldery rapids, but makes an interesting touring trip. When the river is high, there is a good surf wave / hole on a grade 3 rapid below Loch Poulary.

047 **Garry**

Grade	**3+**
Length	**4km**
OS sheet	**34**

Introduction The Garry drains the hills to the west of the Great Glen, entering Loch Oich below the village of Invergarry. It is a scenic river offering solid grade 3 rapids and good play opportunities. Its short, sustained play section makes this an ideal one-car trip.

Water Level The dam on Loch Garry releases one day a week from April to October. The timing of this release varies. The dam may also spill when there is a lot of water around in the winter.

Gauge The best place to gauge the flow is at White Bridge, the take-out for the main section. The last rapid is immediately above the bridge. Alternatively, to spare yourself the drive up Glen Garry, you can get a good idea of whether the river is flowing by peering through the trees as you turn off the A82. 0.6 on the SEPA gauge should be considered a minimum level.

Access To get to the main take-out, turn off the A82 Fort William to Inverness road, towards the village of Invergarry. Follow this road, the A87, through the village and past the shinty pitch, looking for a signpost to a Forest Enterprise car park and picnic site on your left. There is a car park by the bridge. To get to the put-in either walk up the path on river right inspecting as you go or drive back to the Glen Garry road and follow it uphill for a further ½ mile to the next left turn. Park by the Council's works yard (please do not impede their access) and walk down to the river. The path to the river is blocked by a large gate, which may be locked. If you wish to extend your trip, the lower take-out is reached by driving back to the A82. Turn left and then first right towards Invergarry Castle / Hotel. Park at the bridge by the War Memorial. Please show consideration for the family living here. There is considerable history relating to access on the Garry. The landowner is keen to see the land working for him and favours paying guests such as rafters and fishermen.

Description The Garry is a wonderful river that caters for both intermediate paddlers, challenged by the many grade 3 rapids, and playboaters, desperate to get wet in the summer months. The top section contains 5 main rapids, all with play possibilities. The main hole is not too big and has a huge eddy below it, for those with a shaky roll. There are also good eddy lines and cartwheel spots for those with short boats. If you still paddle a larger boat, don't worry, this river has awesome pop-out potential! Below the first bridge, which is the usual take-out, there are three main rapids separated by long flat stretches. Each one has a twist in the tail for the unwary: watch out for trees in the bottom rapid. It's easiest to take out immediately beyond the second bridge.

Contributor:
Mags Duncan Stirling

Allt Ladaidh 048

Access Paddle across Loch Garry and walk up the path on river left for around 2km.

Grade	**4/5**
Length	**2km**
OS sheet	**34**

Description This challenging run offers a variety of drops of all shapes and sizes – expect some portaging.

Contributor: Dave Waugh

Allt Abhiora 049

Introduction This burn flows under the road to Skye and on into the north side of Loch Garry. The Allt Abhiora is not so much a river as a single line flume with the occasional plunge pool.

Grade	**5**
Length	**1/2km**
OS sheet	**34**

Water Level Very wet. With an almost instantaneous run-off, it will need to be raining on the day for this one.

Contributor:
Dave Waugh

Gauge It is easy to check the flow from the bottom of the run.

Access Turning off the A82 at Invergarry, take the A87 towards Skye. After 5 miles turn left onto a minor road that heads along the lochside towards Tomdoun. You reach the burn after 1½ miles at a humpback bridge. This is the take-out. The put-in is found by returning to the main road and turning left up the hill. Yes, that tiny ditch you cross after 1 mile is the river! Parking here is very limited and care should be taken as this is a fast piece of road. The best you can manage is to drop off the boats and park further up the hill.

Description A good example of old school Topo paddling, this burn has got it all. Everything has been paddled but some of it is very sketchy. Make sure you bring a full face helmet and elbow pads.

050 Garry Gualach / Allt Garaidh Ghualaich

Grade	**4/5**
Length	**2km**
OS sheet	**34**

Introduction The Garry Gualach is found at the west end of Loch Garry, south of Inchlaggan, (171 005). This is an interesting trip of an exploratory nature involving a paddle across the loch followed by a walk-up. A new hydro scheme is to be built on this run. At the time of writing it is not known what effect if any this will have on the section described.

Water Level Wet. If the majority of the popular runs in the area are in good shape, this should be OK. Avoid it at really high levels.

Gauge The burn from Lochan Torr a Gharbh Uillt at Inchlaggan will give a good indication of the level. If there is a good flow here, the river should be OK. If it's stonking, maybe you should go elsewhere. In high water the river becomes a serious undertaking with some powerful hydraulics. In the past, these have dissuaded some very strong teams looking for a first descent.

Access Turn off the A87, Skye to Invergarry road, onto the minor road signposted to Kinloch Hourn. Continue to just past Inchlaggan where a path down to the loch provides access to an old foot ferry. There is some parking and a gate leading to a small path down to the loch. Once on the loch, follow the old road signs (the now flooded road lies beneath you!) across to the south side of the loch. At Garry Gualach a path on river left leads south-west. Follow this for around 2km until the valley flattens and a deer fence crosses the river.

Description Hopefully the adventurous nature of the approach has not put you off and having found the put-in, you should be nice and warm and ready to paddle. The river is mixed in nature, starting out quite open and bigger than expected. Ledge drops and slides are the order of the day, some steep with big pools along the way, some long and shallow, all good fun though. One ramp in this upper section has a shallow and rock-infested pool and is probably a portage. At high flows there are some meaty holes. The main rapids of concern come next as the river narrows down to a twisting tight gorge. A double slab is hidden within, and inspection is recommended as the line varies with water level. Below this the river accelerates round a left-hand bend with a large and broken fall just below. This has been paddled via the staircase on river right. After this the river eases, although you should look out for a fence and one more drop, as well as a weir feature and wires which may still cross the river towards the end. All that's left is to follow the signs back across the loch. Hopefully you got the water level right!

Contributor:
Stew Rogers

Other important points This is a little paddled river, quite remote in nature, suited to small self sufficient teams. Have a good method sorted to carry your boats.

Loyne 051

Grade	**4(5)**
Length	**3km**
OS sheet	**34**

◯◯◯

Introduction The River Loyne flows alongside the A87, Invergarry to Kyle of Lochalsh road. From the viewpoint overlooking Loch Garry, the road drops down to the north with the dam of Loch Loyne away on your left. The Loyne is dam controlled, which makes it a treat to catch. The slow build-up of intensity draws you nicely to the biggest rapid, which is close to the end. Ancient Scots pine trees line the banks of this river, although they are sadly depleted in number and provide little shelter for man, beast, or kayaker.

Water Level Very wet. The loch has to be full and then it needs to rain some more.

Gauge Obviously the dam should be releasing! At the road bridge where you put on, the river should appear to be bank-full.

Access Access to the river is at the road bridge on the A87, just below the dam. There is a pull-in to accommodate vehicles next to the bridge. Egress from the river is on the A887, Invermoriston to Kyle of Lochalsh road, 1 mile below the junction of the two roads. Again there is some parking to be found here.

Description Putting on at the road bridge gives you a kilometre of grade 1/2 water to warm up those cold muscles. Watch out for the fence hanging in the river in this stretch. It can be paddled through, but care is needed. Eddy hopping will bring great rewards as the river picks up to grade 3 for a couple of drops, then up again to grade 4. By now the river has got definite charm and you are scampering for eddies as each horizon line arrives. There are a couple of grade 4 drops, the first having an undercut left wall at the bottom and the second being a raggy double drop into a narrow hole, before you reach McRaes Falls (Gd 5). Named after a Scottish freedom fighter who was allegedly gunned down by the security services on the road nearby, this impressive staircase of falls have been run on both sides, with the obvious chicken shoot (Gd 5-) being on the left. From here the river eases to offer some interesting grade 3 water before the confluence with the River Moriston. The Moriston is also dammed and is usually dry. In exceptional flood, it's worth continuing downstream: however that's another story.

Contributor:
Alastair Collis

Other important points The Loyne gives a feeling that you are away from the rest of the world but is actually never too far from the road.

052 Doe

Grade	**5**
Length	**2km**
OS sheet	**34**

Introduction The Doe is a medium-sized river forming part of the headwaters of the Moriston. At a high flow it's quite a powerful run with some good bedrock falls. A good option on a really wet day.

Water Level The Doe needs a lot of water as it is heavily affected by the intakes for the Glen Moriston power scheme. You need a big enough spate to fill these and leave some water for the river, perhaps similar conditions to those needed to bring the nearby Loyne into nick.

Gauge The last few drops behind Ceannacroc Lodge are a good place to judge the flow.

Access You need to tread a little carefully here as the river is accessed by the private road leading to Ceannacroc Lodge. We drove past the lodge and parked near the estate houses by the river. The estate staff were happy to give us permission to drive on up the road but I suspect this will very much depend on who you ask. You could avoid this being an issue by parking at the main road. This would add another 1km to the walk in. The put-in will be at the first road bridge over the river or via the tributary just downstream depending on the water levels.

Description A couple of bedrock rapids lead quickly to a large twisting slab. This is a real cracking drop but you want to make sure you stay upright as the pool has a very shallow look about it! Further downstream a 20m fall is an obvious portage, best on river left. The final ledges on the run-in to the lodge can contain big powerful holes at a high flow. In flood conditions the first of these below the old footbridge may need to be portaged.

Contributor:
Andy Jackson

Allt a Chaorainn Mhor 053

Access Driving east from the Cluanie Inn, the Allt a Chaorainn Mhor is the second burn you cross. Follow the obvious track to the east of the river, dropping down to begin the run at the start of the gradient.

Grade   **4(5)**
Length   **3km**
OS sheet   **34**

Description This short run is worth a blast if you are passing. The best drops are towards the end, with the last one just downstream of the A87 making a superb finish.

Contributor:
Andy Jackson

054 Shiel (Upper)

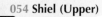

Grade **4(5+)**
Length **13km**
OS sheet **33**

Introduction On the road to Kyle of Lochalsh and the bridge to Skye, the Shiel drains west into Loch Duich. This is an easily accessed river for those who fancy a little exploring, with some flat water, some hard falls and an awesome cascade, which may or may not have been run.

Water Level Wet.

Gauge The river flows right next to the A87 and the flow is easily assessed.

Access Driving west from Loch Cluanie and the famous Cluanie Inn, the river starts to come together after about 3 miles. A trip can be started in a number of places. Take out at the lay-by opposite the path for the Forcan Ridge, about a mile downstream of the cascade.

Description The first half of this river contains some interesting features and a portage or two may be prudent depending on where you start and the level of the river. Watch out for the short tunnel seen easily from the main road. Immediately below the road bridge lies the main cascade. This is an awesome rapid, with a long staircase of falls. Sadly the final drop lands in a rather rocky pool. Although this looks eminently 'doable' I haven't spoken to anyone who has actually run this bit. It is an easy portage on river left and is followed by a nice boulder section before the river mellows on the way to the take-out. This trip probably has the most to offer to a group of experts who fancy their chances at the falls in the upper half and want to have a go at the cascade. Others will enjoy it for the journey alone and find the portaging none too arduous.

Contributor:
Andy Jackson

054 Shiel (Lower)

Grade **1(2+)**
Length **2km**
OS sheet **33**

Description The lower section starts at the take-out for the upper. It's a good beginner's trip with cracking scenery. There is a small gorge at Achnagart Farm (Gd 2+), and a weir just downstream of Shiel Bridge. There is also a playhole, where the Allt Undalain joins the river, particularly if this burn is in flood. Turn right where the river meets Loch Duich and take out at the slipway by the Kintail Lodge Hotel.

Contributor:
Bruce Poll

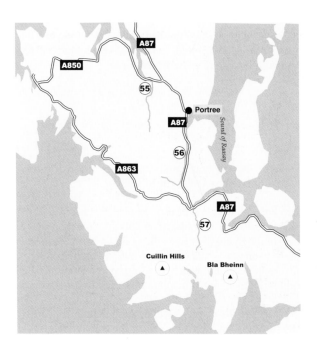

approx. scale 1cm = 5km   N

Skye's the Limit

Skye's the Limit

A few rivers have been paddled on the famous Isle of Skye. They all need a good amount of rainfall, so if it's wet and you wish to explore, this could be a good place to escape to.

055 Snizort

Grade   **3/4**
Length   **5km**
OS sheet   **23**

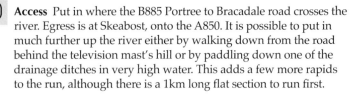

Introduction The Snizort flows in an open glen, over several bedrock falls.

Water level Very wet. Plenty of rain is needed as the river runs off quickly, although not as fast as the Sligachan.

Access Put in where the B885 Portree to Bracadale road crosses the river. Egress is at Skeabost, onto the A850. It is possible to put in much further up the river either by walking down from the road behind the television mast's hill or by paddling down one of the drainage ditches in very high water. This adds a few more rapids to the run, although there is a 1km long flat section to run first.

Description The river flows over several bedrock falls, the largest of which is around 3m high. One fall, at the end of shelved S-bend rapids, squeezes the entire river into a narrow drop which lands in an extremely deep pool. A must-make boof when the river is high, the hole that greets you can be rather 'engaging'. There is a rapid under the bridge at the take-out. Alternatively, carry on down the river until you reach the back of Skeabost Bridge Hotel. Egress onto the hotel road and walk back up to the bridge. Occasionally a playwave forms after the rapid beneath the remains of a footbridge.

Contributors:
Neil Farmer and
Andy Sime

056 Sligachan

Grade   **4/5**
Length   **800m**
OS sheet   **32**

Description This river lies halfway between Broadford and Portree on the A87 (A850), at Sligachan. Walk upstream from the Sligachan Hotel, for as far as you see fit.

Contributors:
Neil Farmer and
Andy Sime

Varragill 057

Description This run needs plenty of water and needs to look high. The river starts some 3 miles north of Sligachan and runs alongside the A87 all the way to the sea, just short of Portree. Scout from the road and choose your own stretch.

Grade	2/3)
Length	6km
OS sht.	23/32

Contributors:
Neil Farmer and
Andy Sime

Steep Creeking Workshops

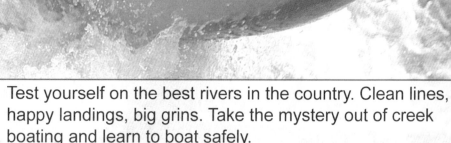

Test yourself on the best rivers in the country. Clean lines, happy landings, big grins. Take the mystery out of creek boating and learn to boat safely.

Creek boat coaching
Swift water rescue training and assesment
River guiding including instruction
Low water alternatives - canyonning and white water rafting

verticaldescents.com

Inchree Falls, Fort William   TEL: 01855 82159?

The West

Contents

Nevis - Fort William Area - Donald Patterson

Outflow - Fort William Area - www.breadandbutter.me.uk

Fassfern - Fort William Area - Andy Jackson

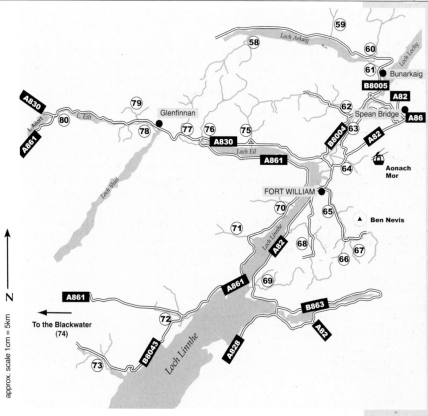

Fort William Area

The rivers around Fort William

From a paddler's point of view, Fort William is very much the capital of the Wet West Coast of Scotland. With rainfall recorded here on an average of 250 days per year, it's easy to see why. The rivers here are generally spate runs which are quick to rise and fall, sometimes frighteningly so! If you are unlucky and find dry conditions then perhaps Glen Spean to the north or Glen Etive to the south will be a better bet. When the rains come and the rivers rise the white water paddler is spoilt for choice. Go scare yourself on the Upper Nevis or Allt Chia-Aig, or try a more controlled trip on the Loy or Arkaig. There is something here to suit all tastes. In the town itself you will find plenty of choice for food and drink with the Nevisport Bar the most popular hang-out for boaters. There is also a good selection of outdoor gear shops, a climbing wall and swimming pool, and in the right season ski-ing or mountain biking at the nearby Nevis Range.

058 Allt Camgharaidh

Grade	**4(5)**
Length	**1km**
OS sheet	**33**

Introduction Tucked away on the 'wrong side' of Loch Arkaig, the Allt Camgharaidh is one of three rivers that drain into the loch at its western end. A short fun trip with the odd hole to keep you on your toes and a great drop to finish. It is well worth the trip up the tortuous road from the milk run on the River Arkaig.

Water Level Wet. No tiny burn, it should hold its water reasonably well, worth a peek after a period of moderate rainfall.

Gauge The best you can manage is to peer across the loch, 'Um' and 'Ah' thoughtfully, then toss a coin to decide if the paddle across the loch will be worth the effort. You will need to get a feel for how wet the day is from elsewhere.

Access From the put-in for the River Arkaig, drive west for what seems like forever, on the minor road beside the loch. At Rubha Giubhais (024 923), just before the road climbs away from the loch, you will find limited parking in a lay-by. It is a little under a kilometre to paddle across the loch, then a 1km walk up, best on river left. The tributary that cascades into the river on the far bank marks the most obvious put-in. The fit and keen could walk higher.

Description The river has a beautiful setting. It runs through an unspoilt and seldom visited glen, where remnants of Caledonian Pine forest provide a taste of Scotland long since gone. The river is not super steep, and without the toil of the walk in, you will be able to appreciate the beauty of the surroundings. Once on the river, occasional small ledges define the fun, with at least one hole which has a punchy feel. The best is saved till the end, with the last drop falling into the loch itself. This is Grizzly, a grade 5 with a tight line to avoid the cave behind the fall. The waters of the loch welcome you at the bottom; a great way to finish the trip. Well not quite, you still have to paddle back across the loch.

Contributor:
Andy Jackson

Allt Mhuic 059

Introduction A great little river with a nice series of clean drops followed by a slightly more adventurous section that awaits a descent.

Grade	**4(5)**
Length	**500m**
OS sheet	**34**

Water Level The Allt Mhuic can be run in any decent sized spate, but might be a little scrapey unless it's really going well. The level shoots up and down in no time at all!

Gauge This burn needs a similar flow to the Allt Chia-aig.

Access Follow directions for the put-in for the River Arkaig. You will find the river 4 miles further along the Loch Arkaig road where there is a small Forestry Commission car park. The best access is up the river left bank starting at the forest road bridge.

Description The first 6 or 7 drops offer the best of the action. They are generally clean and at high flows give a fast and action-packed run. All too soon the Big Shallow Drop appears and you will want to make sure you find a suitable eddy in good time. This drop does exactly what it says on the tin. The pool at the bottom is only 1.5m deep! We didn't run it. From here the river gets a bit more 'sketchy' with what looks to be at least two more meaty drops. It could still be good with enough flow, but this section needs more exploring. If you choose to end the trip here, it's just a quick scamper back to the car.

Contributor:
Andy Jackson

060 Allt Chia-aig

Grade	**4(5)**
Length	**2km**
OS sht.	**41/34**

Introduction The Allt Chia-aig is a tributary of the mighty River Arkaig. It is situated close to Fort William just north of Spean Bridge. Described as a true 'Highland epic' by those foolish enough to paddle this burn, the Allt Chia-aig is more of an adventure than an everyday kayaking trip.

Water Level Medium. The rivers need to be above their base level for this run.

Gauge Looking upstream from the road bridge, you want to have enough flow coming over the falls to float. Don't be put off by this cascade, some of the run is a little nicer!

Access See directions to the Arkaig. Park in the Forestry Commission car park just before you cross the Allt Chia-aig. Head up the forest walk, which leads steeply up through the trees. At the forest road, turn left and continue up the glen. When you can't be bothered to walk any further and the river upstream appears to be flattening off, cut down through the forest, aiming to get on below a large ugly fall (the entrance to the Alamo Gorge).

Description The first descent of this river had much to do with a dry spell in Fort William (in itself an unusual event), a drunken night in the commando bar and far too much testosterone floating around. All that you need to know about this river can easily be gleaned from a few quotes from the epic that followed.

> **❝** If I ever get out of this, I'm going to kill you."
> "Oh my God, I need a shorter boat."
> "Ouch."
> "He just went down!", "Yeah, which way?"
> "This isn't !?!?!?!?!? canoeing."
> "Remember the Alamo."
> Thump.
> "Did anyone bring a climbing rope?"
> "That was a nice drop, what's that doing on this river?"
> "It's getting dark. How many have we lost?",
> . . . "How many did we start with? **❞**

Contributors:
Andy Jackson and
Andy 'Blobby' Burton

Other important points Surprisingly this has now had several descents and even return visits.

Arkaig 061

Grade 2+(4)
Length 2km
OS sheet 41

Introduction A considerable river, the Arkaig drains a wild and remote mountain area close to Fort William. It links Loch Arkaig to Loch Lochy. The splendour of both lochs can be enjoyed from the put-in and take-out. The river offers only one difficult rapid, which can be portaged. The rest of the run has some surf waves, but nothing of great note. The banks in its lower reaches are overhung by the dreaded rhododendron bushes. Despite this, it is an entertaining paddle and a good run to do if time is short.

Water Level Mildly wet/Extremely wet.

Gauge Looking upstream from the road bridge at Bunarkaig (187 878), the last rapid can be seen. If this rapid is mainly rock with only one line, river left, the run will be low. No rocks here and the run will be high. The Arkaig rises slowly, due to the size of Loch Arkaig. It peaks the day after the rain has stopped and is often still worth visiting even several days after rain.

Access The Arkaig can be reached from just north of Spean Bridge, by turning onto the B8004 at the Commando Memorial. After crossing the Caledonian Canal, turn right and follow the signs to Bunarkaig. The obvious road bridge shows the last rapid. Parking is available at the bridge itself or at the take-out located beside the loch, some 200m before the bridge. To reach the top of the river, follow the road and turn left at the next collection of houses. Cross the Allt Chia-aig and park at the loch end.

Description From the put-in, paddle the short distance along the loch and under the road bridge. The pillars create some good eddy lines to warm up and play on. Heading on downstream, the river is flat until you come to a left-hand bend, where the river picks up. It is possible to get out onto a small island on the right to inspect the only major rapid of the trip (Gd 4), although getting out here may be interesting when the river is big. At high flows this rapid is quite impressive with big rolling holes and an alpine feel. Check out both sides of the island; if the river is high you may be tempted to carry back up to run the other side as well. A small surf wave in the pool gives everyone something to enjoy. The river from here slowly winds its way through the rhododendron bushes. There are more surf waves downstream but most are 'one shot wonders'. The last

Contributor:
Alastair Collis

rapid above the bridge comes all too soon. It is an easy grade 3 in all levels of water. You are now on Loch Lochy. The SCA agreed egress point lies just along the loch shore on river right.

Other important points The Arkaig is a run that obviously winds its way through someone's back yard. The banks are beautifully tended and ornate paths wind alongside the river to a summer-house. Please keep noise to a minimum, respect your surroundings and you will be made very welcome.

062 Loy

Grade	**3/4**
Length	**2km**
OS sheet	**41**

Introduction The River Loy flows south-east out of Glen Loy and into the River Lochy, some 3 miles north of Fort William. It is a short spate river, with a number of rapids and small drops, which provide great entertainment. Narrow and tree lined, fallen trees can end up in the river! The single-track road up Glen Loy is adjacent to the river bank for most of its length, making it easy to scout in advance.

Water Level Wet/Very wet. Needing lots of rain! Not altogether rare in these parts, but the relatively smaller catchment area of this river makes it slower to come up than the likes of the Roy. At very high levels the river gets into the trees and eddies disappear. At this flow the river should be considered a solid grade 4.

Gauge Inspect from the B8004 road bridge. When a lot of boulders are showing upstream of the bridge, then the run is low. These rocks need to be covered/almost covered for the river to be up enough to paddle. If the Lower Nevis is up then the Loy probably is too.

Access To reach the river, follow the B8004 (the back road between Spean Bridge and Fort William) until you cross the river at an obvious humpbacked bridge. Drive up the road beside the river until you reach the next bridge at Inverskilavulin (125 831). It is also possible to start the river further up the glen, but beware of fallen plantation trees, which in places block the entire width of the river. Take out at any point along the river, or just downstream of the B8004 road bridge at (148 818).

Description After a straightforward first kilometre, a series of drops
are encountered. The largest has 3 chutes. The usual line is down
the middle, but the landing pool is fairly shallow and boats have
become temporarily pinned here. If you start further upstream than
Inverskilavulin, the small island should be passed on its right-hand
side. Beware of river-wide strainers from adjacent plantations in this
upper section. It is also possible to continue downstream, through a
tunnel under the Caledonian Canal returning to the road via a small
side tunnel. This is a great fun way to end your trip and is highly
recommended. At very high water levels headroom in the tunnel
might be limited!

Other important points This fun paddle twins well with a trip to
the Arkaig. Parking at the take-out is a bit limited, so please try
not to obstruct the narrow road.

Contributor:
Rory Stewart

Lochy 063

Introduction The River Spean becomes the Lochy at Mucomir
Power Station and flows sedately to Fort William. This run provides a gentle introduction to moving water.

Water Level The river always holds water, but can become fast in
spate conditions.

Gauge You can check the flow at the put-in. The first shingle
rapids give a good indication of the trip. 0.6 on the SEPA gauge
should be considered a minimum level.

Access The best put-in is half a mile downstream of Mucomir
Power Station (184 838), on the back road from Spean Bridge to
Fort William, B8004. Take out just before Fort William at Inverlochy. Driving south towards Fort William, turn right off the A82
just past the junction with the A830 opposite the petrol station
(signed Inverlochy Castle). Take the first right, then immediately
left and park just through the railway bridge.

Description The run consists mainly of grade 1 shingle rapids with
one grade 2/3 on a left-hand bend at Eas nan Long (The Waterfall of
the Ship), more commonly referred to as Torcastle. At low water this
rapid is a straightforward shoot into a pool. With more water it

Grade **1 (2/3)**
Length **10km**
OS sheet **41**

becomes a powerful rapid with several alternative shoots, surging boils and powerful eddy lines. The take-out is marked by the outflow from the aluminium smelter. Depending on the river level and the state of the tide, this tailrace can provide a fine playspot but is more normally a boily mess. The river has a tendency to collect tree debris, which may become a hazard particularly at high flow.

Contributor:
Mags Duncan Stirling

Other important points It is possible to make a round trip by paddling up the Caledonian Canal from Neptune's Staircase, and portaging into the river at Gairlochy; possibly not the most exciting white water option!

064 Allt Daim

Grade	**5**
Length	**2km**
OS sheet	**41**

Contributor:
Alastair Collis

Access The first 3km of the approach to this run is up a forest road. After that there is a further 2½km walk to the top of the river. As the Alcan intake dries the lower half of this burn you really need permission to use the Forestry Commission road to make this run feasible.

Description Some classic slab paddling is on offer here. The first slab at (177 744) is a bit messy but the second, found ½km downstream, is a real classic! From here on, there is a mix of bedrock and boulders. A shallow drop forces a short portage where the river enters a mini-gorge. It gets steeper towards the end. Take out at or before the diversion weir at (167 757).

065 Nevis (Upper)

Grade	**4(5)**
Length	**3km**
OS sheet	**41**

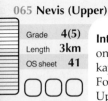

Introduction The River Nevis flows through a spectacular glen and on into Loch Linnhe at Fort William, the centre of white water kayaking on the west coast. With its hospital and hectic (!?) night life, Fort William itself caters for all eventualities. At a high flow, the Upper Nevis is one of Lochaber's test piece grade 5 runs: a rite of passage, giving entry into the 'big boys league'. There are few places on the run where you can afford to allow your concentration to slip from the task in hand and, until you are at the bottom of Polldubh Falls, your thoughts are constantly on what's coming up next.

Water Level Wet/Very wet. Typical Lochaber weather will bring the Nevis into good condition. The river comes up incredibly quickly, and in the frequent local monsoons it is often at or above a runnable level! In fact, if it's raining hard, the level may change dramatically whilst you're actually on the river. Any melting snow also helps the flow greatly. During the autumn and spring the Nevis runs frequently, but unfortunately not for long. It can be raging one afternoon, but then dry the next morning.

Gauge The Nevis rises and falls very quickly and so gauging it can sometimes be tricky. One option is to look up Meall an t-Suide, the hill at the foot of the glen. If two or more of the 'gauge burns' are running then the river could be at a good level. Driving up the glen, it is easier to judge the flow once at Polldubh Falls. There should be enough water to float the easy stretch above the falls: no rocks showing at all and you are in for an exciting time. 0.65 on the SEPA gauge should be considered a minimum level.

Access The Glen Nevis road is obvious from the roundabout by the Woollen Mill at the north end of Fort William on the A82. The road winds up the glen, crossing the river once at Polldubh Falls (145 684). The take-out is just below these falls on river right. There is a large car park just before the bridge, and a few spaces right beside the fall. To reach the put-in, continue on up the glen to a car park at the end of the road. From here it's on foot with your boat on your shoulder, following the path towards Steall Meadows. After 400m you cross a side stream via some steps cut into the rock. Turn off the trail onto a small path that leads down towards the river. You will arrive at the foot of the Steall Gorge, which is totally unrunnable. It is possible to put in at a small pool at the point where the river turns left and spills down an impressive boulder field.

Description Attempting a description of the first rapid, Boulder Blast (Gd 5), is useless. Suffice to say that it is probably the most continuous rapid of its grade in the area. Several lines are possible but a swim will hurt. From here the river is open and fast flowing, carrying you quickly to the start of the top gorge, signalled by the water pipe on river left. This gorge gets progressively harder and ends with Dave's Hole (Gd 5). Here the water pushes right, feeding you nicely into the hole and the

ride of your life. It is best shot on the left! The river now eases a little, but beware, the infamous Scimitar Gorge (Gd 5) is soon upon you. If you have any sense you will have found this from the road and memorised both your run-in and line through the gorge, or your take-out eddy. It is a place that demands respect, with 3 difficult drops in quick succession. Note well the dangerous sump, which lies on river right on the 2nd drop. If you need to be told the line in this maelstrom of water, you shouldn't be here! Once out at the bottom, don't let the euphoria take over, you are not out of the woods yet! Good grade 4 water (with one grade 5-) continues as you flush through the Mad Mile. As the rock turns from grey to pink, it is time to think of the next set of falls, unimaginatively named Leg Breaker after an incident at the annual sponsored raft race down the river - on lilos! This is followed closely by Dead Sheep Falls. A snappy roll may well come in useful if you flip at Leg Breaker, as it's hard to find a line down this grade 5 that doesn't involve being upside down. The hole at the bottom is often kinder than it looks and surfs are generally short but violent! The Nevis now saves its energy on the run into Polldubh Falls (Lower Falls). These falls have two shoots split by an island supporting the road bridge. It is wisest to run the main right-hand channel on the left. However, the other shoot, Spid's Slot, has had at least two descents, both unintentional and backwards! Take out 50m downstream on river right.

Other important points In recent years, the Upper Nevis has been the scene of a local speed challenge. At the time of publication, the record for a solo descent stands at 22 minutes 30 seconds. However, attempts to break this record come with a health warning. As they say on the TV, 'Don't try this at home'. At high flows it is worth checking the eddy above Scimitar Gorge before getting on if you plan to scout or portage it. Spid's Slot isn't recommended, and if you are here and backwards you have made a serious mistake!

Contributor:
Alistair Collis

065 Nevis (Lower)

Grade	2(4)
Length	8km
OS sheet	41

Introduction The Lower Nevis winds its way down the glen from Polldubh Falls, meanders through the lower stretches of Glen Nevis and continues on into Fort William. After the maelstrom of the Upper Nevis, this section is all in a nice open glen with riffles and waves giving most of the excitement. There is however, one major rapid near the bottom; portaging is simple.

Water Level Wet/Very wet.

Gauge As for the Upper Nevis, the 'gauge burns' on Meall an t-Suide, should both be visible for best results. A look over the A82 road bridge at the Woollen Mill in Fort William will give a good indication; few rocks - then go for it.

Access Turn off the A82 at the roundabout to the north of town next to the Woollen Mill. Follow the road up the glen passing an obvious rapid, the Roaring Mill after approximately 1 mile, and reaching Polldubh Falls after 4 more miles. The put-in is below Polldubh Falls on river right at a small eddy. The best egress point is from the large pool below the Roaring Mill, although it is also possible to kayak further down the river and into Loch Linnhe.

Description Putting in below the falls, the river is in a small gorge for a very limited time with several small waves and ledges. The banks soon fall away and you are left in the open glen with the river rushing on towards the sea. There are lots of places to practise ferry gliding and eddy turns. The new Visitor Centre passes by, and soon the noise and spray warns of the approaching Roaring Mill (Gd 4). Inspection here is necessary and portaging is easy on the left bank. This makes a good end to the trip as the last 2km are more of the same, but without the scenic views. If you continue into town be aware that as the Nevis drops into Loch Linnhe, there is a man-made weir that has a formidable towback in some conditions.

Other important points When the river is very high, trees start to crowd the eddies, making breakouts and rescue more difficult. In these conditions make sure you scout the take-out above Roaring Mill and get out in plenty of time if you don't intend to paddle it.

Contributor:
Alistair Collis

066 Allt a Choire Dheirg

Grade	**5**
Length	**500m**
OS sheet	**41**

Description Joining the Nevis below Polldubh, this run has been described as mountain surfing. Fast, shallow and lots of fun, it includes Sonic Slabs, which are quite a giggle.

Contributor:
Alistair Collis

067 Allt a Choire Mhusgain

Grade	**?**
Length	**500m**
OS sheet	**41**

Description Joining the Nevis at Polldubh Falls, this burn can be viewed by walking up the path to Stob Ban, part of the Ring of Steel. The drops are a little less clean than those on the Allt a Choire Dheirg, but this one is equally way out and virtually ungradeable.

Contributor:
Alistair Collis

068 Kiachnish

Grade	**4(5)**
Length	**7km**
OS sheet	**41**

Location The Kiachnish flows from Lochan Lunn Da-Bhra (lundavra), entering Loch Linnhe 3 miles south of Fort William. The Kiachnish is a great run, on a par with but slightly easier than the Upper Nevis. It begins in an open glen, flowing over a mixture of bedrock and boulders. The river then enters a steep-sided wooded gorge with good bedrock rapids. The last part of the river is less steep, and the rapids become more shingly towards the end.

Water Level Very wet.

Gauge The base of the bridge at the put-in has three large angled concrete steps (downstream, river left). If no more than 30cm of bottom step is showing, the level is too low. Ideally this step should only just be showing. As a rough guide if the Nevis is running at or above a medium level the Kiachnish should be runnable.

Access Driving north on the A82, you will cross the River Kiachnish 3 miles before Fort William. To get to the put-in, turn right at the roundabout as you enter Fort William (signposted to Upper Achintore). Follow this road, which soon becomes single track, until once again you can see the river off to your right. Put in at the large lay-by 200m before the bridge over the river (069 665). Take out back at the bridge over the A82 (067 691). Parking is limited here so try and leave the minimum number of vehicles. If you are a big group your best option would be to park in one of the lay-bys just south of here on the A82. This would mean a short paddle on the sea at the end of your trip to get back to your car but it would avoid any hassles with parking on the private road end.

Description 300m from the road bridge there is a 1m ledge drop. From here, the next 1½km is really good grade 3/4 paddling, best at a high flow when the odd river-wide hole spices things up. The river then eases to grade 2/3 for another 1½km, until a tributary joins on river right (094 687). Take care at the small weir just downstream which has some metal-work protruding from it. Barbed wire can be a hazard here. Those who have enjoyed this stretch but don't fancy the gorge below can carry up through the fields on river right to the road. The gorge starts with a good grade 4 and the rapids come thick and fast. It should be considered 4+ at high flows and could contain the odd tree. Scouting and portaging is generally straightforward and you should always be able to climb out if required. An extremely narrow slot stands out as being worth protecting (Gd 5). 200m below this comes the biggest fall on the river. Scout/portage this one on river left. Two lines are possible, the left being the most likely. Beware of the pinning potential on this drop, as there is an old fish ladder here. The river now eases to grade 3, but keep your wits about you as one last grade 4/5 waits for the unwary. The hole at the bottom of this one is a bit 'grippy'! From here it is a straightforward paddle to the take-out with the exception of a fence across the river which could be dangerous at high flows.

Contributors:
Callum Anderson and
Gregor Muir

069 Abhainn Righ

Description The Abhainn Righ flows into Loch Linnhe at Inchree, some 8 miles south of Fort William. The waterfalls here have been paddled more than once, each successive group thinking they were the first! However, they do not come recommended for those who value their body or their sanity, except as a nice place for a stroll, gorge walk or canyoning trip. The largest fall is about 16m high, followed by one of 12m and a couple of smaller ledges.

Contributor: Bridget Thomas

Grade	5
Length	**300m**
OS sheet	41

070 Abhainn Sron a' Chreagain

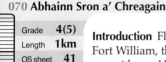

Grade	**4(5)**
Length	**1km**
OS sheet	**41**

Introduction Flowing into Loch Linnhe on the opposite shore to Fort William, the Abhainn Sron a' Chreagain is a steep and narrow run with good bedrock slabs, that eases in its lower half.

Water Level Wet/Very wet. Best when high, catch this run if you can - it drops off quickly!

Gauge The shingle rapids upstream of the road bridge should be paddleable with water to spare.

Access Coming from Fort William take the A830 towards Mallaig. At the head of Loch Eil turn left onto the A861 for Strontian. Opposite Fort William you will come to a river (071 725). Park in the large lay-by just before the bridge and follow the path upstream on river left. After about 1½km the path begins to peter out and it is time to drop down to the river. You could start higher up, but the best white water is now below you. Take out above or below the drop under the road bridge.

Description Initially the river is narrow with bedrock rapids and overhanging trees. You soon come to a good steep section, which at high flows would be pushing grade 5. A gnarly folding fall where the river S-bends is worth scouting. This fall is easy to check during the walk in, as it is close to the path. From here the river is a little less steep overall, but there are still a couple of eye openers. The drop under the road bridge is the sting in the tail. It looks a bit unfeasible but seems to go OK.

Contributor:
Callum Anderson

Other important points If the last fall looks beyond your abilities you might find the upper stretch a struggle.

071 Scaddle

Grade	**4**
Length	**1km**
OS sheet	**44**

Description A good small diversion if you're passing by or looking for something different, the Scaddle has 3 main rapids, the last being the biggest. Flowing into Loch Linnhe opposite the Kiachnish, this run needs lots of water. The Coe and the Kiachnish were both running the day we did it. To find the Scaddle, drive north on the A861 from the Corran Ferry to Aryhoulan.

Drive/walk about 1km up Glen Scaddle to the point where the
river valley flattens out and get on.

Contributor:
Neil Farmer

072 Tarbert

Introduction This is the river that runs east from the pass between
Strontian and Loch Linnhe. A short fun trip with convenient road
access, it is handy if you are on the far side of the loch and there is a
lot of water around.

Grade	**4(4+)**
Length	**1km**
OS sheet	**49**

Water Level Very Wet

Gauge A section of the old road runs next to the river and this
makes it very easy to check out the run before getting on. This
is to be recommended, as the main drop would be awkward to
scout once on the water. The river will need to be fairly full for
this run to be anything other than a rock-fest.

Access From the Corran Ferry, drive south on the A861. Just past
the junction with the B8043 the road turns inland. Half a mile
beyond this junction, the main road crosses a small stream and
it is possible to turn left onto the stretch of old road mentioned
above. This is the take-out. You could put in anywhere convenient further up the A861, or alternatively make use of the old
stretch of road to drive the short distance upstream.

Description A very small river, the Tarbert flows fast and flat
over shingle rapids for most of its journey down the glen. The
last kilometre of the river is contained in a small gorge, which
hides some grade 4 water. The rapids are very tight and, if the
river is only just high enough, they will involve a fair amount of
rock contact. As the gorge narrows the crux of the run appears.
This 2m fall is slightly blocked in nature and requires a committed move to avoid the cliff on the left (Gd 4+).

Other important points This short trip is worth combining with
something else. Perhaps the Blackwater, the Abhainn Sron a' Chreagain or the Abhainn na Coinnich. If this run looks harder than
you fancy, you might want to check out the Carnoch River which
flows down the west side of the pass towards Strontian.

Contributor:
Andy Jackson

073 Abhainn na Coinnich

Grade **4/5(5)**
Length **1km**
OS sheet **49**

Introduction The Abhainn na Coinnich drains the small Loch Uisge in Ardgour and runs east into Loch Linnhe. It is a cracking little river that lies well off the beaten track. Steep and rocky in its upper reaches, the Coinnich feels very much like a mountain burn. In its lower half the river has more power with stoppers and holes providing the main challenge.

Water Level Very wet. A new hydro scheme is to be built on this run. This will include a small dam at the end of Loch Uisge. It is expected that the extra water storage in the loch will mean that a bigger flow will now be required to bring the run into condition. Big spates should remain unaffected so if it's wet enough to bring the Coe into good nick, this could still be worth a look.

Gauge Check the flow where the river first drops down to the road from Loch Uisge (813 548). This is perhaps the rockiest section and you should be able to tell if you have enough water from here.

Access Drive south from the Corran Ferry on the A861. Take the left turn at Inversanda and follow the minor road along the shore, an adventure in itself. At Loch a Choire, the road heads inland and as you leave the forest at Kingairloch House, you can see the river to your left. Carry on upstream to check the level as described above and park by the shore of Loch Uisge. The trip ends at the bridge at Kingairloch House. The road into the estate is private and the easiest way to avoid getting into trouble is to carry the boats a short distance back upstream to the public road. Follow the path round the estate buildings, through the forest and up to the public road where there is a gate and passing place (835 535).

Description Paddle across the loch to its eastern end where a rocky weir marks the start of the trip. Hold on tight as you are straight away into the section that you saw from the road, and it will probably be steeper than you had expected! Take care as the river swings east down the valley, a large 3-tier waterfall (Gd 5) comes up quickly. The remains of a fish ladder lurk below the water on the 3rd drop so swimmers should keep their legs up! One more steep boulder strewn rapid on this upper stretch takes some thinking about, before easier water leads to the forest edge. A long section of grade 3/4 starts at a footbridge and gets more exciting as it goes. A tree wedged high above the river gives warning of a water level best avoided and marks the start of the best rapids. Scouting here is awkward but not to worry, everything goes at about grade 4/4+, with a couple of holes that you will want to punch. Keep a good eye out for trees, as there is some debris in and around the river. A rhododendron tunnel leads to the bridge and take-out.

Other important points Please try not to upset the occupants of Kingairloch House, who may be a little surprised to look out of the kitchen window and see you emerging from 'their' river. Small groups and a low profile will work best.

Contributor:
Andy Jackson

074 **Blackwater**

Introduction The Blackwater changes character along its length, with peaceful flat water leading to full-on bedrock falls and a final continuous bouldery gorge. It runs in a loop away from the road and gives a feeling of isolation very different from the popular runs of the Fort William area. Expert paddlers who want to do something 'a little different', will have a great time on this one.

Grade	**4/5**
Length	**8km**
OS sheet	**49**

Water Level Wet/Very wet. The river needs a lot of rain, but don't wait for flood conditions as the gorge section at the end could be a little too exciting at very high flows.

Gauge At the take-out, the river is less confined and should look a little bony, but with enough water to float between the rocks.

Access Driving south from Fort William on the A82, take the Corran Ferry across Loch Linnhe, then turn left and drive towards Acharacle. Take the left turn onto the A884 towards Lochaline. About a mile past the turn off to Kingairloch the tributaries of the Blackwater can be seen coming together on your right. To reach the put-in, park at the top of the hill before the road turns away from the river, and walk down the steep hillside. To get to the take-out and check the flow, continue towards Lochaline. Just as the river comes back to the road, there is a turn off to the right which leads to a house. There is plenty of room to park before the old stone bridge.

Description From the put-in, the river is almost completely flat for about 4km, with a wilderness feel and plenty of deer and

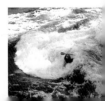

bird life. You'll be starting to wonder if there's any white water on the river at all, when you come cross the first rapid, Out of the Blue (Gd 5). A short run-in leads to an obvious horizon line and a steep shallow ramp into a boily pool. A potential pinning spot, this rapid warrants careful inspection. The river now eases again until you reach the next major grade 5, Black Beauty, marked by a bridge over the river. Inspect/portage on river left. This is the start of the white water proper. A fun grade 4 section quickly leads to Primrose Falls (Gd 5+), a serious set of drops that may go at the right level, although protection would be difficult. Portage river left. After the falls, the water is continuously interesting. You need to be on top of your game as the banks steepen through this final section. Some precision eddy hopping is required to make sure you don't get swept into one of several trees lodged in the gorge. Some can be avoided, whilst others require portaging. We managed this at river level. As the gorge walls drop away, a stone bridge appears which marks the take-out.

Other important points Although most of the paddling is grade 4, the river holds considerable hazard. With more than a handful of 'must make' eddies, this is not a place for a large or inexperienced group. If you can't see what's coming next, make sure you get out and look! If you wish to inspect the river before you commit or just want to paddle the last 2km, which has most of the action, there is a track which leads up from the take-out on river left. Paddling from the top does however give the trip a special wilderness feel.

Contributors:
Ryan Clements and
Bridget Thomas

075 Fassfern (An t-Súileag)

Grade	**4(5-)**
Length	**3km**
OS sheet	**42**

Introduction The Fassfern is found by the A830 at the small village of Fassfern approximately 6 miles west of Fort William. This scenic glen offers some nice boating and some long walking. The Fassfern, or An t-Súileag to give it its full name, is a mainly bedrock run with a tree-lined bank. There is on-going bank erosion and so there are often trees obstructing the run. The lower section is of the pool-drop nature and the upper section is a lot more continuous, with a lack of eddies making for some panic-stricken decisions.

Water Level Wet. It would help if the Nevis was big to get this baby running.

Gauge Standing on the road bridge in the village looking upstream, the river bed above the bridge is open and boulder strewn. The river is low if only a handful of the largest boulders are visible. If all that can be seen is bouncy water then the grades go up and the lower section becomes continuous.

Access From Fort William take the A82 north before turning off onto the A830. After approximately 6 miles a small sign points right towards Fassfern. Stop just over the bridge in the large car park. The road up the left side of the river before the bridge is a private road and is usually locked. If the gate is open the chances are that there is work going on. Taking a vehicle in here will result in it being locked in, possibly overnight. The only option is to walk up on river left. A brisk 30/40 minute walk brings you to a bridge over the river; 100m further on is a small mountain stream that crosses the road, this is your access point. Take out directly below the bridge on the right.

Description Straight from the put-in stream the river immerses you in its intensity with a series of small bedrock ledges that bring you out at Tango (Gd 5-). This triple fall is the hardest rapid in the lower section and can give a variety of interesting lines. The collection pool below this is huge, so any detritus is easily gathered before progressing further. The river is now bubbling along merrily and some swift moving grade 2 brings you to your next mission - 7UP (Gd 4-). This rapid is the longest one and as such deserves respect. The tricky start is followed by seven small ledges, the idea being to 'play' in each ledge. The river now wanders off with a couple of innocuous rapids. The next horizon line shows, as you approach it, a large roostertail. Running just to the right of this will land you in the hole at the bottom of Slider (Gd 4-). Just around the corner from here a chute brings you into the home straight. The last horizon line before the road bridge gives Backwards Slab (Gd 4). As the name suggests this is begging to be run backwards; failure to do so brings bad 'Juju' for the rest of your paddling trip. It is only a short way to the road bridge and its own rapid of grade 3. Most people take out river right below the bridge. Alternatively, just around the corner downstream is

Master Blaster, (Gd 4+); this has a big towback on the left side, beware! It is possible to run this and continue on down to the sea, where the main road crosses the river. There is one more rapid on this stretch.

Other important points The upper river can also be paddled after heavy rain, but due to the long walk in is not so regularly run. This section of water is much more continuous, it is also a good grade harder, and has one possible portage.

There is a year-round culling programme that is in operation on the Fassfern estate and as such there is always the possibility that you could be mistaken for a deer and shot. There are more adventures than just paddling here.

Contributor:
Alistair Collis

076 Fionn Lighe

Grade **4(5)**
Length **2½km**
OS sheet **40**

Introduction The Fionn Lighe flows into the west end of Loch Eil close to where the A861 branches off the A830, Fort William to Mallaig road. Yet another spate run on the north side of Loch Eil, this river has some nice grade 4 water, and one or two dodgy rock formations.

Water Level Very wet.

Gauge From the take-out, the river should look high, bank full and fast flowing. This is not a good river to try and scrape down.

Access To reach the river drive west on the A830 towards Mallaig. About a mile after the end of Loch Eil you will cross the river. Parking is available at the end of the track on your right, beside an old bridge. Walk up on a good track for about 2km, to where a footbridge crosses the river. Put on here.

Description From the put-in bridge, the first 500m is easy going grade 3. The rapids start to pick up until the first major challenge is reached (Gd 5). This is a dog-leg that moves from left to right. As the river starts to drop into a small gorge there is a slightly ugly 2m fall into a slot which is easily portaged. The rapid exiting the large pool below here has a nasty sump lurking below the water. Take care! This is followed by a 3m river-wide ledge creating a stopper with a strong towback. More interesting rapids follow, with the final kilometre being a gentler grade 3.

Contributor:
Richard 'FOZ'
Salmond

077 Dubh Lighe

Grade	**4(5)**
Length	**2km**
OS sheet	**40**

Introduction The long finger of Loch Eil points west from Fort William. Just short of the historic landmark of Glenfinnan, the river Dubh Lighe drains south from the mountain of Streap. A little run river in a quiet neck of the woods, the Dubh Lighe is a great trip, which is often 'in nick'. Stretches of flat water and a couple of portages do not spoil what is a fun river, with a surprising number of good rapids.

Water Level Although wet weather is required, the Dubh Lighe does not require as much water as many other spate rivers. It could be a good bet if other trips aren't quite in full flow. That said, the river has a rattly feel at lower levels and is definitely better after some good rain.

Gauge All the rocks upstream of the road bridge should be covered with a good flow right up to the banks to signal that a runnable flow has been reached. If the river is very full and flowing powerfully, other options could be considered.

Access Take the A830 from Fort William. About 2 miles beyond the junction with the A861 you cross the river. Take an immediate right and park at the foot of the track that leads up the glen. Walk up a good forest road to the put-in. Just when you are getting hot and sweaty (after 2km), take the right-hand fork which drops quickly down to the river at a bridge crossing a narrow gorge.

Description The narrow gorge at the put-in contains a couple of drops. The first of these needs to be scouted, and it could be worth doing this before you get on at the top of the gorge. This drop has some pinning potential, but goes fine at the right level (Gd 5). If you don't fancy this harsh start you can eddy out a few metres above the constriction and make a short portage on river left, regaining the river by a narrow gully just above a nice 1m ledge. Just as the first gorge ends you need to keep a good look out for a sump lurking in the middle of the river! A nasty configuration of boulders is a trap for the unwary paddler in an otherwise innocuous looking rapid. This ugly feature is covered at higher levels. There now follows some really sweet water with a couple of 'engaging' drops which make for some nice boating (Gd 4/5). This section is all quite runnable, mainly from the boat,

with 1 or 2 spots that may require extra care. Easier water leads to the lower section where the character of the river changes and the nice stuff is mixed up with a 'bit of rough'. This change is signalled by a tree blockage just above an equally blocked fall (portage both at once and seal launch on river left). Further downstream, a 2m fall ends with a nasty pothole completely enclosing the plunge pool, with most of the water sumping through underneath! Yuck! If you paddle this be sure to boof. The next 4m fall is onto rocks and can be portaged on river right, clambering down into the gorge just above a nice hole. Despite the portages, the paddling is still fun as you pick and choose between that which you fancy and that which you don't. Don't miss out on the last clean 4m fall, which is a real hoot.

Contributors:
Alastair Collis,
Andy Jackson and
Iain 'the freak' Murray

078 Abhainn Shlatach

Grade	**4(5)**
Length	**2km**
OS sheet	**40**

Introduction The Abhainn Shlatach drops steeply into Glenfinnan, next to the A830, known locally as 'The Road to the Isles'. The river offers two sections, both quite short: an open upper run with a couple of classy multi-stage drops and a lower gorge with some messy slabs set amongst overhanging rhododendrons! No prizes for guessing which is the favoured stretch.

Water Level Wet/Very wet for the upper. The lower stretch can be run with a little less water, but still needs a fair amount.

Gauge Just upstream of Glenfinnan there is an ugly weir that separates the two stretches of river. This is just a short walk down the track that leaves the A830 just beyond the village and before the bridge over the railway. At a good flow for the upper section the river should be bank full, with the rocks just downstream of the weir covered. Basically lots and lots! If the river looks just about floatable, then the lower section would be the more suitable choice.

Access To reach the upper put-in, drive west on the A830 from Glenfinnan; the drops on the river are easily visible from the road. After just over ½ a mile, the river flattens off and there is room on the north side of the road to park. Just don't get run over by a train on the short walk to the river. The run is split in two by the weir, described above, which serves as a useful put-in and take-out point. The take-out for the lower section can be found by turning right at the foot of the hill in Glenfinnan. Follow the road past the hotel and find a spot to park near the bridge or pier at the lochside.

Description Flat water soon leads to the first fall, which gets much better with more water. Stretches of braided and flat water continue for another kilometre, interrupted by some long 'full-on' bedrock rapids; definitely worth a scout in places. At one point you have to make a committed move above a nasty roostertail. Directly below here the river splits round another island; both channels have good white water. Take care not to be swept into the ugly weir already mentioned. Portage river left. Below the weir you are quickly into the lower gorge. The first major horizon is a large jaggy fall - one to walk. At higher flows the ledge below here has a large hole! The last twisting slab has several options, all of which may involve some tangling with the rhodies! Take care if you are scouting this fall from river left; you might be straying into someone's back garden.

Contributor:
Andy Jackson

San-bag Burn 079

Description This burn joins the Abhainn Shlatach at Cross (875 817), a place which is well named in this context. Due to its unpronounceable Gaelic name, Allt Feith A Chatha, local paddlers refer to it simply as the 'San-bag Burn'.

Grade	**5**
Length	**500m**
OS sheet	**40**

Contributor: Andy Jackson

Ailort 080

Introduction The Ailort flows from Loch Eilt into Loch Ailort, about 10 miles beyond Glenfinnan, on the Fort William to Mallaig road. This is a short paddle of only 2km, but continually interesting - much better than a casual sighting from the A830 would suggest.

Grade	**2/3**
Length	**2km**
OS sheet	**40**

Water Level Wet/Very wet. Although a small river, which needs to be reasonably high, it holds water well as it drains from Loch Eilt. This is a great run at huge flows when it may be considered a grade harder.

Gauge The river flows close to the road just after leaving Loch Eilt and levels can be easily checked here. Most rocks should be well covered if the river is to be worth paddling.

Access Access is via a short carry from one of the roadside parking places (791 828) at the west end of Loch Eilt. If like me you depend on a wheelchair, access is difficult for your paddling partner who has to carry you from the road, and then go back to get the Topo-Duo. Otherwise it is a simple and short carry with your boat from the car to the river. Egress is easiest at the bridge where the A861 crosses the river at (765 820). Find this by taking the left turn at Lochailort, next to the hotel.

Description There is a broken weir shortly after the start, which provides the most difficult part of the trip. It is easy to inspect, and an obvious line presents itself. Shortly after this, a couple of steep grade 3's may prove a touch rocky but are straightforward from an upright perspective. The river progresses with several rapids, shoots and generally interesting paddling. Most of the easy water flows well and passes quickly. Although a small river and a short paddle, this is an enjoyable trip in its own right. It would also make a great second river when daylight does not make a longer paddle a sensible option, or a superb summer evening paddle when water levels allow.

Contributor:
Adrian Disney

Other important points This is a popular salmon fishing river so a small discreet group would definitely be the way to go.

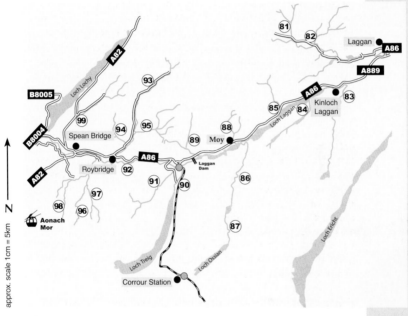

approx. scale 1cm = 5km

Glen Spean

Glen Spean

The Spean is by far the biggest river in this 'neck of the woods'. It offers paddling at all water levels. In even the driest conditions you can enjoy navigating the narrow bedrock channels of the Spean Gorge and in times of extreme flood there is plenty of action to be had on the Upper Spean as the Laggan Dam releases its watery load. The many tributaries of the Spean also provide great runs. The Roy is the most popular, and deservedly so but check out the Treig and Cour, fantastic in the right water conditions. The villages of Roy and Spean Bridge are a good base for kayaking operations with a good choice of bunkhouses, campsites and chalets for accommodation. The Commando Bar is a favourite watering hole and a good place to warm your toes in front of the fire.

081 Allt Fèith a Mhoraire

Grade	**4**
Length	**1km**
OS sheet	**34**

Water level Very wet. You'll need lots of water - we ran it when the Feith Talagain looked too big and it was raining at the time.

Gauge Don't be put off by the small size of the two braids running across the road where you park, as 100m into the wood you'll find one of General Wade's bridges and see the full picture!

Access Turn off the A86 Newtonmore to Roybridge road in Laggan village and head towards and beyond the Spey Dam. From Garva Bridge, where you park for the Feith Talagain, drive another 3 miles until you cross the Allt Fèith a Mhoraire (468 960). Here the tarmac changes to the dirt road of the Corrieyairack Pass, just 600m short of Melgarve bothy. From the bridge, head up the approach path that runs up the west side (river right) for just over 1km, to where a major tributary, the Luaidhe, joins. It is possible to scout on the way up by bushwacking down through the trees to the river.

Contributor:
John Mason

Description This is an awesome granite slide run, like a smaller version of those Californian classics. Some rocky grade 3/4 rapids lead to a harder rapid before heading under the deer fence for the main event, 500m of super slide action.

Feith Talagain 082

Grade	**4/5**
Length	**2km**
OS sheet	**35**

Introduction Tucked away in the Upper Spey valley, this burn flows south to join the Spey at Garva Bridge. This is a classic spate burn with a good selection of bedrock and boulder rapids. There are several nice drops and mini gorges that will give either a fun but rocky bounce, or a full-on day out, depending on water level.

Water Level Very wet. The Feith Talagain has only a small catchment area above the put-in, so it will probably need to be raining on the day to make it 'a go'.

Gauge Just before the river joins the Spey there is a hard twisting fall. This makes a good place to judge the flow, but don't be put off, the rest of the river is nicer than this one! Make sure there is enough water to float the boulder section just upstream.

Access Turn off the A86 at Laggan and follow the minor road to where it ends at Garva Bridge. This is part of General Wade's road, a communication network built in an attempt to subdue the Jacobite forces. The road degenerates into a rough track from this point eventually crossing the Corrieyairack Pass and following the River Tarff down to the Great Glen, but that's another story! Leaving cars at the bridge over the Spey, it is a short walk to the river. If the water level looks OK, cross the bridge and continue upstream. It's probably best to follow the forest track up the hill, skirt the edge of the forest and contour across the boggy hillside. After 2km a tributary (540 967) marks a flattening in the river and a good spot to put in.

Description The first steepening marks a nice series of drops starting with a 1m boof ledge. A clean 4m fall and a double slab make some really nice boating. Next comes the main event, which comprises a couple of 5m ramps. At big flows this comes complete with a weird rooster tail and a very large hole! The action continues with more drops and chutes before a kilometre of easy water to the bridge. Already mentioned is the slightly unappealing nature of the rapid below the bridge, but if you do decide to run it, watch out for the water sumping out under the boulder in the right-hand shoot.

Contributor:
Andy Jackson

Other important points Expert paddlers who run this river at high flows will have a real stonker of a trip and find it's good grade 5 action almost all the way!

083 Pattack

Grade **3/4(5)**
Length **2km**
OS sht.**43/35**

Introduction Flowing into Loch Laggan and thence down the Spean, the Pattack drains from the northern slopes of Ben Alder. This is a good intermediate trip, with many fine grade 3+ rapids and a couple of harder sections that can be easily portaged.

Water Level Moderately wet / Very wet. At high flows the smaller rapids become washed out, and the trip is only worthwhile if you intend to run the main rapids.

Gauge The last rapid drops into a pool beside the A86, Spean Bridge to Kingussie road, at a popular picnic spot close to the upper end of Loch Laggan. If there is enough water to run this rapid the trip will be on. If this rapid is pumping, expect a very fast trip.

Access To reach the take-out, follow the A86 to the picnic spot mentioned above, some 24 miles east of Spean Bridge, where there is a large Forestry Commission car park. To get to the put-in drive back towards Spean Bridge. After about a mile, park in a lay-by opposite a farm track and walk the 2km up this track past the farmyard to a locked gate at the edge of the forest. An obvious small path leads down to the river. Alternatively, you could try your luck at the estate office, which is another ½ mile back towards Spean Bridge on the right-hand side, (547 897). If you ask them in advance they will normally provide you with the combination to the lock on the bottom gate to allow vehicular access. The estate office phone number is 01528 544300, or email ardverikie@ardverikie.com.

Description The path from the forest gate brings you to the top of a steep gully. From here it is possible to scramble down to the river at the bottom of the Falls of Pattack (Gd 5). If you are silly enough to wish to paddle this 10m monstrosity, follow the path upstream and choose your put-in. At low flows the pool at the bottom of the Falls is shallow, at higher flows the run in becomes progressively more interesting, but at least the pool fills up (a little). From below the Falls, the river is grade 3 for the first kilometre, with lots of small drops and eddy lines to enjoy. A horizon line warns of the first harder rapid. At grade 4, this can be run down either side at most flows. The river then returns to grade 3 with some more nice playspots. The sides of the river begin to rise as you approach the first gorge. Despite a feeling of impeding doom, the rapids get no harder and the river banks soon open out again. However, you are now not far from the second gorge (Gd 4). This contains 4 really sweet rapids, finishing in the drop seen from the road. The stopper here is shallow and isn't quite as bad as it at first seems. There is a good path on river right from which to inspect the drops. If you don't fancy them, it's only a short walk back to the picnic area.

Contributor:
Bridget Thomas

Other important points Please don't attempt to drive up the access road without first getting permission. The guys at the estate here have been very supportive of paddlers and are happy to help. Lets all make sure it stays that way.

Monarch of the Glen Burn 084

Introduction This river may have a proper name, but if so it's not marked on the OS map. It runs out of Lochan na Earba into Loch Laggan, close to Ardverikie Castle, featured in Monarch of the Glen. The stealth mission across the Loch is a rewarding approach.

Grade **4+(5)**
Length **1 ½km**
OS sheet **42**

Water Level Very wet. We paddled it with plenty of rain plus snow melt.

Access Park in the Creag Meagaidh car park off the A86 Roybridge to Newtonmore road, and then paddle over Loch Laggan to the river left (west) side of the river mouth (498 873). The river is hard to spot because of fallen trees at the point where it joins the loch. Walk up using the network of tracks to Lochan na Earba, stopping at the first stone bridge to check the level and inspect.

Description The river runs out of the loch and is mainly grade 3/4 until a good 500m section of grade 4 leads to a rocky grade 5, which may be a portage. After that more grade 4 rocky action leads to a military bridge. It actually got dark then so we never got to paddle the steep slabby section that is hemmed in by rhododendron bushes and leads down to a stone bridge. After the bridge, slabby drops lead to the trees that block the river as it enters Loch Laggan. All that remains is a paddle back across the loch to your car, unless you want to check out the spooky island featured in an episode of Monarch of the Glen.

Contributor:
John Mason

085 Allt Coire Ardair

Grade	**4(5)**
Length	**2km**
OS sheet	**34**

Introduction The Allt Coire Ardair flows down the main U-shaped valley on the southern side of Creag Meagaidh and drains into Loch Laggan. This is a fast continuous spate run, with little time to catch your breath or admire the stunning scenery.

Water Level Very wet. You need max flows for this one - we did it with snow melt in the rain, topo-bogganing down the snow into an icy grey torrent.

Gauge The river should look bank full with all but the larger boulders covered.

Access Turn off the A86 Spean Bridge to Laggan road at the hill walkers' car park for Creag Meagaidh. Carry up the obvious walking track on the right side of the glen (river left). Put in as the valley starts to level out. Take out above the braided lower section and follow the path back to your car.

Contributor:
Paul Currant

Description This run is made up of bedrock slabs strewn with boulders over a steady gradient. There's one ledge which stands out and may create a large river-wide hole. Not far below this, there is a steep and slightly rocky slab. Otherwise it's a very simple recipe: strap your boat to your back for a hike into a beautiful location and crash out of control back down again. Once on the move you might drag in a few holes, but otherwise it's all go till the end.

086 Abhainn Ghuilbinn

Grade	**3/4(5+)**
Length	**6km**
OS sheet	**42**

Introduction The Abhainn Ghuilbinn feeds into Loch Laggan on its south side, close to Moy Cottage (427 826). Although it is possible to walk up from the bottom and run the lower gorges, the whole river is better paddled in conjunction with the River Ossian. Run in its entirety, the Ghuilbinn is a tremendous trip. It starts from Loch Ghuilbinn with a long boulder field that cheers the soul. After a small upper gorge the river opens then hurtles through a couple of technical drops and so out onto the flat. A lower gorge follows and to cap the day off, the ugliest fall is saved until last.

Water Level Wet/Very wet (Medium for the lower gorges). A prolonged period of heavy rain is generally required to get this river
at its best. With less water, it is possible to have a good day out in
the lower gorges, but the longer trip will feel like a slog.

Gauge The only way to gauge the flow on the Ghuilbinn is by
walking in from the A86 and looking at the last large fall on the
river. If this fall has very few rocks showing it may be worth considering the full run. If there is a choice of chutes, many of which
do not run, the lower gorge is probably the only option.

Access The lower gorges can be accessed from a large lay-by on
the A86, close to Moy Cottage, where a bridge crosses the narrow
neck of Loch Laggan (433 830). Follow the track across the bridge
and turn left before the houses, to reach the Abhainn Ghuilbinn.
Walk up the right bank until the river goes flat. You are now
above the lower gorges. For details of the upper put-in, see the
Ossian description. After the trip, paddle across the loch and back
up the channel to your car.

Description Loch Ghuilbinn exits into easy water that is a nice
warm up for the section to come. After about 1km, the flow picks
up to give a long section of good grade 3 paddling. A short section
of flat precedes the first horizon line, Acid House (Gd 4). Soon
after this is the start of the first gorge. The two entry falls are close
together (Gd 5), and the second is undercut at the bottom. The last
rapid in the gorge is a hoot and goes by the name of The Drainpipe (Gd 4+). Run the first hole then collect your thoughts to boof
the pour-over ledge. Failure to make this line spells trouble. There
is however a large pool for flotsam to gather in, if you manage
to escape the stopper. 1km of easier paddling is followed by the
bottom gorge, which is best inspected. A couple of sweet drops
bring you to the main event, a twisting undercut 3m fall. The
main shoot has been run at grade 5+, although a much friendlier
chicken shoot is fair game at high flows. From here, a short paddle
brings you to the last delight: a set of fragmented slabs with many
routes, but only one or two real possibilities. There are a couple of
nasty sumps which are not obvious at high flows. From here it is
an arduous (read flat) paddle down to the loch, and then across to
the A86. If you haven't enjoyed this day out then stay in the city,
truly one of the great adventure paddles in Scotland.

Contributor:
Alastair Collis

Other important points There is a stalkers track along the left side of the Ghuilbinn which will be easier to use than the bank if you are in difficulty. More water will undoubtedly raise the grades of some of the rapids on the Ghuilbinn.

087 Ossian

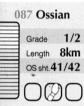

Grade **1/2**
Length **8km**
OS sht.**41/42**

Introduction The Ossian drains north from Loch Ossian through an isolated stretch of mountains to the east of Loch Treig. Sitting on the edge of Rannoch Moor, some will recognize the nearby Corrour Station from the cult film Trainspotting. Just getting to this river is an adventure in itself. There are no roads and the only access is by train, foot and flat-water paddle! This is really the first half of a two river journey from Rannoch Moor to Glen Spean via the Rivers Ossian and Abhainn Ghuilbinn. The trip on the Ossian is one of splendour rather than white water, that comes on the Ghuilbinn. The low gradient and shallow bed make this run technically easy.

Water Level Very wet. If you are trying to squeeze this run in without due notice to the weather, and the river is dry, there is no road to ferry boats down to the next river. 8km with your boat on your back is a long way.

Gauge As the Ossian is in the middle of nowhere the only way to gauge the run is by considering the amount of rain that has fallen in the last week and especially the last 72 hrs.

Access This is probably the only train-accessed run in the country. To get to the river you need to sweet talk the railway people into carrying boats. This will be easiest if the train has a guards van and you are a small group. At time of writing this means that you have to travel north, probably from Bridge of Orchy on the evening train. Plan to 'bivvy' out or make use of the Youth Hostel or bunkhouse at Corrour. From Corrour Station it is a half-hour walk to Loch Ossian. It's then a 5km paddle along the loch to the river mouth. Egress, at the end of the Abhainn Ghuilbinn, is on the banks of Loch Laggan approximately ½ mile east of Moy Cottage where a concrete bridge crosses the narrow neck of Loch Laggan. Parking is ample here in a large pull in off the A86.

Description Once on to the river you will find the Ossian a float trip. As you leave the trees behind, a small rocky tributary comes in

Abhainn Ghuilbinn - Glen Spean - Lynne Walker

Spean Gorge - www.KayakoJacko.co.uk

Allt Ionndrainn - Glen Spean - Chris Dickinson

Pattack - Glen Spean - Chris Dickinson

Spean Gorge - Bridget Thomas

from the right, to paddle or not to paddle it (hmm...). This signifies the start of the grade 2 stretch; don't blink or you'll miss it. This may not be the best white water that Scotland has to offer, but it is an awe inspiring journey. You are cutting through huge mountains in a narrow valley with some nice surfing if the river is high.

Contributor:
Andy Jackson

Other important points Remember that this river is out in the boonies and as such you should be prepared to deal with more than your usual float alongside a road. The whole trip back to the road takes a full 8hrs, without too much inspection. Be aware of the amount of daylight you have, or you could become a prince of darkness.

Moy 088

Introduction The Moy Burn slips under the A86, 3 miles east of Laggan Dam. It is a tiny creek that runs into Loch Laggan and plays a small role in the formation of the mighty Spean. A steep rocky ditch, the Moy provides a short but boisterous run. There are no big drops but several which will keep you on the edge of your Topo's seat.

Grade	**4/5**
Length	**½km**
OS sheet	**34**

Water Level Moderately wet / Wet.

Gauge From the road bridge it is easy to assess the flow. The run-in to the final falls should look easily floatable as opposed to a bump and scrape. This run improves with water but can get over-high when in flood.

Access The Moy crosses under the A86 on a very fast section of road so care needs to be taken when parking or checking the level. It is best to park where there is access to a section of old road near the ruins at Moy Cottage. Carry up river left to a slightly blocked ramp with an overhanging tree on river right. This is about 300m beyond the deer fence. Take out back at the road bridge.

Description This trip is a succession of small but challenging drops and ramps. The biggest drop is around 3m high and falls into a deep pool. Take care though, as the water tries to push you up against the slightly undercut and oh so smooth cliff. The drop below the deer fence has a rocky feel to it but should go OK. As

the burn winds its way through the final tree-lined section things get quite continuous and you soon arrive at the falls you saw from the road bridge. This shallow and jaggy drop was created when the river bed was blasted during road improvements. In the olden days the last fall on the Moy was the hardest and probably the best on the run. A super clean plunge into a deep hole. What lurks now is probably still the hardest but in no way the nicest drop on the run. You may want to stop just above this final cheese grater if you value the bottom of your boat.

Other important points Please take care not to damage the deer fence as you cross it on the walk up.

Contributor:
Andy Jackson

089 **Rough Burn**

Grade **3/4(5)**
Length **2km**
OS sheet **41**

Introduction This burn joins Loch Laggan just above the dam, and thus feeds into the River Spean. A strange trip with nice bedrock slabs split round large islands in the river. The upper reaches are hidden away in the forest but generally the river is clear of trees. The run ends with a very obvious boulder rapid flowing into the loch. Right next to the main road, this is probably the most looked at and least paddled rapid in Scotland.

Water Levels Wet / Very wet. A controlled but slightly scrapey run can be had if the river is up a bit, but it is undoubtedly best when it is stonking. It seems to take a little more rain than you would expect to bring this one up.

Gauge If there are rocks showing directly under the road bridge, the river will be too shallow. The river could be paddled at most high levels but will be powerful and harder if it is very high.

Access The Laggan Dam, at the put-in for the top section of the Spean, can be found 7 miles east of Roy Bridge on the A86. The Rough Burn flows into Loch Laggan a few hundred metres further east again. Park at the bridge (377 814). This car park can be busy with hill walkers and the like so it might be necessary to leave cars at the car park by the dam. To get to the put-in (364 822) cross the stile and carry up the forest road leading upstream. Take the left fork after 1km and wade through the mud at the end of the track to put on beyond the forest edge. Take out at the road bridge or in Loch Laggan if you are feeling brave.

Description Flat initially, the river soon splits around a large central island. Here the rapids pick up with nice bedrock slabs giving grade 4 boating. The channels join then split again, this time for several hundred metres. Both channels give good paddling with perhaps the right-hand one being best. If you enjoy one channel why not portage back upstream to experience the other? Shortly after the two forks join the gradient eases and the rapids are more bouldery. There is however one large slab still to come, which is quite powerful at a high flow (Gd 5). Watch out for the metal spikes hidden below the water on river right near the top. You can't canoe under the road bridge due to a fence spanning the river. While you portage nip down the river right bank and check the boulder section leading to the loch. It gets gradually harder and depending on the level of the loch it may have a nasty grade 5 boulder drop near the bottom.

Contributor:
Callum Anderson

Other important points You can start your trip further upstream on the **Allt a Chaorainn.** This is worthwhile if there is a lot of water. It gives another kilometre or so of very tight grade 4/5. If you paddle into Loch Laggan stay well clear of the Laggan Dam as you risk being sucked into the pipe leading to Loch Treig.

Treig 090

Introduction The Treig flows into the Spean, halfway down the upper section just below the railway bridge (357 799). Its water is held back by Loch Treig which is almost always low, as this is the primary working reservoir of Alcan, feeding the outflow in Fort William. This short run provides 3 or 4 good ledges and slabs when in spate, and is well worth the walk.

Grade	4+
Length	1km
OS sheet	41

Water Level Very wet. Your best chance of running the Treig is when it has been extremely wet and the dam is overflowing or the small tributaries which join the river are bringing the run into condition.

Gauge The best gauge is to paddle down the Spean and look at the last rapid on the Treig, just upstream of the confluence. If this 1m ledge has a river wide curtain of water spilling over it, you are in luck. The dam rarely releases and generally the Treig rises and falls very quickly.

Access Best arrived at in conjunction with the Upper Spean, the Treig is the first river past the railway bridge on the left. If the Treig is high enough, a 10 minute walk up on river left will bring you to the top of the grade 4 rapids. Alternatively the Treig can be reached by vehicle by turning off the A86 at Fersit, approximately 2½ miles west of the Laggan Dam. Drive past the take-out for the Upper Spean and follow the road over the Allt Coire Laire. Continue until the road becomes a dirt track and you will find the obvious road bridge. Egress can be at the end of the Upper Spean run.

Description Due to the years that this river has been devoid of water, it has started its own regeneration of Caledonian forest. Putting in at the road bridge will find you in a river bed that is equipped with its own 'growing strainers'. The top section of the river is a true tree infested rocky ditch, (Gd 2/3). As the tributaries join to swell the flow, the river shows what it has to offer. The last series of drops are all bedrock and provide quality rapids at grade 4+. Particle Accelerator is a V-shaped slab that shoots you down over a 1m ledge and through two holes. The river now splits and the next rapid is directly downstream. Eddying out here can be a problem in high water. The left-hand channel brings you to Atom Exciter, a fun 3m ledge that gives airborne boofs. Next comes Rear End falls, a ragged double step fall. Finally, Gauge Ledge brings you back into the maelstrom of the Upper Spean.

Contributor:
Alistair Collis

Other important points It took some of the worst weather that I have seen in the 6 years that I have lived and paddled in the Lochaber area to bring the Treig to a paddleable state. Many are the times that I have paddled the Upper Spean on 4 pipes and looked longingly up at the Treig. Only when the Laggan Dam was releasing on all 6 pipes and flood warnings were being issued did I get to fulfill my dream. The next day the river was low.

091 Allt Coire Laire

Grade	4/5
Length	2km
OS sheet	41

Introduction The Allt Coire Laire lies some 20 miles north-east of Fort William. It is a tributary of the Spean, joining the main river about 1km above Inverlair Falls, the take-out for the upper run. This little known classic is best saved for when one of those Big Water days that we all pine for, actually arrives. If you've just had a blast on the Upper Spean with all 6 pipes open and a whole lot more, you'll want to start thinking about getting off the Spean at about where the Allt Coire Laire flows in, well before the scary lead-in to Inverlair Falls. The run starts off fairly flat, braided, and gravelly, in a steep sided, forested glen, but quickly picks up until one twisting bedrock and bouldery rapid links with another. A Topo isn't essential but is probably best suited!

Water Level Very wet/As much as possible. Run off is pretty quick due to the steep sides and shallow soil of its catchment. A small dam at the top of the run means that it needs to have been very wet (torrential rain, or heaps of snow melt plus lots of rain). If the Spean's on 6 pipes and lots more, the Laire may well be running.

Gauge Where the road crosses the burn (or from the confluence if you're on the Spean), if it looks pretty 'scrapey', with lots of rocks showing through – don't do it. If, however, the water under the bridge looks like it can't wait to join the Spean and go nuts at Inverlair – have a couple of mars bars and get that boat on your shoulder. Completely ignore any murmurs of 'I can't be arsed walking, man'. Its not very far . . . honest!

Access Turn off the A86 (Fort William – Kingussie road) towards Fersit. Drive over the railway, over the Upper Spean and continue round past a few houses for about a mile. Once out of the forest, the road goes over the Laire. This bridge, or the confluence with the Spean, is the take-out. To get to the put-in, backtrack to the first house beside the road on the right. Park here and walk for about 2km up the private track to the left. You are in forest all the way, with the odd view down through the trees to the river. When the track goes back down to the river, there is a quarry and a dam – put in here.

Description After the initial boulder section, where the main challenge is to pick the deepest channel between endless rocks, the Laire becomes quite constant. Running through a mini bedrock gorge it is steep and tight for a while with lots of twisting chutes, boulder splats, and all that is fun in a short boat. The more water, the more fun! Keep eddy hopping and look out for trees. There are no portages, but strainers may be a problem and there are definitely a few things worth looking at if you're unsure. All too soon, the river opens out again and gets a bit more volume for the last ½km – float down this reminiscing and giggling until you reach the bridge.

Contributor:
Kenny Biggin

Other important points This trip is perfect in combination with the Upper Spean and the Treig. It is best for a small group, since the river is narrow and the eddies tiny.

Spean

The Spean is one of the larger rivers on the west that is easily accessible for the kayaker. It is never too far from the A86 Spean Bridge to Kingussie road. Glen Spean is a broad open glen that has the mountains of Ben Nevis to the south and Creag Meagaidh (craig meggy) to the north. The views from the upper stretches of the river remind you why you come to the outdoors. The river has four distinct sections. On 6 pipes, the upper section offers the biggest volume white water run in the UK, particularly if water is also spilling over the dam. At more reasonable releases, it is still a great fun and continuous run. The Monessie section has an adventurous feel before you even get on the river. Its combination of gorges and long rapids leave the kayaker begging for more. Open water from here gives good boating on the middle section at an easier level. The Spean Gorge is a classic trip, which can be run at low flows. A technical run, it is away from roads for much of its length. The river has been tamed by Alcan's Laggan Dam, built in 1934. It now only provides entertainment for the big water junkie when Lochaber district is in one of its wetter moods. However, with the Roy as its major tributary, the middle and gorge runs often have good volumes of water. The river has not yet, to our knowledge, been run in its entirety from the dam to Mucomir Power Station in one push, without portages, maybe something for the next generation of kayakers?

092 Spean (Upper)

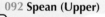

Grade	**3+/4**
Length	**4km**
OS sheet	**41**

Introduction The Upper Spean starts at Laggan Dam (372 807), 9 miles east of Spean Bridge on the A86. It follows this road at a discreet distance until it is crossed by the minor road to Fersit. The Upper Spean is probably the largest volume white water run in Scotland. When all 6 pipes are blowing and there is a large flow coming over the top of the dam, this is the closest thing that you will get to monsoon boating in the Himalaya. Getting in just below the dam is a belittling experience as the amount of water cascading out of the air is phenomenal. The open nature of this run gives excellent boating with continuous white water for the first 2km.

Water Level There is no point in coming to the Upper Spean if the Laggan Dam isn't full. During the summer a sudden downpour will make no difference to this section of river. During the latter half of the winter and in the spring when the heavens open, the dam will fill and suddenly you will find that the pipes are on. 2 pipes gives an interesting run at grade 3+. 4 pipes gives an Alpine-like grade 4 run. 6 pipes gives monsoon like conditions (full-on grade 4!). No pipes means no run and no fun.

Gauge The best gauge is the Laggan Dam. However if you are approaching from Fort William or Inverness then a look over the bridge at Spean Bridge (222 817) will give an indication as to the amount of water. There is a gauge on the downstream left side of the bridge. Above 4 on the gauge and you may be in luck. Remember that the Roy is a major tributary upstream of here and may account for most or all of the water you see.

Access Access is off the A86, with parking at the dam being ample. Walk down the road for 100m, cross a fence and continue down a steep bracken covered slope. Egress is just above Inverlair Falls on the Fersit road, accessed from the A86 approximately 2½ miles downstream of the dam. There is ample parking on the right after the small bridge that spans Inverlair gorge.

Description The run changes hugely in character depending on the flow. Good for intermediate paddlers on 1 pipe, it is a total blast on all 6! There is a large boulder that produces the infamous pour-over ledge in the middle of the river about 150m downstream of the dam. Once past this the river is fast and continuous for the next 2km, and in the biggest flows moves like grease lightening-swimming here is bad. At this level the trees, usually on the banks, are in the water and escape is going to be hazardous. Generally there are few holes to avoid so relax and enjoy it. Once at the railway bridge the river eases to give you a break. There is one more grade 3+ rapid, that can be boat scouted, before the gorge. The next time the banks close in signifies the lower gorge. It is at its most technical on 2 pipes and the entry hole is followed by a large whirlpool that can swallow the smaller boats. Don't let this put the playboaters off, this spot can give lots of fun if you have a nose clip!

The split rock at the bottom can be run on either side with the right being easier. Inverlair Falls has been kayaked (very rarely), but to swim this monster fall is a one way ticket out of here. There have been many tales of people being rescued on the lip of the falls and even an epic tale of a paddler being plucked by helicopter from the island that splits the falls. Don't let this be you.

On 6 pipes, it's best not to attempt the gorge. If you do, it is possible to eddy out just above the road bridge in a small boiling eddy on the right. Please, don't even think of carrying on below this.

Contributor:
Alastair Collis

Other important points If you think that a swim in the last gorge is a possibility then get out and walk the last 150m to the bridge. If you end up swimming in the last gorge then our advice is dump everything and swim for shore as if your life depends on it... it does!

092 Spean (Monessie)

Grade **3/4(5)**
Length **3km**
OS sheet **41**

◯◯◯

Introduction Monessie gorge is a hideous cataract blocked by sumps, huge holes and guarded by a large waterfall. This gorge has been run at low flows but would be very serious with the dam releasing. The section described begins immediately below this monster! The Spean has just spent its energy forcing its way through a tortuous gorge and is trying to relax. There are however a few last surprises before Roy Bridge. This is a varied piece of white water, with all the right ingredients. The combination of gorges, flat pools and long open rapids makes for an interesting trip.

Water Level Wet. To make the most of this run you need at least 2 pipes releasing from Laggan Dam. However, 6 pipes may be too much for the uninitiated as the grade 5 comes up all of a sudden.

Gauge As for the Upper Spean, the best gauge is the dam. Looking over the bridge at Spean Bridge may give a false indication about this run, as much of the water here may be coming down the Roy, which joins the Spean below the Monessie section.

Access Drive upstream from Roy Bridge for 1½ miles to a small turn off into the woods on the left by a gate. It is possible to drop people off here, but parking is limited to two cars. If you see the river on your right then you have gone too far. Access is over the road and down the field until you come to the railway line. You can now drop into the small stream bed on your right and pass under the railway via the 'Tunnel of Fear'. The stupid will trespass on the railway and down climb the muddy bank. Egress is at Roy Bridge where you can get out at the caravan and chalet park, carrying your boats to the village. It is however a long carry to any decent parking, so why not continue on down the middle section to Spean Bridge?

Description Emerging from the tunnel under the railway, intrepid paddlers will find themselves at a small pool with a strong jet of water crashing out of the Monessie gorge and into a cliff. Across this is your warm up playwave. Out of this pool and you are straight into the first gorge (Gd 3). There are no 'must make' lines and a short stretch of easier water is enough for the collection of any debris. Next, the river throws in a long grade 3 rapid and then a shorter stretch of flat water before it rounds a left corner and over Split Decision, a severe grade 5. Get out to inspect on the right at the top of the bank defences. Lines down the left or right are possible at different water levels; it's your choice. To put in directly below Split Decision is tricky, but worth the effort as you're straight into the second gorge, which offers fast and furious grade 3+ water. From here down to Roy Bridge, the river is open and relatively flat. A close watch on the bank as you near Roy Bridge is necessary to spot the small sandy beach that marks the egress.

Contributor:
Alastair Collis

Other important points The egress point at Roy Bridge is a private caravan park and not a car park. Please respect the local populace and carry back up to the main road (¾km) and a public car park. It is definitely easiest just to carry on down the Middle Spean to Spean Bridge. This will be a ½ hour blast if the river is high.

Spean (Middle) 092

Introduction The Middle Spean is the section from Roy Bridge (270 813) to Spean Bridge (222 817). There are shops at both put-in and take-out for those who are ever hungry, and public toilets at the take-out. This section of river is wide and open and has a very benign feel to it. The river comprises of boulder and bedrock sections, but these do not give rise to many difficulties.

Grade	2/3
Length	5km
OS sheet	41

Water Level Fairly dry / Very wet. This section of river can be paddled at almost any level. On lesser flows it provides great fun for beginner parties. In flood, the section becomes fast and continuous, but never desperate.

Gauge Look over the bridge at Spean Bridge. If the gauge on the downstream side is between 1 and 4, then this section is at its best. Below this level the section can be run but is a bit of a scrape.

Access Access is the same as for the Lower Roy's egress. Turn off the A86 in Roy Bridge beside the Roy Bridge Hotel and Grey Corries Lodge. After the road passes beneath the railway bridge it bends to the left. Here there is a stile, and a path to the river. As there is little space on this road it's better to move vehicles to the public car park in Roy Bridge and walk the short distance to the river. Egress is on river left to the car park in Spean Bridge behind the woollen mill.

Description Having spent its energy in the upper sections, the Spean is now content to relax. With easy water until it reaches Railway Bridge Falls (Gd 3), about halfway through the run. Here, depending on the water level, the group will find either a 1m ledge to be shot with ease or a more powerful hole, which is easier on the right. The excitement over, it is now possible to concentrate on learning white water manoeuvres and strokes. The end soon comes, and people may want to go on through the gorge or take advantage of the shop and restaurant here in Spean Bridge.

Contributor:
Alastair Collis

Other important points The Middle Spean can be combined with several other runs to create longer trips that cater for the wide range of skills within a group.
Parking on the side road at the put-in is actively discouraged, so please use the public car park by the bridge over the Roy. Thanks.

092 Spean (Gorge)

Grade **3/4(5)**
Length **6km**
OS sheet **41**

Location Starting at Spean Bridge, this section is the only part of the river that is not in close proximity to the A86. It only nears the road again at Mucomir Power Station (183 838). This deep-walled gorge is a beautiful place to be whatever the flow. The start of the river has an open feel to it but after 3km the gorge closes in and the paddler will feel as if they are at the bottom of the world.

Water level Dry to very wet. Because of the confined nature of the run, all the rapids vary greatly depending on water level. Generally, the lower the water the more technical the river becomes. The Spean Gorge is navigable at even the lowest levels in summer. Though at these levels you may find yourself wondering why! Surprisingly it's not a hard run when the river is high, as all but the two main rapids disappear, but it is definably quite powerful, pushes along quickly and 'funny water' and boil-lines abound.

Gauge Below 0 on the gauge in Spean Bridge, located river left, downstream of the main road, the river should be considered low. 1 is a good fun medium level. Above 2 the river should be consider high. 0.7 on the SEPA gauge on the River Lochy should be considered a minimum level.

Access At Spean Bridge there is a public car park behind the Woollen Mill, where a small muddy path in the corner leads down to the river. For the take-out, drive towards Inverness. Turn left onto the B8004 at the Commando Memorial and follow the road to Mucomir Power Station. Egress is just downstream of the outlet on the right, next to a small wooden hut. If the river is busy you can help avoid access problems here by paddling another ¼km downstream. The river is very close to the road and there is a good egress point just before Gairlochy. Definitely consider this if you are a big group.

Description The section starts as a wide and shingle-braided river. The remains of General Wade's High Bridge mark the first grade 3 rapid, Fairy Steps. A line down the right works, although this rapid also offers many interesting moves in a playboat. Below this, there is a tree stuck on river right; it has been there for many years and will be for many more. You are now entering the gorge. Exit at this point is possible on river left to the Kilmonivaig road, but strenuous. In premium flows there are two rapids of note, the second with a cool cartwheel spot, before the Witches Cauldron (Gd 5). Easily washed out, only in low flows does this rapid warrant the grade 5 status when people have become pinned or disappeared beneath the undercut left wall for many anxious seconds before rescue. Take care to protect/portage as necessary. Just below this lies the most continuous section. It starts with a narrow gap that feeds you into a small boily area with a leaning wall on the left. There is a small eddy just below this, which holds only one or two boats. This next rapid is no more frightening than the last and

gives fewer problems. You have almost escaped the clutches of the gorge now and only have to negotiate the famous Constriction. A challenge at high flows, it is a squeeze and a scrape when the river is low. There are only two more rapids left now. The first is obvious (Gd 3+), just avoid the large cushion wave on the right. The second has two options, one of which used to have a tree in it. You are now leaving the gorge and there is only the long flat paddle out and fond memories of rapids run to amuse the tired paddler.

Contributor:
Alastair Collis

Roy

The Roy is one of the busy rivers on the west coast due to its classic rapids and easy road access. The river splits neatly into three sections, the upper, the gorge and the lower. There is also some good paddling on a couple of tributaries. The river is slow to rise, but will be runnable for a few days after heavy rain. The best time to try the Upper Roy is during spring and autumn downpours. Glen Roy was carved by the glaciers that once covered this part of Scotland. Their retreat left behind 'parallel roads' visible on the sides of the glen. Ask any local boater about them and you will no doubt be told about the Roman invaders that started to build a road around the glen from either end. The two teams of slaves missed each other in the mist and the first dual carriageway was made. The real story of how they were formed is on a visitor information board in a small car park on your way to the upper put-in.

093 Roy (Upper)

Grade	3(4)
Length	2km
OS sheet	34

◯◯◯

Introduction The Upper Roy lies at the head of the glen. The first few kilometres from Brae Roy Lodge are fairly flat and most paddlers will choose to get on at 'the elbow'. The Upper Roy is undoubtedly a classic grade 3 run when the river is high. This easier section is a good warm up for the more sustained gorge downstream. The two main rapids in the open glen give spectacular pictures and easy rescue.

Water Level Very wet.

Gauge Looking over the A86 road bridge, the river should be bank full and flowing powerfully for there to be sufficient water to try the upper section.

Access The best put-in is at the large bend in the river, 'the elbow' (313 895). This is about 2 miles before Brae Roy Lodge, at the point where the river picks up. Take out at Rooster Tail (301 877), the last rapid before the river drops away from the road and into the gorge.

Description The open upper section is a nice warm up of easy going grade 3, with gentle steps and walls that don't tax the mind too heavily. The river flows along nicely and brings you quickly to the first of the upper glen's idyllic falls, Wish You Were Here (Gd 4). A flat paddle brings you to the next open fall, Rooster Tail (Gd 4). This shallow drop is normally paddled via the rooster tail on the central chute. From here the river enters the main gorge.

Contributor:
Alastair Collis

Roy (Gorge) 093

Introduction This middle section of the Roy lies in a gorge far below the road. If you have a problem, it will be a long and strenuous climb out on river right in search of the road. This is a fantastic paddle with interest throughout, but never too scary. Tight bedrock rapids follow one another in quick succession, and although the run eases in its second half, it is still good fun.

Grade **3/4(5)**
Length **3½km**
OS sheet **34**

Water Level Moderately wet / Very wet.

Gauge The middle gorge can be scraped at most flows. Upstream from the road bridge at Roy Bridge, you will see a band of quartz rock on river left. If the river is up to the level of the quartz the gorge will be at a good medium / high level. In very high water the Roy Gorge is fast and unrelenting, a swim here is punished severely.

Access Driving up Glen Roy, the road climbs to an obvious viewpoint and car park. The gorge can be seen far below. The road then descends to the river and after 2 miles the best put-in is reached. Park at the muddy gateway and walk across the field to find Rooster Tail rapid. Egress from the river is at the dilapidated bridge at Cranachan (297 846). From here a steep track leads up the hill to the road, not for those with a heart complaint. A small stone pillar at the side of the road marks the spot where exhausted paddlers will emerge from their ascent. If the river is high you might avoid this trauma by continuing on down the Lower Roy.

Description From Rooster Tail a section of grade 3+ rapids gets the trip under way. The white water gradually becomes more continuous with the banks coming in to restrict the paddler's view as the gorge begins. Take care as Head Banger, a nasty grade 5, appears suddenly on a left-hand bend. Inspect or portage on river left. Immediately below this badly undercut rapid lies The Brothers Grim (Gd 4+), a ledge split by a large boulder. The action continues around the S-bend downstream. There is lots of good grade 3/4 water in the next kilometre or so. The main event, once a tricky diagonal ledge, has all but disappeared after changes to the river bed, leaving a steep ramp into a flushing wave. A river wide ledge stands out as the next highlight and just begs to be run blind. Once past this the gorge opens out and the grade eases to allow for more playful kayaking. With one last effort the river squeezes through a 1m gap in the cliffs and the gorge section is over. Cranachan Bridge is just around the corner and now with your last dregs of energy the walk out is started.

Contributor:
Alastair Collis

Other important points In very high water the Roy Gorge is a continuous and committing run. What in low to medium water were fun rapids with small holes become unrecognisable and boils and holes abound. Swimming above Head Banger at this level is a dangerous sport.

093 Roy (Lower)

Grade	**2/3**
Length	**5km**
OS sheet	**41**

Introduction This section brings you down to Roy Bridge, just above the confluence with the Spean. The Lower Roy has the confines of an open gorge but the technical difficulty of an open river. The constant gradient gives paddling at grade 2/3 all the way to Roy Bridge. Below here to the egress point there is a rapid that touches on grade 3.

Water Level Moderately wet/Very wet. For playboating the wetter the better.

Gauge As with the Roy Gorge the quartz band of rock upstream of the road bridge gives a good indication of the fun to be had. If the level is below the rock shelf it will be a bit of a scrape.

Access The Lower Roy starts 3 miles up the Glen Roy road, parking is as for the egress for the Roy Gorge. With high usage the parking at the top of the trail down to the river (297 846) can be congested. Access is down the dirt track to the old bridge. If you can't park at the dirt track please have a thought for the local farmers when selecting a secondary parking place. The egress point is downstream of the A86 road bridge, below the last good rapid. An obvious eddy on the left allows you to walk out on level ground. Following the path will bring you to a fence with a stile. Walk from here under the railway bridge, up past the Grey Corries Lodge and out to the main road. The public car park is just over the road bridge.

Description The Lower Roy starts with a small flat section to warm up on before the gradient picks up at a series of S-bends. It is here that the Allt Glas Dhoire enters from the left to swell the volume. As the river continues on its way to Roy Bridge at a constant gradient, a second tributary enters from the right, this is the same one crossed on the drive to the put-in, (the Allt Ionndrainn). In high water, there is a playhole on the right side of the island just above here. In a couple of places, care needs to be taken and trees can also create a hazard from time to time. The river has a small kick in its tail below the main road bridge in the way of a fun grade 3 rapid. This is overcome right of centre. The egress point is directly below here where the river flattens out. Alternatively carry on down the Middle Spean to Spean Bridge.

Contributor:
Alastair Collis

Allt Ionndrainn 094

Description Joining the Lower Roy on river right, the Allt Ionndrainn can be a giggle in high water. You can nip up from the confluence, best done on river left, and put on just above the road bridge. There are 3 main drops on the journey back to the Lower Roy.

Grade	**4/5**
Length	**250m**
OS sheet	**41**

Contributor:
Alastair Collis

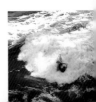

095 Allt Glas Dhoire

Grade **4**
Length **2km**
OS sheet **41**

Introduction The Allt Glas Dhoire is a tributary of the Roy. Joining the main river on the left just below the take-out for the gorge. This is a super little river, which is usually at the right level when the Roy Gorge is on the high side to run comfortably. Solid grade 3 initially, it becomes pushy grade 4 further on with little time for rest.

Water Level Very wet. If there is a lot of water in the Roy, this trip could be on.

Gauge At the confluence with the Roy, the Glas Dhoire should be bank full. If the river is high enough, there will be a good grade 3/4 rapid at this point, with a couple of powerful holes. The upper half of this run would be a real rock bash without enough water, so it's probably not worth the walk if conditions look marginal.

Access The neatest way to do this trip is to access the river by paddling down from the start of the Lower Roy. Check the level at the confluence and if all is well, walk up the river left bank. It is a steep haul at first up a long grassy slope before you gain a forest track, which leads up the glen. After 2km the track leads down to and crosses the river. This is the put-in.

Description The river starts as a gentle boulder run. The first noticeable drop is soon upon you and has a nice playhole at the bottom. Take care at the point where the river splits round a central island, as there is a fence across the river just below.
The gradient now increases and the river becomes progressively more difficult, climaxing at a gnarly fall with a channel down the left side. This can be surveyed from the eddy on river right, just above the fall. Most of the action is tucked away in a deep tree lined gorge, and you need to watch out for strainers and other debris. Generally eddies are small and at higher flows they will be in short supply. Not a good place for a big group! The confluence with the Roy signals the end of a good run. From here it is easiest to carry on down the lower section, which will have the odd surf wave to play on.

Contributor:
Gregor Muir

Other important points The road on the south side of the glen is private.

Cour 096

Grade	**4/5**
Length	**5km**
OS sheet	**41**

Introduction Draining a large portion of the Grey Corries, the Cour runs through the Leanachan Forest to join the Spean just upstream of Spean Bridge. A magical trip of slabs and falls, tucked away in the forest. The highlight is a pushy gorge, which starts with a tasty 4m fall. Sadly, this river is a bit of a hassle to get to and rarely at the right flow . . . Ahh!

Water Level As with all the streams on the southern side of the Spean, the Cour is severely affected by water abstraction for the aluminium works at Fort William. The section described here lies below the dam, so there needs to be enough water around to meet their requirements and some! Generally heavy rain combined with snow melt gives the best chance of a runnable level. In extreme flows the upper half of the run feels very continuous.

Gauge The small burn next to the Ben Nevis Distillery at the A82/A830 junction east of Fort William gives a good indication of whether the rivers coming from the Grey Corries are over-flowing their dams. If there is a good flow here, the Cour may also be up. A more accurate place to judge the flow on the Cour is the metal bridge at the take-out. A tributary that joins the river below the best of the white water contributes a good deal of the flow here, so the river will have to be full and flowing hard at this point for the run to be on.

Access To get to the put-in, take the A82 from Spean Bridge towards Fort William. After about 1 mile, turn left onto the minor road leading south to Leanachan Farm. Park here and follow the path that links with the old tramline from the aluminium works. The best put-in is where the tramline crosses the river via a rickety old bridge (230 767). It is about a 2km walk (35 minutes). You can take out at the metal bridge just before the river joins the Spean, or continue downstream for another 3km to Spean Bridge. To reach the upper take-out, turn off the A82 in Spean Bridge next to the Commando Bar. Follow the minor road through the village and along the south side of the Spean, until you reach the bridge over the Cour.

Description The gnarly slab immediately below the bridge at the put-in is perhaps the nastiest feature on the river and you

may choose to get in below it. From here, there are a couple of nice ledges before the river 'goes off'. The main event is a gorge that has some powerful holes at a high flow, but it's all good clean fun (Gd 4/5). After a couple of kilometres, the drops become more spaced, but you are still carried along nicely. The Allt an Loin joins from river left, and you need to keep a watch out for the lower falls, which are the sting in the tail. Definitely inspect this drop, which is shallow for most of its width. If you really like walking with your boat, the Cour has been paddled from 4km further upstream. Here the river is a roughly even mix of portages, flat water and nice rapids.

Contributor:
Andy Jackson

Other important points An OS map will be useful to find the put in for this run.

097 Allt Choimhlidh

Grade	**5**
Length	**1km**
OS sheet	**41**

Description A tributary of the Cour, this burn is worth a paddle, but is a mission to get to. Follow the approach to the Cour but walk a further 1km to the dam on the Allt Choimhlidh at (239 765). An OS map may be useful to help find the spot. The 1km section above the dam is a blast at high flows, grade 5 with 2 portages.

Contributor: Andy Jackson

098 Braveheart Burn (Allt Coire an Eoin)

Grade	**steep**
Length	**500m**
OS sheet	**41**

Introduction This remote and inaccessible burn is tucked away in the most beautiful and delicate valley behind Aonach Mor. You can see its huge upper waterfalls and paddleable sections clearly on a wet day from the war memorial above Spean Bridge. This wee burn epitomises Scottish steep paddling and it's a great place to walk up to with or without a boat. It has only been completed by a handful of paddlers and will probably take you most of the day to do, so leave plenty of time. (You will be too tired to do anything else after this).

Water Level This burn does need a fair amount of water and is best done in the sunshine just after summer rain.

Gauge You should be able to see white streaks coming off the surrounding hillsides, but don't wait for too much water.

Access We'll leave this up to your own ingenuity, but the forest tracks leading away from Aonach Mor car park may be your best bet. For the car park, turn off the A82 halfway between Spean Bridge and Fort William following signposts for Nevis Range Ski Centre.

Description As you walk your boat up the left-hand bank past some of the steepest paddling in Scotland, you'll know when to put in. You see a set of drops that don't look 'worth it' at the end of a relatively flat section running out from the huge waterfalls further up the glen. From the put-in it's straight onto a 'helter-skelter' slide, past (or into) a rock above a drop with a shallow pool. Try to avoid slamming yourself into the left-hand wall. A narrow slot then leads you into a pool with a truly impressive horizon line. It's only with the prior knowledge that the next drop is a perfect parabola into a deep pool that one ventures forth. But hold your horses and be ready to grab the right bank to make a sharp exit for a walk round the next monster! Put back in directly below and off you go again. Some will opt to walk the next long slide with its scooped out landing. The cavernous drop above the forestry fencing is awe inspiring, twisting into a narrow pool with, at good flows, a surprisingly sticky hole waiting at the bottom. The next set of smooth slides are an absolute delight, with a speed splat halfway down. A few smaller drops then lead to a flatter section and the end of the run.

Contributors:
Paul Currant
and Gregor Muir

Other important points Take out before going down Alcan's water intake.

Gloy (Upper) 099

Grade	**3/4(5)**
Length	**4km**
OS sheet	**34**

○○○

Introduction Just north of Spean Bridge, the Gloy emerges to flow next to the A82 and into Loch Lochy. This section is the upper half of the river down to the narrow road bridge. The Upper Gloy is a secluded river trip in an open glen. The river has an isolated feel and is continuous in nature.

Water Level Wet/Very wet. The river rises rapidly during heavy rain and doesn't hold water for very long.

Gauge The Upper Gloy is paddleable when the river above the narrow bridge at the start of the glen is bank full, i.e. all the rocks

upstream are covered. When the river is in full spate the upper section is quite fast and full-on.

Access Approach by the A82, Spean Bridge to Inverness road. The turn off is signposted Glen Gloy, 2 miles from the Spean Bridge Commando Memorial. The river can be inspected from the narrow bridge on this minor road or from the bottom of my garden. Egress here, river left below the bridge. The single-track road continues on to Upper Glenfintaig. Put in here. Do not be tempted to go any further past the farm buildings.

Description The Upper Gloy is continuously interesting, especially in higher flows. A short gorge leads from the put-in, with the river running at grade 3 for most of its length down to the take-out at the narrow bridge. In one or two places the river narrows producing short action packed rapids. These can creep up on the unwary. The only rapid of major note is about halfway down. Here a ledge drop can reach grade 5 at higher flows. It is best inspected from river left, and the holes in the centre and the left avoided by a nifty move from left to right. Watch out for low trees, which can become a bit of a nuisance when the river is high enough to run.

Other important points Large groups with minibuses/canoe trailers etc. would be advised to be discreet at least. The glen is in continuous use, and has a potentially sensitive access situation. The local farmer has concerns about paddlers scaring livestock into the river when it is in spate. Unfortunately the run is only feasible in such wet conditions so the best advice is to travel in small groups and take care not to be causing general disruption, or chasing any sheep! Leave the canoe trailer at home - it saves it getting stuck on the bridge!

Contributor:
Stew Rogers

Gloy (Lower) 099

Introduction The lower half of this popular trip runs parallel to the A82 for much of its length. The Lower Gloy is a great run in a somewhat 'industrial' gorge. Continuously interesting, it has the potential to become quite serious.

Grade	**4**
Length	**1km**
OS sheet	**34**

Water Level Wet. The Lower Gloy can be paddled at a slightly lower level than the upper section. The river rises rapidly during heavy rain and doesn't hold water for very long.

Gauge Best conditions are to be had when all the rocks below the bridge are covered and the river is bank full. Caution is advised at high spate flows, when the river may reach grade 5.

Access Approach by the A82, Spean Bridge to Inverness road. Take a right turn, signposted to Glen Gloy, 2 miles from the Spean Bridge Commando Memorial. Turn into the glen and put in below the narrow bridge on river left. It is best to get out above the main road bridge on the A82 where there is a large lay-by on river left.

Description The Lower Gloy is a superb section of water, which although short in length, will feel a lot longer. The river runs alongside the A82 in a narrow gorge, before passing under the road bridge and disappearing down an impressive and dangerous gorge to end up in Loch Lochy. Once on the water, the gorge starts almost immediately. The rapids are all pretty similar in nature, narrow in places with some tight lines. The eddies are plentiful and although you should expect to share them with the carcass of a washing machine or other junk hurled down from the main road, don't let this put you off, the boating is continually good. At the time of writing the gorge was home to a few trees across the river. Careful scouting should see you clear of all the major obstacles, however, things change, not least trees in this section of water. Keep an eye open for blockages, especially at the bottom of some of the narrower sections. At higher flows the drops become less technical, but faster, with stronger hydraulics, and there are fewer eddies. It's quite important to get the take-out right. If in doubt, get out above the bridge and scramble back up to the lay-by on the A82. Beyond the road bridge, the river continues for a couple of drops before coming to an abrupt end. To paddle further

Contributor:
Stew Rogers

is death on a stick. The river weaves a steep tortuous descent through sumps and ledges to the loch. If you wish to paddle the drops below the bridge there is a take-out on river right on the lip of this monster. However this is definitely not recommended at high flows. Carry up to the path, then walk the boats back up to the A82. Please don't drive down as this is a private road through the holiday homes.

Other important points Don't go past the road bridge in high flows or if you are unsure of the take-out!

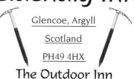

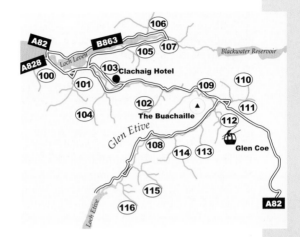

N

approx. scale 1cm = 5km

Glen Etive & Glen Coe

Glen Etive & Glen Coe

Surely the home of Scottish Steep Creeking, Glen Coe and Glen Etive offer between them some of the finest burn bashing to be found in this guide. To get the most from this area you will need to be adept in the art of short boat paddling and also not be adverse to the odd bit of shouldering your boat.

The waters of the Leven and Coe offer excellent and challenging grade 5 boating while the many tributaries of the Etive feature some fine rock bashing action. That said, the falls on the Middle Etive are not as daunting as they look and the upper and lower sections on the Etive mean that there is something here for everyone. In times of low water the Middle Etive is usually scrapeable but the area comes into its own when the small burns are running. In very high flows try the Lower Coe or perhaps the Coupall, you'll have a blast.

Glencoe village has all the amenities for the travelling kayaker and the Clachaig Inn boasts a good array of beers and whiskeys. Although wild camping is now discouraged in the area around the pub, there are ample campsites, bunkhouses, B&B's and self catering chalets in and around Glencoe to suit all pockets. Wild camping is permitted in parts of Glen Etive, although campfires are not permitted. This beautiful area is now more in the minds of the young adventurous kayaker after the films Highlander, Braveheart and Rob Roy. It is also more importantly the site of the clan massacre of the Macdonalds by the Campbells in 1692. Fine scenery caps it all off and the area is ideally suited for a boating weekend with many options lying in easy reach.

100 Gleann a Chaolais Burn

Grade	5
Length	1km
OS sheet	41

Access From the Ballachulish Bridge, turn left at the roundabout onto the A828. After half a mile you cross the burn. Left turn and drive up the glen to a car park by the side of the river. Access from here is via a private Forestry Commission road. It may be possible to get permission to drive up the road by contacting the Lorne Forest District office on 01631 566 155. Otherwise it is a 1km walk up to the put-in just upstream of the bridge over the river.

Description This is the burn running down the glen immediately behind the Ballachulish bridge. Not to be confused with the Allt

Gleann A Chaolais on the road to Kinlochleven. The river is bouldery in nature but it's the 3 or 4 bedrock drops which provide the
fun for the paddler. The best of these is the slab found right at
the start. There is also a slightly ugly weir which may need to be
portaged. When high enough to paddle, the river has a real 'edge
of your seat' feel with small eddies and little chance to stop above
the main drops.

Contributor:
Andy Jackson

Laroch 101

Introduction The sleepy village of Ballachulish is split in two by
the River Laroch. It flows through Gleann an Fhiodh emptying
into Loch Leven just north of Glencoe. As it winds its way down
the glen, the Laroch moves in and out of dark mysterious gorges.
These defiles are split by sections of technical kayaking, demanding nerve and ingenuity to overcome the worst of the obstacles.
This river is not exactly designed for kayaking, but it makes for
an interesting journey.

Grade	**5**
Length	**500m**
OS sheet	**40**

Water Level Wet / Very wet.

Gauge Looking upstream from the footbridge in the village, the
view should be of a shallow boulder field that you can weave
through without too many problems. This flow will give a good
level for the gorges but render the rest hydraulically challenged,
with a generally 'bony' feel. More water means less rocks, but
fewer eddies and overall a harder, more pushy trip.

Access Turn off the A82 into Ballachulish and drive to the most
southerly end of the village. At this point there is a road bridge
with associated footbridge. From here a private road leads south
out of the village past the school. There is space at the bridge to
park one car; any more vehicles should be parked elsewhere.
From here it's shanks's pony time, following the road through
the farm and onto the footpath to Glen Creran. After 2km you
cross a small tributary by some handy stepping stones. Half a km
beyond here look out for the spot where the river drops from an
open and shallow channel into a dark, tree lined gorge.

Description The start of the top gorge is guarded by Entry Falls
(Gd 5). This fall is a benchmark for the river. From here a series

of small drops ends at a cool boof ledge, deep in the gorge. The river is now a mixture of tight squeezes and narrow chutes. The most notable of these being 'What You See Is What You Get' (Gd 4+). At times the river is almost laughably narrow, quite a giggle as long as you don't get jammed somewhere you shouldn't. The river now has you in its spell; and the drops are flashing past as you become adept at reading the water from your boat. Just as you are settling in, the river picks up and throws in a multi-drop grade 5. Shortly after this is the most serious drop of the run, 'Sick & Twisted' (Gd 5+), a five stage slot/shelf drop. If you decided to give this one a miss, it is possible to seal launch back in from the left bank and run the super cool ledges just downstream. From here the river remains narrow for a while, as it passes through several slate rock bands. A small tributary, the Allt Socaich, enters from river right. Just below this there is a clean and picturesque double drop (Gd 4). The river is now more open and boulder strewn as it picks up size on its way down to Loch Leven. There are however still plenty of drops and ledges to keep you entertained. Take out just below the footbridge on river right. At bigger flows the lower section, from the Allt Socaich, would be a good run of grade 4+.

Contributors:
Alastair Collis,
Andy Jackson and
Iain JC Murray

Other important points There are plenty of overhanging trees on this run and as usual these tend to end up in the water. This is an intense little run with more rapids than you could shake a stick at. Expect some equipment damage.

102 Allt Lairig Eilde

Grade	**4/5**
Length	**2km**
OS sheet	**41**

Contributor:
Bridget Thomas

Description The Allt Lairig Eilde drops into the Coe at the Falls of Glen Coe, a popular tourist stop beside the A82. It's an exciting wee tributary with some crazy falls and slabs. Some unlikely drops do go, although elbow pads and old blades are a good idea. There is a clean looking 10m drop near the end of the run, but watch out as the pool is shallow. The run ends with the Falls of Glencoe. This fall has been run, but only by the certifiable.

Coe (Upper) 103

Grade	**5**
Length	**500m**
OS sheet	**40**

Introduction The Coe flows beside the A82 as it comes down off Rannoch Moor and into the mountainous area of Glen Coe. The river is divided into two sections by Loch Achtriochtan: the upper being steep and rock infested, the lower having a powerful feel and an impressive gorge.

Water Level Moderately wet. For a first run down and to get a feel for what is a very demanding and dangerous run a medium flow is recommended.

Gauge At the put-in below the Falls of Glen Coe, the river should look a little bony.

Access Access is from the lay-by on the corner of the A82 where the Allt Lairig Eilde tumbles into the river over the obvious three tiered Falls of Glen Coe. It is also possible to start further up the River Coe as it runs parallel to the road at this point. Take out at or before Loch Achtriochtan (140 568). Parking here is scarce and it may be that the paddlers will want to paddle across the loch to where there is adequate parking at the put-in for the lower run.

Description The Upper Coe is hemmed in by a very restricted gorge, which is at times only as wide as a kayak. This gives a threatening and bizarre feel with most of the rapids having only one route of dubious quality. Whilst the upper part is a true portage fest, the river eventually widens and produces some interesting deeper gorges, with some enjoyable grade 4 water.

Contributor:
Alastair Collis

Other important points Comments from those who have run the river include; 'This run is a true rocky ditch and is only recommended for those who have a ticking fetish' and 'I have run the river once and have no desire to run it again'. On the other hand some people do like this run!

103 Coe (Lower)

Grade	**4/5**
Length	**4km**
OS sheet	**41**

Introduction This lower section of the River Coe is situated just outside the Clachaig Inn, a handy place to toast success or ponder disaster! The Lower Coe is a mixture of delights. It starts with an open section that is clearly visible from the road. A good spot to massage your ego, as tourists stop to stare at the crazy people in the rain. From there it drops into a vertically sided gorge with no escape. Then as suddenly as the gorge started, it is finished and you are catapulted between overhanging trees and out into a wide flood plain. The finish comes with a narrowing of the river and then the open loch.

Water Level Wet / Very wet. For experts to get the best out of the Lower Coe, you must have walked away from all the other rivers in the area, as they are far too full to be run. At lower flows the river is less powerful and still entertaining.

Gauge The upper part of this stretch can be viewed from the A82. If the river looks a little bony, the gorge can be run by itself and gives a pleasant run at about grade 3+. If there are few rocks showing and the river is a series of waves, the run will be a full on grade 4+ experience.

Access Access is from the lay-by off the A82 where the river flows out of Loch Achtriochtan (140 568). There is an easy take-out at the Glen Coe Bistro. This can be found immediately beside the A82 half a mile before Glencoe village. You are welcome to park in the Bistro car park, but please pop in and say hello to the Bistro staff if you are leaving your vehicle. When you get off the river please follow the steps up from the river and round to the car park. Alternatively it is possible to continue down to Loch Leven (098 592), but note the dangerous pothole drop in this stretch.

Description Getting boats and gear off the roof of a vehicle can be the hardest part of this trip; when there is big water in Glencoe it is usually accompanied by gale force winds. Once you've warmed up it's away and under the road bridge - make sure you pick the correct arch! The crashing wave that waits soon lets you know what's in store. From here to the first rapid it's grade 3 boating with a couple of 'class' surf waves. The river has considerable power given its relatively small size. Get out after the surf waves as Back Door Man (Gd 5-) awaits you around the corner. There are a couple of lines that can be run, both with varying degrees of success. The next rapid, Entry Falls (Gd 4+), has a Himalayan feel and has a line down the right. Next stop the Lower Gorge. Eddying out above it gives you a chance to collect your thoughts and take in some oxygen. This ½km section is basically solo boating at high flows, when rescue from the bank is out of the question due to the speed of the water and the vertical sides. Enter here and receive the Coe experience. The river is pushy grade 4+. Its huge waves and boils fire you along its length like a bullet out of a gun. At high flows there is only one eddy to make about half of the way through the gorge. Stopping here allows you to breathe again and watch the rest of the party enthuse about their experience. If your eyes are not out on stalks by this point then you either have no feelings or the river is too low. To contemplate swimming the gorge at this level is not an option. The gorge ends soon after the eddy and all feelings of pleasure and relief are overtaken by the worry that the river is now overhung by trees and moving like an express train. There is the odd tree to negotiate then one more major rapid of grade 5-, which comes up very fast. There is a line on the left and another centre-right if you can find it. The rapid has a strange fold and a powerful stopper that sucks in boats and gives them a sound thrashing. Scout if you can get out in the trees or take the consequences. From here the river opens out into a wide braided section with several channels. Below the usual take-out there is one final rapid just beyond the road bridge. Glencoe Village Falls (Gd 5+) is narrow with a sump in it. Care is needed here and it is not a recommended place for a swim. The river now spews out into Loch Leven. Egress is possible at the lower road bridge.

Contributor:
Alastair Collis

Other important points Although none of the rapids are rated individually above grade 5-, when in flood all normal white water rules are out of the window. It is not a good idea to get on this river without a 'bomber roll', as the force and speed of the water will be your downfall. You can run the Coe at a lower level, but at high flows it is an awesome experience.

104 Allt na Muidhe

Grade **4/5**
Length **1½km**
OS sheet **41**

Contributor:
Andy Jackson

Access Park in the lay-by on the A82 just east of the burn. Walk up the track on river left for 1km, crossing the bridge and putting on a further ½km upstream beyond the farm buildings.

Description Classy grade 4/5 action intermingled with some scary rock features can be found on the Allt na Muidhe, a tributary which joins the Lower Coe just after the end of the gorge. Take good care where a tributary joins from river right in the latter half of the run. A nasty boulder sump is well hidden at the foot of a rapid just above here with more unrunnable water just below! It is best to portage on river left, regaining the river just downstream of the confluence by an awkward seal launch into the narrow potholed channel.

105 Allt Gleann A Chaolais (Caolasnacon Falls)

Grade **4/5**
Length **1km**
OS sheet **41**

Introduction Tumbling from the Aonach Eagach ridge, this burn crosses the B863 midway between Glencoe village and Kinlochleven. This is a short and steep section of river, ideal for getting some drops under your belt. Narrow and twisting with plenty of rockslides and drops, the Allt Gleann A Chaolais has it all, with easy access and rescue. Bring your own camera crew!

Water Level Moderately wet/Wet. Spate conditions are needed to bring the best out of this gnarly little section.

Gauge If you can see rock through the lower drop there is only just enough water.

Access Parking consists of two very small lay-bys on the downstream side of the bridge. Please do not move the white stones, and be aware that you are on a tight bend. As you walk up beside the river, you can choose your own put-in. Most paddlers get out just above the bridge. In very high water, it is possible to continue down to Loch Leven with one portage.

Description The action starts about 1 km above the road with a largish fall into a shallowish pool! From here the drops come thick and fast. Broaches, rocksplats and nose scrapes are the dangers and from time to time trees block the route. One extremely narrow slot is normally portaged and you would be wise to find this in advance. The last two main drops on this section both have hard entries at high water. Overall the run is very easy to inspect, almost from the car!

Contributors:
Roger Palin and
Andy Jackson

Nathrach 106

Grade **5(6)**
Length **1½km**
OS sheet **41**

Introduction The Nathrach runs off the Mamores, next to the West Highland Way, and cuts a gorge down to the loch, close to Kinlochleven. This river has everything: tight, technical paddling, big falls and much, much more. Situated in a deep gorge with high wooded sides, tree jams are common and rescues extremely difficult.

Water Level Medium. However, if you're in the area and there is no water, a gorge walk inspection of this run will provide good entertainment.

Gauge If the fall by the road looks picturesque, and has a good steady flow then the section will be in condition. The fall itself is too shallow to run. If the river is in thunderous spate condition, look elsewhere.

Access The take-out is at the B863 road bridge, just over a mile from Kinlochleven, on the north side of the loch. To reach the put-in, drive up to Mamore Lodge Hotel, parking £1, and then walk along the West Highland Way.

Description The start point (163 629) gives a narrow twisting journey down to the obvious confluence. This section is pretty extreme with some definite portages which will probably need some rope work! At the junction of the two tributaries, the flow increases but the run does become a little more reasonable. That said the run from here is incredibly exciting, with every possible problem and no let up. After a log jam there is a huge double fall of over 20 metres! The second drop (10m) has been run, but the bigger one still awaits a challenger. This is really a day for extreme adventure paddlers wanting a challenge. If you portage round you will find the action continues below until yet more unrunnable drops above the bridge.

Contributors:
Roger Palin and
Andy Jackson

Other important points A full gorge walk inspection is recommended before attempting this run as you can drop into non-reversible pools. Failing this you will need bank support with abseil equipment and good knowledge.

107 Leven

Grade **5/5+**
Length **1½km**
OS sheet **41**

Introduction The River Leven is tucked away at the head of Loch Leven and neatly splits the town of Kinlochleven in two. The Blackwater reservoir was built at the beginning of the 20th century to harness the power of the Leven. The water that should be in the Leven was instead used to generate electricity for the production of aluminum. The smelter is now closed but the water has not been freed! It is still harnessed and electricity fed to the smelter in Fort William. The Leven runs through a series of water worn gorges giving fine bedrock rapids. These are all committing and several give good sport at grade 5+. The central section of the river is the hardest and most temperamental in terms of water levels.

Water Level Wet/Very wet. There needs to be a reasonable amount of water around to counteract the influence of the dam, unless water is being released.

Gauge Looking upstream from the footbridge across the river at the west end of the village, the river should cover approximately 50% of the river bed. A small playhole just upstream of the bridge serves as a good gauge. If the hole looks playable the trip is on! Much more water and the trip is still possible but the biggest falls will be verging on ridiculous! It may be wisest to walk up and check out the last big fall, MacKays Falls, as this is one of the harder drops.

Access From the road bridge in the village, find the minor road that leads up river right. Park where it is no longer navigable and a short walk in the same direction, on a dirt path will lead you out at the gauge bridge. To walk to the put-in find the footpath which leads up river right. It is marked to the dam. After the wooden bridge across the Allt na-h-Eilde tributary, it is only a matter of following the path for a short distance until you draw level with an obvious spill gully below a concrete building, high

Allt a Chaoruinn - Glen Etive & Glen Coe - Chris Dickinson

Coe - Glen Etive & Glen Coe - Jennifer Berry

Allt a Chaoruinn - Glen Etive & Glen Coe - Alex Coon

Etive - Dallness Falls - Glen Etive & Glen Coe - Ryan Clements

on the opposite bank. A short bush walk brings you back to the River Leven and the top of the first rapid, Three Falls to Agrippa.

Description The warm up rapid, Three Falls to Agrippa (Gd 5), is a peach for a starter. The two bedrock ramps, each 3m in height with pools to land in, lead to a vertical entry of 2m into a funky twisting narrow slot with rocky exit fall. Upon leaving the collection pool a small gorge of grade 3+, Cockstone Gorge, brings you to the start of the exciting stuff. From here until the tributary enters from the right the river is grade 4+ or harder. Notable rapids include Boof It, an obvious must-boof ledge, and The Gutter, an easy grade 3. These are followed by The Drain Pipe, a low angle slab with a powerful hole at its base, and The Plug Hole (Gd 5+), a nasty twisting drop that looks ugly in anything but low flows. It is possible to avoid a portage by taking the chicken chute which joins the tributary by using one of the small clefts branching from the right side of the river on the lip of The Plug Hole. From here a short grade 4 section leads you back to the main river just on the lip of one of the most impressive cataracts in Scotland.

At grade 5+, End of the World is easily the most 'full on' rapid on the river. This eye-opening cataract has four large falls, which once committed to must be finished. The first two falls are both 4½m, and can be protected with difficulty. The last twin fall, and biggest at a combined height of 11m, lands in what can be a nasty corner hole. By down climbing the left side of the gorge it is possible to set up protection for this last show of bravado. The cataract finally spills out over a 2m ledge then into an awkward 90⁰ left corner, I Feel Fine. At Grade 5, this is a class way out of the gorge. It is possible by some delicate climbing to run this rapid if you have walked the End of the World.

A short boulder section, grade 3, now brings you to another narrowing where some interesting grade 4 lurks. Just past this is MacKays Falls. This obvious horizon line hides a 6m free fall, which sounds cool until you check out the cave behind the left side of the fall. A seemingly unavoidable flat landing will convince the prudent to walk this one. Now the river calms down until the gauge bridge is reached.

Other important points Elbow pads and a full-face helmet are the ticket on this baby. Be sure to book the hot tub before the run, as this one is hard on the back. This river is one of the test piece rivers of the area and with water in it, will frighten the pants of even the best of boaters. Come mentally prepared!

Contributors:
Roger Palin and
Andy Jackson

There is some creeking to explore on the tributary near the End of the World, the **Allt na-h-Eilde**. This can be a useful alternative put-in.

Etive

Glen Etive is situated off the A82 near the Kingshouse Hotel. A lonely glen just south of Glen Coe, this is a great place to spend time. It is surrounded by the majestic beauty of Buachaille Etive Mor (1022m), Meall a Bhuiridh (1108m) and Chasaig (862m). The glen is best visited during the spring or autumn, as during the summer the midges here make the ones on Skye appear friendly! The outstanding beauty of Glen Etive has led to an increase in its popularity, especially with the kayaking fraternity. The clean bedrock falls and tight delightful gorges with twists, shoots and freefall give rise to a kayaker's paradisiacal playground on earth. The river has something to offer from beginner to extreme play-boating river god. To give close bank support for this playground the road runs alongside the river for most of its course through the glen. The river offers three sections, all of great character. The white water in the middle section in particular can rival anything else on the face of the planet. The upper and lower runs still offer the solitude but cannot match the intensity of the middle section. As a consequence, the middle run is bombarded with large groups of kayakers especially on weekends and during holiday times. At such times, the feeling of isolation is no longer here.

108 Etive (Upper)

Grade **2(5+)**
Length **4km**
OS sheet **41**

Introduction The run on the Upper Etive starts at the Kingshouse Hotel. The beauty of Buachaille Etive Mor (buckle etiv more), often known simply as The Buachaille, is best admired from the small bridge behind the hotel. With its gentle boulder bed, this stretch of river is ideally suited to the intermediate kayaker; there is only one fall that will have to be portaged.

Water Level Very wet. The Upper Etive is a scrape unless the river is high.

Gauge If as you pass over the river on the A82, there are no boulders showing, then the upper section will be a grade 2 float with one portage or grade 5+ fall.

Access Access is from the Kingshouse Hotel (253 547). Sensible parking here is important as the narrow road is in constant use with patrons of the hotel and walkers. You may need to drop off your gear and park away from the river. Egress is at the start of the Middle Etive. Parking can be congested here so the use of the large lay-bys a kilometre upstream may be advised. Cars parked here can easily be seen from the river.

Description The Etive is very benign in its upper stretch and meanders over the bouldery river bed. The only fly in the ointment for the beginner is Buachaille Etive Falls (245 543). This grade 5+ fall tumbles over slabs for about 9m then takes a 3m plunge into a rock infested pool. Once around this there is more grade 2 water until the vehicles are seen in the lay-by or you pass under an old sheep trolley 200m above the Triple Falls. Taking out well above this is recommended in high water.

Contributor:
Alastair Collis

Other important points If attempting this section in high water be aware of the portage and take out well above it.

Etive (Middle) 108

Introduction This section of river is located off the A82 on the Glen Etive road, clearly signposted. The Middle Etive starts approximately 2½ miles into the glen, at the first bedrock falls, Triple Falls. This is possibly one of the most famous pieces of white water in Scotland. The middle section contains the bulk of the white water with a series of bedrock rapids. These bedrock beauties are linked together by easier bouldery flat sections.

Grade	**4+**
Length	**3km**
OS sheet	**41**

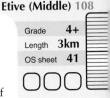

Water Level Moderately wet. Water levels rise and fall quickly on the Etive due to its short nature. In autumn/spring the river will come up in a couple of hours. In a dry summer, it may take a day of persistent rain.

Gauge If as you cross the Etive on the A82 there are no rocks showing in the river, then the middle section is going to be out of order. A better gauge as you drive down the glen is at the first rapid, Triple Falls. If a boulder splits the second fall then the river is low. If this rock is gone then we are talkin'. If there is a large ugly pour-over ledge here, it is wiser to look elsewhere.

Access Put in at the first rapid, Triple Falls, (219 520). There is limited vehicle space here and kayakers usually park in one of the passing places on the single track Glen Etive road. Egress is opposite the Allt a Chaoruinn. Parking is also limited here so please pull well off the road.

Description Triple Falls is a good test of nerve and your extreme playboating skills. With a combined height of 3m for the first two drops, this is classic grade 4 territory. Just around the corner is the final fall in this combination. A generous pool allows the collection of any flotsam. You don't have to go far downstream to come across the next horizon line. Letterbox is slightly stiffer at grade 4+. A line close to the left bank, and going left, with a hefty boof will get you past. Beware of the undercut boulder on the right. Immediately downstream is the Ski Jump (Gd 3). This is probably the easiest fall on the river and lands in a pleasant pool. A short and beautiful gorge leads you out and down through some easier water to the first real test of your journey. Crack of Doom (Gd 4+) is a narrow slot that is guarded by a bouldery run-in. Many top boaters have had deep experiences here. Two tight corners follow and a large drop into a deep pool. If you are starting to get into the river then you will be pleased to know that you are soon to fall upon the Crack of Dawn (Gd 4+). Many years ago this used to be a favourite place to practise rescuing people from vertical pins. However with the introduction of short rounded boats and more recently a shift in the bedrock, this has become less frequent. Although not the biggest height loss this is definitely the shallowest pool you will encounter. Easy water with a couple of surf waves brings you to the Rock Slide (Gd 4). This granite slab gives a thrilling run on either side. The left side gives the playboater some fun in a shallow, but retentive, hole halfway down.

The short flat stretch that follows ends at an ominous horizon line. This is Eas an Fhir Mhóir, the Big Man's Falls, also known as Right Angle Falls (Gd 4+). The height of this fall depends on the amount of beer consumed whilst telling the tale, but is generally accepted to be in the region of 6m. For many this will be their first taste of free-fall. Enjoy it, for it doesn't last long. The following gorge is a nice rest from the strenuous activity upstream and leads out to the boulder run down to the Allt á Chaoruinn and the last classic grade 4+ fall. Inspection here is advised. From here it is a short run through the narrow gorge to the usual take-out just below the private road bridge (197 512).

Other important points To continue from here to the Dalness Falls is a pleasant grade 2 run. There is only one rapid of note which runs at grade 4. A distinct plume of spray and a large beach on the right marks where you can get out and inspect the approach to this rapid.

Contributor:
Alastair Collis

Etive (Dalness) 108

Introduction Dalness Falls (172 511) are a serious undertaking and have the added problem of 'no canoeing' signs and barbed wire.

Grade	5
Length	**500m**
OS sheet	**41**

Water Level The grades given are for what is considered to be a medium flow. In dry conditions the grades get easier. The river has awesome power at high flows and the grades would go up.

Access The Dalness section starts where the road loops briefly away from the river, some 2 miles beyond the take-out for the usual run.

Description Double Falls open the run. At grade 4, this 2½m fall has two options. Next comes an ugly narrow slot (Gd 5), where a well-trained bank team is a must. Now you are at the start of the final section. A clean boof left off the next fall will avoid contact with the opposite wall and set you up for the narrow slot. A small rapid brings you into a cosy eddy above the 7½m Dalness Falls. A right line is a must as the left side lands on a rock ledge that is visible in very low flows. Once in the pool your troubles are not over as the right wall is undercut. It has been known for a person and boat to disappear under the wall and, with much effort on behalf of the bank support team, reappear downstream.

Contributor:
Alastair Collis

Other important points Deer fences have been erected to try to promote regeneration of Caledonian Pinewood along the river bank. Please be careful not to damage them getting to and from the river.

108 Etive (Lower)

Grade **2(4)**
Length **10km**
OS sheet **41/50**

○○○

Introduction The Etive spends the last of its real energy at Dalness Falls (166 508). From here the mountains pull back their skirts and let the Etive flow over shingle beds and through the occasional gorge. You finish by falling into Loch Etive (116 455). The lack of hard white water is made up for by the splendour of the passing scenery.

Water Level A high level leads to a more exciting trip with the main rapid becoming a grade harder. This is not one to do at low flows.

Gauge As for the Upper and Middle Etive runs. If the middle section is too high this could be a good option.

Access The best access is about ½km below Dalness Falls, at a point where the road comes close to the river on a bend. Egress is to the road on the right just before the river enters the loch.

Contributor:
Alastair Collis

Description From the recommended access point, there is about 2km of easier water until you reach Lake Falls (Gd 4), which is visible from the road just upstream of an obvious detached lake. This fall is somewhat technical and leads into a small gorge. At high flows this rapid becomes harder and the gorge disappears. From here to the egress, there are some interesting sections with higher water being best.

Other important points This stretch can be combined with some 'trib bashing' as a couple of tasty runs join it along its length.

Tributaries of the Etive

A lot of fun can be had exploring the small side creeks in Glen Etive. A short boat and a sense of adventure are definitely required to enjoy this 'mountain surfing'.

Coupall 109

Grade	**4(5)**
Length	**2km**
OS sheet	**41**

Introduction The Coupall flows below Buachaille Etive Mor and can be seen from the A82 when travelling north towards Glen Coe. This short run has just a 'Coupall' of good rapids! One long steep hard section and a second nasty fall, all in outstanding scenery.

Water Level Very wet. This river needs plenty of rain.

Gauge The main rapid is visible from the A82. It should look white and not too rocky.

Access To get to the put-in, drive along the A82 and park at Jacksonville Hut (the black one) just north of the Kingshouse Hotel. Park and cross the road carefully. To reach the take-out, drive back towards the Kingshouse and take the first right down the single track Glen Etive road. Egress is at the confluence with the Etive.

Description Flat water at the put-in leads to a horizon line. Thus begins two steep and intense rapids. It is possible to scout from the river, but caution is required at higher flows. Flatter water then leads to a nasty fall about 50m above the Glen Etive road. This grade 5 can be tackled down the guts or via a chicken chute on river left. Portage left to the car, or right to continue to the confluence with the Etive.

Contributors:
Neil Farmer
and Greg McColm

Other important points On a high flow day this makes a nice start to the upper reaches of the Etive. From the confluence bouncy grade 2/3 water, with one portage, leads to the waterfalls at the start of the Middle Etive.

110 Allt Bhlaidach

Grade	4/5
Length	1km
OS sheet	41

Contributor:
Callum Anderson

Access Walk up the private road (see Top Etive) for 100m until you see the river on your left. Continue up the hillside on river right until you reach a small island. Put in here, or if the river is very high, continue on.

Description This very steep mountain stream on the northerly hillside above the Kingshouse needs heavy recent rain to bring it into condition. The top section from the higher put-in is the steepest, involving several big rock slides.

111 Etive (Top)

Grade	4
Length	1km
OS sheet	41

Contributor:
Neil Farmer

Access From the A82, turn off opposite the Glen Etive junction and drive back towards the Kingshouse Hotel. Park at the private road gate and walk up the road for about a mile to an obvious flattening.

Description Some fun can be had on the upper reaches of the Etive behind the Kingshouse Hotel. With wide open boulder rapids, this stretch requires flood conditions. The first rapid on a right-hand bend (Gd 4) is both steep and photogenic. The river then eases slightly to give good grade 4-.

112 Allt Cam Ghlinne

Grade	4
Length	1km
OS sheet	41

Description This trib spills into the Upper Etive on the south side, and requires a good amount of water to be worthwhile.

Contributor: Andy Jackson

113 Allt Fionn Ghlinne

Grade	4
Length	1km
OS sheet	41

Description Known as the Cresta Slabs, this ridiculous burn has been run in its entirety. Take a walk up and ask yourself why? You only need just enough water for lubrication to make this run 'paddleable'.

Contributor: Andy Jackson

Allt a' Chaoruinn 114

Grade	4+
Length	1km
OS sheet	41

Introduction The Allt a' Chaoruinn (owlt a' choorun) is one of the better known tributaries of the Etive. This charming little creek joins the main river at the take-out for the Middle Etive. It is a dream river for the fanatic of the extreme. Its bedrock chutes and slides are something out of your wildest fantasy. At over 80 m/km this is a taste of what all steep creeks should be like.

Water Level This burn needs only one night of good rain to make it runnable. Too much and it quickly becomes a raging torrent. It may be a good option in a summer downpour, or with a spring snow melt. At high flows it is grade 5 territory!

Gauge If the run out to the Etive looks boulder strewn but OK, it's a sure indicator that the drops will be bony but runnable. If the run out has few rocks visible, you're in for a cool run. When there are no rocks visible on the run out, you're in for an epic run. Due to the very small catchment area, this river and its sisters rise and fall faster than a third world dictatorship.

Access Park in the large passing place, on a right-hand bend just past a bridge over the Etive and below the confluence. From here it is possible to boat across the Etive and to walk up the river left of the burn until reaching a wooden bridge - carefully negotiating the end of the fence en route. Cross the bridge and continue up river right on a large boggy track. You are at the top when you reach the fourth drop.

Description The first 6m slide, Speed, is in a deep gutter with only one way down, unless the river is high. It is fast and exciting, but not technically difficult. The wall at the bottom provides a good splat spot. Next is Ecstasy, the longest rapid on the river. Several drops and slides provide the entertainment with some sticky holes at high flows. Don't forget the Tea-Cup Eddy half-way down. The rapid ends in a large pool, where you can collect your thoughts before the next drop. Looking at Pinball it is easy to see how this rapid got its name. Beware of the flipper rock that diverts the water to the right as this has claimed several cag sleeves and elbows. If the river is high, a second line opens up down the left, which is hard to get, but rewarding. The last drop is the Chasm, again there is only one way in. This drop has been

Contributor:
Alastair Collis

run without paddles, as they are or can be a nuisance. The ledge out of here is best boofed on the extreme left. From here the run down to the Etive is an easy respite from the ravages of the Allt a' Chaoruinn.

Other important points   There are people living in the house at the edge of the river. Please be polite and do not trail across their back yard, instead use the river left approach as far as the bridge.

115 Allt Ceitlein

Grade	**4/5**
Length	**500m**
OS sheet	**50**

Description   Another tributary on the south side of the glen, this one is best combined with a trip down the Lower Etive, as both require high water. The first main slabby rapid, Slab Central, is what this run is all about.

Contributor: Andy Jackson

116 Allt Mheuran

Grade	**4+**
Length	**400m**
OS sheet	**50**

Access   This burn is reached by walking down a track from the road, crossing the Etive and climbing up to the white water. You have to repeat this palaver to get back after your run.

Description   More paddleable than some of the other tribs, the Allt Mheuran is worth a visit. Some 'wicked' falls lie tucked away at the head of this burn. They can be paddled at a variety of water levels, from medium low (scrapey) to high (scary). The lower half of the river is a boulder scrape regardless of flow, but it's worth making the effort for the rest.

Contributor:
Andy Jackson

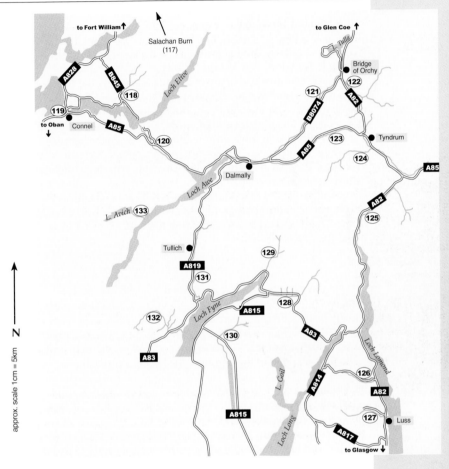

to Fort William ↑

Salachan Burn
(117)

to Glen Coe ↑

L. Tulla

Bridge
of Orchy

A828
B845
118
121
122
A82
B8074
119
to Oban
Connel
A85
120
A85
123
Tyndrum
124
A85

Loch Etive

Loch Awe

Dalmally

L. Avich **133**

A82
125

Tullich

129

A819
131

132

Loch Fyne

A815
128

130
A83

Loch Lomond

A83

L. Goil

A814
126
A82

A815

127
Luss

Loch Long

A817

to Glasgow ↓

N

approx. scale 1cm = 5km

Loch Lomond & Argyll

Loch Lomond and Argyll

This is a large area running from Luss in the south to Bridge of Orchy in the north. The A82 runs the length of the section and allows for easy access to many of the runs. Generally the rivers here require some rain to bring them into condition. If none has fallen recently you may find your options limited, the Awe and Orchy being about your best bet. As the levels rise the Lochy and Lower Falloch soon come into condition and when the heavens really open you can have your pick of any number of classics, the Kinglass, Esragan and Upper Falloch to name but a few. After the storm, as the rivers drop once more, the Orchy shows itself as the 'jewel in the crown' as it holds its water well. It offers both fine playboating and some scary rapids, in a setting which is accessible yet peaceful, and normally windswept too!

117 Salachan Burn

Grade	**4/5**
Length	**2½km**
OS sheet	**49**

Contributor:
Andy Jackson

Access Driving south along the A828 the Salachan Burn is crossed 2 miles beyond the village of Duror. Access is via a private Forestry Commission road. It may be possible to get permission to drive up the road by contacting the Lorne Forest District office on 01631 566 155. Otherwise it's a 2½km walk up to find a suitable start point in the region of the house at Bealach.

Description A fun trip with lots of interest, there are two good sized falls interspersed with some nice bedrock rapids. At high flows it gets quite pushy and you need to go very carefully to keep the trip under control. At a more moderate spate it's still entertaining with fun to be had finding your way from eddy to eddy.

118 Esragan

Grade	**4+**
Length	**2½km**
OS sheet	**49**

Contributor:
Neil Farmer

Introduction The Esragan flows into the north side of Loch Etive at its western end. This is a serious run, with a very isolated upper gorge and a steep, continuous lower boulder section.

Water Level Very wet. This run needs very heavy rain to bring it into condition. As a rough guide, it will be running if the Orchy is on 3+ at Bridge of Orchy and it is still raining.

Gauge Looking upstream from the bridge at the take-out, the river should look runnable but a little 'scrapey'.

Access The take-out for this run is at the road bridge, on the shores of Loch Etive (B845). From here to reach the put-in, drive up the glen away from Loch Etive, until you reach a sharp left-hand bend, where the road leaves the river. To reach the upper gorge, walk upstream for about an hour, until the confluence of three streams. To run the lower boulder section, contour round the hill from where you have left the car, until you reach the river.

Description The run starts with a deep remote upper gorge. The rapids are pool-drop in nature and generally grade 4/4+. The grade would however go up at very high flows and some of the rapids would be very difficult to portage. Watch out for trees jammed in this upper stretch. The lower boulder section is very continuous and much steeper, with an average gradient of 6%. There is one stretch in particular which is steeper than the rest of the run, and almost certainly a portage, depending on the flow.

Other important points This is a serious and isolated run.

Falls of Lora 119

Description This well-know tidal playspot lies under Connel Bridge, some 10 miles north of Oban on the A85. On the biggest spring tides of the year, this site throws up some very large crashing waves, intimidating whirlpools and huge boils. Paddlers with a bombproof roll will have a ball, but note well that this is a more serious place than your average playspot.

Playspot
OS sheet   **49**

Contributor:
Andy Jackson

120 Awe

Grade	2/3
OS sheet	50
Length	6km

Introduction The Awe flows between Loch Awe and Loch Etive. The section that runs alongside the A85 Lochearnhead to Oban road near the village of Taynuilt, makes a classic beginners' trip. The barrage at the Pass of Brander keeps the level fairly constant, making this a good river when all else is low. In these conditions it is however a real scrape as far as the A85 road bridge. More water is currently released overnight on Saturdays, from approximately 9pm - 9am and after prolonged periods of rain. Additionally, in recent years there have been two negotiated daytime releases per year, one in spring and one in the autumn. Details of these are often a last minute affair; the best source of information is the SCA office. The river is at the top end of its grade when the barrage is releasing, particularly if all three sluices are open.

Water Level The Awe can always be paddled, but heavy rain is needed to produce an unscheduled release. Even if the barrage is not releasing, several small tributaries enter the river and the second half of the trip will be more fun if there is some rain or snow melt around.

Gauge The washed away bridge just upstream of the point at which the river is crossed by the A85 is a good place to check the flow.

Access Put in at the Pass of Brander barrage on the A85, halfway between Lochawe and Taynuilt. To reach the take-out at the Inverawe Fisheries and Smokehouse car park, turn right on to the minor road signposted for Inverawe.

Description When the barrage is open a surf wave appears, which makes a convenient place to wait while the shuttle is being run. From here to the road bridge, the river is a series of rocky grade 2 rapids, known as the Graveyard. After the bridge the river enters a gorge with a long grade 2 rapid, ending in a 90° bend, which may be interesting in high water. The best rapid of the river, Magnetic Boulder (Gd 2/3), comes next. At the bottom of the rapid there is a nice playwave at most levels, although it may be shallow when the river is low. A deep pool follows that can be used to collect the pieces. From here on, the gorge is a series of grade 2 drops and pools until the river opens out onto shingle rapids. The take-out is on the right-hand bank by the suspension bridge. A short walk through a cow field brings you to the

Smokehouse. Paddlers from St Andrews University advise that
you should look out for bulls, 'particularly if you have a red boat'.
Alternatively, you can continue down the river for a further ½km.
Here marker buoys and signs warn of an approaching weir, which
should always be inspected. At certain water levels and tidal
conditions, the weir completely disappears, at other times there is
a 2m drop into an unfriendly stopper.

Contributors:
Bill Kersel and
Andy Jackson

Other important points The pool at the put-in, below the barrage
on the River Awe, is an important one for fishing interests as it
can contain some of the best fishing on the river. The tailrace
from the barrage also provides some useful white water and
this means there can be several parties all interested in the same
piece of water. You can help avoid any problems by speaking to
any fishermen who may be present when you first arrive at the
river. Often a friendly introduction helps to reduce any tension
and gives the angler sufficient time to finish fishing the pool and
move downstream before you play at the barrage. Friendly communication can go a long way to ensuring that the needs of both
paddlers and anglers are accommodated.

Orchy

Introduction Half a mile south of the Bridge of Orchy Hotel, on
the A82 between Glasgow and Fort William, is a small signpost proudly proclaiming Glen Orchy. This single track road,
the B8074, leads all the way to the bottom of the glen, where it
meets the A85 Tyndrum to Oban road. The open glacier carved
glen offers superb views both upstream and downstream. Beinn
Dothaidh (bayn daw-ee), 1000m, and Beinn Dorain, 1074m, stand
at the head of Glen Orchy and are not small hills. Nestling at
the foot of these mountains, Loch Tulla supplies the Orchy with
a small reservoir of water. Consequently, the Orchy retains its
water slightly longer than any of the neighbouring rivers.
The Orchy's fame has now spread wide as a top venue for water
sports with rafters now plying their trade on the river. At the
Bridge of Orchy, there are 2 big iron gauges on the river right
downstream side, which give an indication of the river's state.
Most kayakers use the one closest to the bank, which you have
to climb down to river level to assess. The flow can be read as
follows: Below 1 and the river is low, around 2½ and the river is

at medium/high flows. At 5 the river will be on the B8074 in places and must be considered in good spate. The river is divided into three sections of varying degrees of difficulty:

The upper is an easy run requiring high water levels.
The classic middle run has the hardest rapids.
The lower run has some easy white water but is mainly flat.

The upper and lower sections do not receive the traffic that the more popular middle section has to endure. The open nature of the glen, along with its low banking and ever present road mean good access to the river for photographs, portaging and rescue.

After a hard day on the river the Bridge of Orchy Hotel provides a warm respite with friendly staff and a splendid bunkhouse.

121 Orchy (Upper)

Grade	2
Length	**3km**
OS sheet	**50**

Location The Upper Orchy flows out of Loch Tulla and ends at the Bridge of Orchy Hotel. It can be clearly seen from the A82 if approaching from the north. Although not as popular as its more famous sister, the Middle Orchy, the upper section offers the inexperienced a good test of basic skills before moving on to more difficult water. The open nature of this stretch of water, with its shingle rapids, gives easy access to the banks. Combined with eddies in abundance there is never a shortage of places to stop and receive instruction or depart to the waiting vehicle.

Water Level Wet/Very wet. The Orchy holds its water well and this run is often in condition a couple of days after heavy prolonged rain.

Gauge Above 2½ on the gauge at Bridge of Orchy is ideal.

Access Turn off the A82 beside the Bridge of Orchy Hotel, onto the B8005, and drive down and over the river. Follow this road along the right bank of the river until you are at Loch Tulla. It is a short carry to put on at the loch. Egress is back at Bridge of Orchy. There is ample parking space here to leave cars.

Contributor:
Alastair Collis

Description Starting at Loch Tulla, the Orchy has a series of fine surf waves with lots to keep the novice interested. At the Bridge of Orchy, there is a slightly harder rapid to negotiate.

Other important points It is possible to combine this section with the middle and lower sections to give a very long day out.

Orchy (Middle) 121

Introduction With a road running alongside for most of its length, the Orchy is a river where non-paddling partners can watch from the comfort of a heated vehicle. Likewise it makes an ideal group trip since all of the rapids can be portaged one way or another along the boggy banks.

Grade **3/5(5)**
Length **8km**
OS sheet **50**

The Middle Orchy is very similar to rivers such as the Zambezi and Kali Gandaki in that it has very defined rapids separated by long flat stretches. Most of the falls are produced by harder sections of bedrock, which have resisted erosion.

Water Level Moderately wet/Very wet. After prolonged rain the river will retain its water for a day or so.

Gauge The gauge at Bridge of Orchy helps to judge the flow. At 0 the run will be passable but bumpy in places, at 1 it will be fun, at 3 big and exciting, and at 5 or so it will be mind altering. Don't forget that during rain there are many small tributaries swelling the Orchy along its length. The Orchy runs most often during the spring melt or after prolonged rain when the ground has become saturated and Loch Tulla has refilled after the summer droughts. 0.6 on the SEPA gauge should be considered a minimum level for the middle section.

Access There are many access points to the Middle Orchy depending on how much of the river you wish to do. The most regularly used is at the Bridge of Orchy Hotel by the gauge. Another popular access point for more experienced paddlers is where the B8074 first meets the Orchy at the small tributary the Allt Kinglass. Here there is very limited space for vehicles so please park carefully. For large groups with mini-buses or many cars there is a pull-in 500m upstream of Sheep Trolley Gorge with ample parking. This is the obvious rapid close to the road 1½ miles down the B8074. This also provides an access or egress point for shortened trips. The most commonly used egress is where the road meets the river at the Witches Step, just over ½ a mile upstream of the Falls of Orchy. This

again provides limited parking, but there are more passing places between here and the bridge over the river at the Falls of Orchy.

Description Putting in at the Allt Kinglass you only have a short float to get your muscles into boating mode before the first rapid is signified by a big rock in the river. Hence the name, Big Rock. At Grade 3+, this is an ideal warm up for what is to come below. The next rapid, Chicken Shoot (Gd 4), comes after a right-hand bend and in high flows offers good sport. In low water the left side of the island is somewhat easier, (Gd 3). From here there is a long paddle past the occasional interesting playspot before the start of Sheep Trolley Gorge (Gd 3+), the old sheep trolley has long since been removed. The wave at the end of the rapid offers excellent entertainment for the flat hulled boats as well as being a good tail squirt spot. The road is now close to the river all the way to Easan Dubha (essan doo-u), where the river gathers its strength and produces a stiff obstacle. A run off-line here can go unpunished or end in near drowning! The fall becomes easier with more water, as the middle line becomes a monster wave. However, the consequences of a swim become serious and, unless rapidly 'bagged', swimmers may get washed through Sore Tooth (Gd 4) just below. Several people have come out of this experience with scary stories and broken bones.
A small step leads to Roller Coaster (Gd 3). Soon after this the river leaves the road. End of Civilisation, by far the best grade 4 and the longest rapid on the river, appears after a left-hand bend. To make the best of this rapid, take a line down the left through the two holes and into the convenient eddy. The second half of the rapid is easier but still demands respect.
Easier water leads to several playwaves and holes, the most inviting of which is only yards from the last eddy before Eas a Chathaidh (ess a' cha-ay). This is the hardest rapid on the river, and deserves its grade 5 reputation. A large island splits the river giving three choices. In very low water the right offers a 5m vertical fall. At higher flows, this rapidly gains a monster towback and recirculates swimmers very nicely. The left side is more often paddled and offers a double drop that ends in a jagged ramp. In high water a line opens up over the middle of the island. Portaging is simple on the left and the seal launch entry fun.
Below here an island splits the river, and at medium/high flows, there is a playhole on the left side. This hole can recirculate swimmers at high flows. From here, you are soon at the Witches

Step (Gd 4-). Here the river splits again with most water coming down the left. The brave or off-line will drop into the guts of the slot and reappear several metres downstream vacuum packed. Run close to the island on its left-hand side to avoid this under-water experience.

This is an ideal place to get out as a short grassy bank leads to the road. From here, in anything but spate flows, the river is relatively easy until you get to Eas Urchaidh (ess oorachay) or the Falls of Orchy. These impressive falls have been run down the fish ladder on the right in very low water and by an extreme left shoot missing the main rapid in medium flows. Only in spate conditions does the guts of the rapid become runnable and then it is still a full-on encounter well worth the Grade 5+ ticket.

Contributor:
Alastair Collis

Orchy (Lower) 121

Grade	**3**
Length	**10km**
OS sheet	**50**

Introduction Starting at the Falls of Orchy and following the river to its end in Loch Awe, this section is probably accessed with greater ease from the southern end of the glen if it is being run on its own. This slow moving, meandering section brings its own delights to those who prefer their river trips with a little less excitement. The river now has a steady gradient and the rapids that exist are short and sweet.

Water Level Moderately wet / Very wet.

Gauge As for the Upper and Middle Orchy. If approaching from the south end of the glen there is a gauge on the lower run. This is at the old suspension bridge at Catnish. If it reads more than 3 then you will be in for a good time.

Access To reach the put-in from the A85, drive up the glen on the B8074 until you reach the dramatic Falls of Orchy (242 321). Access to the river is from the right bank below the falls, by the metal road bridge. It is possible to get out above Loch Awe, at Dalmally Bridge on the A85 (165 276). However, the paddle out into the loch is worth the extra effort to visit the now abandoned Castle Kilchurn (132 276), which occupies the spit of land jutting out into Loch Awe's north-eastern end.

Description The Lower Orchy is a good run for intermediate paddlers as swims are not generally of a serious nature. Putting in just below the Falls of Orchy, the first obstacle is a weir that has a weakness in the middle where at some flows a good surf wave forms. From here down to the river gauge at Catnish, the river is grade 2+. The next 6km are a mixed bag of shingle and braided rapids where the forest comes and goes from the banks. Shortly after a lonely house on the left bank the river picks up, and a section of more continuous water brings you to Dalmally Bridge (165 276). From here to the loch, the river is grade 1, but if you have navigated the rest of the river from Loch Tulla, why not complete the trip?

Contributor:
Alastair Collis

Other important points In high water this section has some big waves and a couple of juicy holes. In spate conditions it becomes very fast until the last 4km.

122 Allt Kinglass

Grade	4
Length	½km
OS sheet	50

◯ ◯ ◯

Introduction The Kinglass is a small tributary of the Orchy, just to the south of Bridge of Orchy. Short and steep, the Kinglass is a great bit of fun. It is usually done before running the classic Middle Orchy section - something to do whilst the shuttle is being run!

Water Level This run doesn't really need an awful lot of water. If there's enough to do the Orchy, there should be enough for this.

Gauge If the top drop looks OK, the rest of the river will also be runnable. Alternatively, walk up the side and inspect the whole run.

Access There is a small parking place beside the bridge crossing the Allt Kinglass on the A82. Put in on the upstream side of the bridge (298 383). If the road is busy or the parking space occupied, it may be safer to drive to the take-out and walk up the river bank to the start. To get to the take-out, turn off the A82 onto the B8074 just south of Bridge of Orchy. After about 200m you get to a bridge over the Kinglass (295 385).

Description This short section holds a series of three or four falls over bedrock. It can be a bit shallow in places but is well worth doing, particularly as you won't miss any of the main rapids on the Orchy by putting on here. It is possible to stop and inspect each rapid as you come to it, or to walk the whole section before getting on. At higher flows you could start a kilometre further upstream for some nice grade 3/4 warm up rapids. Driving south towards Tyndrum, park next to the A82 at a lay-by on the right and cut across the fields to the river.

Contributors:
Dave Mathews
and Ian Thom

Lochy 123

Grade	**5**
Length	**3½km**
OS sheet	**50**

Introduction The Lochy flows alongside the A85 Tyndrum to Oban road, dropping into the Lower Orchy, close to Inverlochy.

Water level Moderately wet. This trip needs only a splash of run off, and will run the day after rain or showery conditions. Above this level the run would not be an option.

Gauge Go to the A85 road bridge at Inverlochy. Upstream of the bridge on the river left, there are two metal poles sticking out of the rock. When the water is level with the lower of the two poles the run is at a good level – all the drops will go. Any higher and the run would be very courageous.

Access The put-in (229 271) is found at a lay-by on the A85, a little over 2 miles east of Inverlochy. There is a white sign on the railway across the glen. The river disappears into a foreboding canyon at this point. Take out where the river is crossed by the A85 in Inverlochy (197 276). Park just downstream of the bridge.

Description This is a very committing river for established grade 5 knuckleheads. The river is in a fairly deep and constricted canyon, the hard drops being of the waterfall variety. The trip starts abruptly with a slab leading into a grade 5 drop – a quick break out is a necessity to inspect this fall. Then follows three other grade 5 classics. A 4m fall on river right requires a good boof to clear the sticky hole. An ugly split fall, Fubar has been run by the left-hand slot. The highlight of the trip, a 5m fall with a tricky run in, can be inspected from the forest walk halfway down the river. A look at this gives an idea of what the river is like - impressive I'm sure you'll agree!

Contributor:
Greg Nicks

Other important points Some of the drops are awkward to inspect without a bit of climbing and are very tricky to portage without scrambling and boat lowering. If you are up to it, this is a brilliant run, a true test piece of the area. Not for the weak or claustrophobic.

124 Cononish

Grade	**4(5)**
Length	**2km**
OS sheet	**50**

Introduction Running from Ben Lui to the A82 just south of Tyndrum, this is a steep and continuous river, with numerous difficult falls.

Water Level Very wet.

Gauge The river should be at least bank full under the A82 road bridge and ideally halfway up the concrete ledge running under the bridge. Save this one for when levels are too high to tackle the Lochy or Lower Falloch.

Access Driving north on the A82 you cross the river 2 miles before reaching Tyndrum. This is the take-out and limited parking is available, river left on the upstream side of the bridge. To reach the put-in continue north on the A82 for 2 miles, turning left in Tyndrum to find 'Tyndrum Lower Station'. Parking at the station, you need to walk in to the river via the forest track. Cross the railway at the level crossing and follow the track through the forest for just under 2km. Put in where the track drops down to the river.

Contributor:
Neil Farmer

Description Easy rapids lead to the first difficult drop, marked by a fence. Several people have experienced nasty swims in the depths of this stopper! Inspect/portage on river left. Numerous steep rapids follow. Take extreme care as there is a hidden syphon lurking on the left side of a 1m fall. This very dangerous feature is far from obvious. Run a 3m waterfall on river right into a gorge. Beyond the railway bridge, there are a set of falls with several possible channels. Centre left is probably best. One more tricky rapid follows before reaching the A82. Paddlers have been pinned in the dangerous pothole in the central channel here. Portage or inspect on river left.

Other important points The forest track described is a private road.

Falloch (Top) 125

Grade	**4/5**
Length	**2km**
OS sheet	**50**

Introduction The top part of the Falloch is a remote and excellent small burn. It consists of long, continuous slab/slide rapids with occasional small falls. It's narrow, has few eddies and is very steep, making this a hard and serious run, but never desperate.

Water Level Very wet. If the river is paddleable at the put-in for the Upper Falloch, it is worth walking up the extra 2km to do this stretch.

Gauge Look at this one if the SEPA gauge is above 1.5 and the Lower Falloch at the Seven Dwarves rapid is huge/unrunnable.

Access Park in the large lay-by just south of Crianlarich (take care here, walkers' cars have been broken into). Walk across the field, under the railway line, and straight up the Falloch, at 90° to the road. After 1km a branch is reached in the path. Follow this to the river and a small bridge, walk upstream as far as you fancy! Inspect the take-out above the last drop (the water is fast and continuous here). This drop has been run but does not look very nice either with or without water!

Description There are several notable rapids. A long, steep boulder rapid leads down to the bridge. After the bridge, there is a long right-trending shallow slab, soon followed by a set of slides down to a fence over/in the river - there is a single wire and a fence post in the middle of the 'pool' above a small 1-2m fall. There is now a good sized pool to collect yourself. Another fall around a boulder leads to an easier section down to a right bend, and trees. Get out above the bend and trees, and not too late to inspect the last fall from river right.

Other important points There was a tree in one fall in March 2002. At super high flows this section could be very serious. Inspect all of the river on the walk up and be careful. Paul Currant described this section in flood as 'one of the scariest day's boating I've had in Scotland.' Proceed with caution!

Contributor:
Neil Farmer

125 Falloch (Upper)

Grade	**4(5)**
Length	**4km**
OS sheet	**50**

Introduction The Falloch runs parallel to the A82 at the northern end of Loch Lomond. The upper stretch starts some 2 miles west of Crianlarich. Perhaps not as classy as the Lower Falloch, this is still a good trip with some excellent white water. The river runs through short gorges lined with the remnants of the Caledonian pine forest, making you feel a lot further from the A82 than you actually are.

Water Level Wet/Very wet. Try this one when the Lower Falloch looks a little on the high side.

Gauge The river will want to be full and definitely running high and looking scary when viewed from the A82 road bridge on the lower run (see the description for the Lower Falloch). 1.0 on the SEPA gauge should be considered a minimum flow.

Access Driving north on the A82, you will find the put-in for the Upper Falloch about 2 miles before Crianlarich. The river can be seen emerging from the forest and mountains before making a left turn to run alongside the A82. At a straight in the road, there is a large lay-by offering ample parking. Cross under the railway and put in at the left-hand bend. Take out some 3 miles downstream at the Falls of Falloch car park or earlier by walking up from the wooden bridge at Derrydarroch Farm.

Description At high flows this run is fairly shifting, so although the water is easy enough to start off with, you need to take care not to get swept into anything unpleasant. A large slab into a narrow slot marks the start of the white water proper. This is a grade 5 and probably fairly dangerous at very high flows. A long grade 4 section, which is the sweetest part of the river, lies upstream of the bridge at Derrydaroch Farm. From here to the Falls of Falloch is a mixture of easier water and one or two nasty drops that are probably worth a portage. If you don't intend to run the Falls, consider getting out at the farm as it's an awkward walk from above the falls back to the car park.

Contributor:
Andy Jackson

Falloch (Lower) 125

Grade	**4/5**
Length	**3km**
OS sheet	**56**

Introduction The Falloch runs parallel to the A82 at the northern end of Loch Lomond. The Lower Falloch is the 3km run starting with the Falls of Falloch. It is a beautiful run that combines a large photogenic waterfall with a long technical gorge. At good water levels, the river is difficult and serious, but never desperate; one of Scotland's classic rivers.

Water Level Moderately wet / Wet. At high flows this run will be very serious, but some rain is required.

Gauge If the fall visible from the road is just runnable, then the river is possible. The best indicator is to look over the second (most northerly) road bridge, and decide if you like the look of the rapids that run underneath. 0.8 on the SEPA gauge should be considered a minimum flow.

Access Park at the Falls of Falloch car park and walk upstream for 200m. Get in above or below the waterfall. Take out below the fall that can be seen from the road, upstream of Glen Falloch farm. Parking is limited here, so please be considerate and walk the shuttle if necessary.

Description The 10m waterfall at the put-in is run on a fairly regular basis, but is high enough to do some serious damage if you get it wrong. Watch out for the tricky stopper on the lip! For a more mellow start to the trip, seal launch into the pool below the fall, and take some time out to enjoy the scenery. From this point, straightforward rapids lead to a sharp right-hand bend and the first grade 4 fall. The river eases off, then drops over several chutes and increases once more to grade 4. A left turn and looming walls herald the start of the gorge and the Seven Dwarves, best inspected on the left. All the drops are runnable but protection is recommended, especially for The Black Hole, a small drop into a very sticky hole which lurks under the A82 bridge. Flat water leads back under the A82 to a large fall, Twist and Shout, which can be inspected from the huge central rock. It is run left, but there is a chicken shoot / fish ladder on the right. The last fall, visible from the road, has rocks at the base of the main line and is best run over the slabs on the left-hand side.

Contributor:
Neil Farmer

Other important points At high flows, these rapids will become very serious, and you may wish to consider running the top section down to the falls.

126 Douglas Water

Grade **3/4(5+)**
Length **1½km**
OS sheet **41**

Introduction The Douglas flows into the west side of Loch Lomond. It is to the north of Glen Luss. The river starts off flat before dropping into a wooded valley. The rapids are plentiful and inspection easy. The Falls of Douglas, which mark the end of the run, is an impressive yet serious piece of water.

Water Level Medium to high water levels are required.

Gauge If the river below the A82 road bridge looks just runnable, then this river is worth doing. The main rapids are all in a narrow gorge, so high water under the road bridge may be a sign of more excitement than you need.

Access Turn off the A82 onto the Glen Douglas road. Almost immediately you will reach a small car park next to a bridge crossing the Douglas. You can park your car here and walk upstream for a couple of minutes to see the Falls of Douglas. This is the take-out. There are several possible access points as you drive up the glen. The best place to put in is at a lay-by where there is a right-hand bend on the river, 1½ miles upstream from the Falls. Here the river is the closest it gets to the road. It is possible to extend the trip by putting in further upstream, although there is MOD land higher up the glen, which should probably be avoided.

Description The upper section of the river is flat. As the river drops into the gorge, the fun starts, with many short grade 3/4 rapids. These are all easily inspected, often from the last eddy above them. Fallen trees are a potential hazard making inspection worthwhile. One narrow grade 4 about 1km into the run is particularly prone to tree blockages and is usually inspected from the right. Grade 3 water continues down until a longer rapid is encountered. This consists of some 100m of grade 3+ water, ending in a superb slab slide after a left turn. There are plenty of eddies down this rapid.

From here, a few straightforward rapids take you down to the egress, immediately above the Falls of Douglas. Don't miss the eddy! The Falls have been paddled, but not at a level where the rest of the river would go. A short walk is required to get back to the car park by the bridge. This is often a very slippery path with a steep drop down to the river.

Other important points The description given is for medium levels. In high water this river has an alpine feel to it. New surf waves appear, new lines are possible and eddies are fewer, an incredible run. It is strongly advised to inspect the last eddy above the Falls before paddling the river. At certain levels this eddy is not large, and the Falls are not obvious from the river.

Contributors:
Ian Thom and
Neil Farmer

Luss Water 127

Grade	**4(4+)**
Length	**3km**
OS sheet	**56**

Introduction The Luss flows from the west into the bottom end of Loch Lomond. This is a small river in a deep wooded glen. It has many paddleable rapids, but take care to miss the Falls of Luss.

Water Level Wet. The river needs plenty of water, but is a serious undertaking at very high flows.

Gauge Most of the rocks below the A82 road bridge should be covered. 0.5 on the SEPA gauge should be considered a minimum flow.

Access Turn off the A82 and drive to the top of Glen Luss. Put in on the Mollochan Burn, which should look small but runnable. Parking is limited here - there is alternative parking down the glen below Glenmollochan Farm. The take-out is below the old road bridge, in Luss village, where there is a large car park.

Description Most of the rapids are runnable at grade 4. Watch out for the 3m, two-tier fall on the Mollochan Burn, which appears some 200m from the start. The harder rapids (Gd 4+) on the main river are in the first 1km. After 1½km the river drops into a nasty tree choked gorge, The Falls of Luss, which can be portaged either side. The river then eases slightly on the way down to the village of Luss.

Contributor:
Neil Farmer

Other important points This run is similar in style to the neighbouring Douglas Water.

128 Kinglas

Grade **4+(5)**
Length **6km**
OS sheet **33**

Introduction The river follows an open, steep-sided glen from just below the 'Rest and Be Thankful' pass to Loch Fyne. A firm favourite, the Kinglas is a steep and continuous alpine style river. It rises and falls quickly, but is more than worth the effort.

Water Level Wet/Very wet. This is a run to do whilst it's still raining, or has only just stopped. Heavy localised rain the night before is a good sign. A new hydro scheme has been built on the upper half of this run. The new intake weir is at a series of slabs where the river steepens and should be portaged. The amount of water taken by the scheme (1cumec) is relatively small, so hopefully not too much paddling will be lost.

Gauge There are rock slabs under Butterbridge, the old stone road bridge at the top of the glen. If these are covered, the river is runnable. If the water level is up to or over the banks, the top section will be serious, and the gorge harder still.

Access Put on at Butterbridge, found on the A83 from Tarbet to Inveraray, 2 miles upstream from the junction with the A815. Take out where the A83 meets Loch Fyne and the Cairndow village road. There is a convenient bus shelter here in which to await the shuttle. Alternatively a warm drink can be had at the hotel in Cairndow.

Description The first half of the river is pool drop in character, with many grade 4 drops that become much harder in high water. The point where the forest meets the river marks a hard and dangerous drop (Gd 5). After this, the run becomes more continuous, and perhaps half a grade harder than in the upper section. If you weren't psyched enough already, the river now whisks you off into the darkness of the tunnel under the road bridge. But don't worry, so far everyone who has gone in has reappeared, just in time to face the narrow gorge which follows. The final weir should be run centre left.

Other important points Watch out for fallen trees and for a foot-bridge, which may be partially submerged at high flows leaving just a wire to catch the unwary, about 1km above the tunnel, across a narrow slot.

Please do not drive down the private road on river left of the lower section.

Contributor:
Neil Farmer

If the river is very high consider just tackling the upper half and taking out at the island behind the small telephone exchange building.

Fyne 129

Grade	**3(5)**
Length	**8km**
OS sheet	**50**

Introduction This small spate river offers tight technical canoeing in splendid wild country. The first kilometre from Inverchorachan in particular is superb. The road that runs beside the Fyne is privately owned and permission to use it should be sought from Glenfyne Estate; it is most likely to be granted outside the fishing season. Alternatively, it is always possible to walk up.

Access A private road branches off the A83 at the northern end of Loch Fyne and leads on up the glen. The hardest and best of the Fyne is above Glenfyne Lodge, but so is the toughest driving. Where you get in may be determined as much by the state of your vehicle as your paddling ability. If you can make it, put in near a solitary white cottage at a flattening in the glen called Inverchorachan (228 179). Take out at Glenfyne Lodge (214 148) or continue on to Loch Fyne, where the A83 crosses the river's tiny estuary.

Description The opening triple Granite Falls (Gd 5) are technical and spectacular with the 15m deep 'black hole' waiting with open arms below the middle fall. A short way below Granite Falls is the difficult and serious shallow ramped Salmon Ladder (Gd 5) with boulders blocking the exit. After the confluence with the Allt na Lairige, the Fyne is continuously difficult, but never desperate down to the bridge below Glenfyne Lodge. From here it is flat water to the sea.

Contributor:
Terry Storry

Other important points Terry Storry, the author of British White Water and an inspiration to a generation of paddlers, died in a climbing accident in 2004. This river is included in his memory.

130 Cur

Grade	**4/5**
Length	**4km**
OS sheet	**56**

Contributor:
Neil Farmer

Introduction Steep and open to start, the river soon drops into a gorge and care must be taken to avoid trees.

Water Level Very wet. The Kinglas should be running high for this to be worthwhile.

Access From the A83, follow the A815 Dunoon road over the Kinglas tunnel to Strachur. Stay on the A815 through the town, past a petrol station, then turn left towards Succoth. Follow the road past the forestry operations (not taking the left turn up the glen) to find the take-out at a stone bridge over the river. To find the put-in, turn up the road mentioned, drive past Succoth Farm and follow the river-left fork. Park below the obviously unrunnable section!

Description An open grade 4+ rapid leads to a narrowing of the river and then a fast flowing braided section above a bridge. This is where the right fork joins. Portage over the bridge as there is a fence below it. A nice grade 4 rapid forms where the 2 tributaries join, leading to the gorge above Succoth Farm. Beware, there is a grade 5 fall here with a tree across it. The section below is about grade 4, has several trees blocking the river and is fast flowing. A swim would not be nice or very safe.

131 Aray

Grade	**4(5)**
Length	**6km**
OS sheet	**56**

Introduction A good-sized river, the Aray flows into Loch Fyne. Just south of two better-known classics, the Awe and the Orchy, this is a highly entertaining river with some good grade 5 action. The main attractions are 3 sets of falls, which provide a good technical challenge. Even if these falls are portaged, the river will still provide the intermediate paddler with a fun trip.

Water Level Wet. The Aray needs quite a lot of rain to be runnable and tends to run off quickly despite its size. However, take note that the harder rapids get increasingly serious at higher flows.

Gauge It's best to judge the flow by locating any of the major falls described below. This should allow you to decide if the trip is on, as well as noting those 'must make' eddies. If you can easily float between the falls the trip will be fun. A good high flow is best but beware that at super high flows it would be easy to get swept into the falls, which look hideous.

Access Drive north on the A819 from Inveraray. After 4½ miles, there is a braided section of the river that is alongside the road (086 144). Get in here or further upstream if you enjoy dodging low trees! The take-out is very pleasant, keep going to the sea and finish at the Inveraray harbour front.

Description The first part of the run is easy cruising. However, this ends abruptly after about 1½km at the Falls of Aray, marked by a wire bridge. Don't miss the eddy; inspection or a portage will be required here. The right-hand side is a beautiful staircase fall. The river eases up for a while until Three Bridges (Gd 5) after a kilometre or so. This is a hard rapid with some ugly bedrock. A sneak route exists on river right. A couple of kilometres of pleasant grade 4 follow, before the final grade 5 rapid. Carloonan Mill Falls can be taken by a double drop on the right or a narrow high slot on river left. From here to the sea the river features some weir type drops with the occasional nice surf wave until you hit the salt in Loch Fyne.

Contributor:
Greg Nicks

Other important points At the time of writing a tree is partially blocking the entry drop to the Falls of Aray.

Douglas 132

Grade	**4/5**
Length	**5km**
OS sheet	**56**

Introduction The Douglas lies to the south-west of Inveraray on the A83. The Douglas is a remote river with a variety of rapids, and a long walk in.

Water Level Wet, but not flooding.

Gauge Look upstream over the A83 road bridge. There are two ledges on the bridge pillar (river right). If the water level reaches the top step, then the run should be OK. Alternatively, check out the last rapid above the bridge and decide for yourself.

Access From the A83 road bridge, drive west for approximately 1 mile until you see a farm track with a gate, angling back towards the river. Walk up this track for approximately 5km, then cut through the forest to the river.

Contributor:
Neil Farmer

Description The numerous rapids in the upper section are interrupted by 2 large ugly falls, of about 7m and 9m respectively. Caution is required, as the falls are hidden amongst friendlier rapids - portage left. A set of large slabby falls is followed by a difficult S bend drop and a mini-gorge. Finally a weir appears. This can be portaged on the right-hand side, but please be discreet as you are now very near a private house.

Other important points Please be considerate when parking, changing etc.

133 Avich

Grade **4(4+)**
Length **2km**
OS sheet **55**

Introduction This river runs from Loch Avich into the north side of Loch Awe. The Avich is a wee creek, ideally paddled when conditions are wet, but there's not a great deal of water elsewhere on the west. The river is quite steep in places and characterised by rocky shallow drops.

Water Level Moderately wet / Wet. Loch Avich serves as a reasonable reservoir at the top of the run and should help to keep the river at a runnable level for up to a day after heavy rain. This run probably requires a similar water level to the nearby River Lochy (Glen Orchy), where there is also a gauge; 7 or 8 is a good level. The run is easily feasible lower and if most of the rocks above the bridge are covered the trip should be a go. At high flows the low trees in the first half of the run will be a problem. You can get a good view of the main drops by walking up the track (signed the 'river road') on river left.

Access The river is best approached from Taynuilt, (by the River Awe). From here join the B845 south taking the first right turn towards Inverinan. The road follows the north shore of Loch Awe and you come to the river where the road takes a sharp right turn to cross the narrow bridge. This is the take-out. There is room to park just before the bridge. To reach the put-in, return towards

Etive - Glen Etive & Glen Coe - Neil Farmer

Roy Gorge - Glen Spean - Paul McLaughlin

Kinglas - L. Lomond & Argyll - Neil Farmer

Kinglas - L. Lomond & Argyll - Neil Farmer

Falloch - Loch Lomond and Argyll - Neil Farmer

Inverinan taking the 1st left up towards Loch Avich. You can park by the lochside just after the cattle grid.

Description Put in on the loch, and paddle for about 1km along the easterly shore, until you reach the river. A wee river, initially flat with a tree slalom, there are only a couple of rocky ledges before you come to the first major event. This consists of 4 shallow rapids/drops and is worth a look, in case of trees. The one rapid of consequence on the river, definitely worth inspecting, is aptly named Batty Crease (Gd 4+). It's a narrow triple fall, with a pot-hole on the second drop. At lower levels the pothole was OK, as each one of our boats navigated the bottom, and popped up heading skywards! From here it's a bit of a rock bash to the take-out, on river left, just before the road bridge crosses the river.

Contributor:
Heather Smith

The East

The East

Strathspey

Tay & Tribs

Up fae Dundee

Central

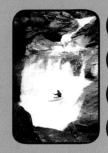

approx scale 1cm = 5km

N

to Inverness

Forres

A96

A940

A939

134

135

Beachans

136

Dulsie

A940

A939

B9102

137

A95

Bridge of Avon

B9007

A95

B9008

B9102

Grantown on Spey

138

A938

B9136

139

A939

A95

B970

Tomintoul

Strathspey

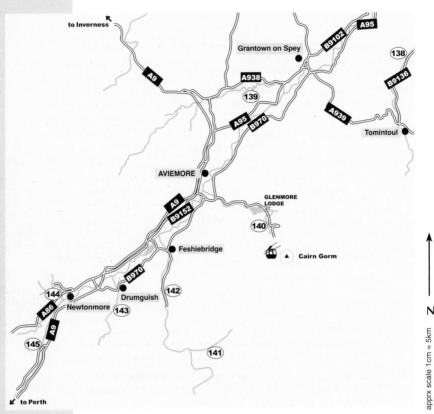

apprx scale 1cm = 5km

Strathspey Continued

Strathspey

The Spey and Findhorn are the two main rivers of this area and to many need no introduction. The Spey is one of the major rivers of Scotland, but it does perhaps offer more to the touring canoeist or salmon fishermen than the white water enthusiast. The Findhorn more than makes up for this. A large river it offers no less than four white water runs. There are some good tributaries in the upper reaches of the Spey such as the Feshie, Tromie and Calder, and Aviemore perhaps makes the best base for exploring these. Outdoor gear shops and a selection of fine 'nighteries' provide all the ingredients for a fine paddling destination. Strathspey is not blessed with as much rain as its western or northern neighbours. Watch out for weather systems sweeping in from the north-east, as these can feed the rivers of this region well. Melting snow from the Cairngorm Mountains can also provide high flows, so its worth watching for any sharp rise in temperature in the months of March or April which might strip the mountains of their wintry cover.

Findhorn

The Findhorn runs north into the Moray Firth near Forres. Draining the Monadhliath Mountains, its upper reaches are largely flat and uninteresting, but in its last 24km, the river contains a series of pleasant gorges giving white water of all levels. There are 4 sections that are regularly paddled, the choice being generally dependent on the ability of the paddlers concerned and the amount of water around.

Top   Good spate boating at grade 3.

Upper   A grade 3/4 section that needs medium to high flows, this is a great section for developing river running skills.

Middle   This section requires a similar water level to the upper stretch, but is a grade easier.

Lower Gorge   This is a classic stretch of river. At Grade 4/5 it's considerably harder than the other sections and can be run with less water.

Parking is generally quite limited with other users, such as walkers, also looking for space. This is particularly the case at Randolph's Leap, which often attracts a number of visitors. Please keep the number of vehicles to a minimum, park considerately and change discreetly. This is a tranquil area and general noise and disturbance should be kept to a minimum.

134 Findhorn (Top)

Grade	**3(4)**
Length	**3km**
OS sheet	**27**

Introduction The top section runs from Banchor to Dulsie, just off the B9007 well north of Carrbridge. This is a wonderful, short and exciting trip through open gorge scenery.

Water Level Moderately wet / Very wet.

Gauge Check the level at Dulsie bridge; if there is enough water flowing down the right-hand side of the large rock slab on the bottom fall of the Dulsie rapid to paddle this channel, the river is high and this section will be a super paddle. A full river-width stopper above the final drop tells its own story - the river is stonking at this level. 0.4 on the SEPA gauge should be considered a minimum flow.

Access From Dulsie bridge, find the minor road on river left. At Banchor, where the road descends to the river for the first time, there is limited parking on a grassy area at the bottom of the hill on the left-hand side of the road. Put in down a steep slope from this area. Access through this area should be maintained for estate vehicles. Take out on river left below Dulsie.

Description The river starts off through shallow shingle banks, but quickly closes in to flow through an open gorge for most of its length to Dulsie bridge. Rapids are frequent and playspots plentiful. All the rapids can be run by eddy hopping, but if the need arises inspection and safety are easy to arrange. Inspection of Dulsie Rapid (Gd 4) from the right-hand bank is possible but can be awkward. It may be simpler to check it out from the top of the bank prior to commencing the trip.

Contributor:
Jim Gibson

Other important points Please note the points made in the introduction about parking and changing, thanks.

Findhorn (Upper) 134

Introduction Dulsie to Ardclach Churchyard (Ferness). A longer trip, this stretch is excellent for both the intermediate paddler and developing leader to expand their skills.

Grade	**3/4**
Length	**7km**
OS sheet	**27**

Water Level Moderately wet / Very wet.

Gauge As for the top section. If the rapid at Dulsie bridge looks low, the river will become 'scrapey' and less worthwhile. 0.3 on the SEPA gauge should be considered a minimum flow.

Access At Dulsie bridge, a path leads down to the river on river left. To put in above Dulsie, take access across a grassed area through a gate at the parking lay-by. Care has to be taken to cross a barbed wire fence on this pathway and the subsequent steep descent to the river. Paddlers have occasionally been challenged gaining access directly above Dulsie rapid. It is possible to take out at Ardclach Church, or Logie bridge.

Description This trip is mostly grade 3 with shingle banks and little drops. It has one little gorge section, Levens Gorge (Gd 4), where the river sweeps round a left-hand bend and the water is channelled into the gorge entrance via a drop on river left. There is a beach on river right from where inspection and safety can be carried out. The line is fairly obvious: the pour-over on the right-hand side of the drop should normally be avoided. The gorge section should generally be run towards the left-hand side, as there is a hidden sump in the rock formation on river right. After this gorge the river opens up again with enough variation to maintain the paddler's interest. One other drop in an open gorge section is located about 2km above the take-out and may require inspection, depending on the capabilities of the group. This can be done from the shingle banks on river right.
Following this rapid the river opens up again, and a leisurely paddle follows, down to the take-out at Ardclach Church. Paddle down to the large eddy on the left and walk up the river bank to find a pathway up to the church car park. Do not get out above this, as it will involve walking across a field to the car. The farmer has expressed serious concerns about paddlers causing disturbance to his animals grazing in this field. An alternative egress is at Logie bridge a further 2km downstream.

Contributor:
Jim Gibson

Other important points Car parking is limited at Dulsie bridge
and the surfaced car park at the church is for people visiting
the church graveyard. The graveyard is still in use and burials
continue to happen despite the church being derelict. It is best to
avoid this area during funeral services.

134 Findhorn (Middle)

Grade **2/3**
Length **9km**
OS sheet **27**

Introduction Ardclach-Logie-Dalltullich-Randolphs Leap. A long
trip, which can be broken down into shorter sections, this
is an excellent stretch for the developing river paddler and for
experienced paddlers to polish up on their technique. It is also
a good section for developing leadership skills with a variety
of rapids, all of which can be run from the river. If required,
inspection and safety can easily be achieved.

Water Level This trip is best done at medium to high levels. A
trip at low levels can be fun but a bit of a scrape on the shallower sections.

Gauge Have a quick level check at the put-in. If the river is floatable here the section will be passable. As for the upper section,
0.3 on the SEPA gauge should be considered a minimum flow.

Access Access and egress is possible at:
• Ardclach Churchyard
• Logie Bridge - a small parking area on the south side, at the
   east end of the bridge; the farmers access must be maintained
   at all times.
• Dalltullich Bridge - limited to two vehicles.
• Relugas Bridge - to the south side and east end of the bridge
   just below Dalltullich.
•Randolph's Leap - a large parking lay-by beside the road.

Description From Ardclach, the river starts off at grade 3, and
remains steady at this grade until just after Logie bridge. It then
runs through some shingle/rocky grade 2 rapids for about 3km.
After a right-hand bend the river gathers in a large pool just before
a noticeably bigger drop and rapid, known locally as either The
Wall of Death or Dragon's Teeth. This rapid is normally run on river
right, from which side it can easily be inspected. Shortly after this

rapid, in high water a green wave is formed across the river, which can give fantastic surfing. Following this wave is the approach to Carnage Corner just above Relugas Bridge. This rapid is normally run on river left, avoiding the natural weir type rock formation across the remainder of the river. The left-hand shoot can give good pop-outs and is worth a play. Egress to the bridge is river left on the south side of the bridge. A further 2km of grade 3 paddling takes you to Randolph's Leap. Egress to the road is from river right in a large eddy just at the narrow entrance into the next gorge section. Carry up the steep and rocky path to a wooded area through which you gain access up to the parking lay-by on the public road.

Contributor:
Jim Gibson

Other important points Two headstones beside the path, within the wooded area, indicate the height the river rose to in the 1829 floods.

Findhorn (Lower Gorge) 134

Introduction Randolph's Leap to Sluie Farm. This is a classic stretch of river. It makes an exciting and quite demanding trip for the experienced leader and intermediate paddler ready to progress onto heavier and more technical water. The feeling of remoteness deep in the gorge gives an added edge to the paddle, but a number of playspots on the way down allow some relaxing moments and the opportunity to appreciate the beauty of the gorge.

Grade	**4(5)**
Length	**5km**
OS sheet	**27**

Water Level Medium to high are the best levels. The gorge can be run when the river is low but becomes a bit rocky in places. In extremely high conditions it will be a grade harder and probably better left to experienced paddlers who enjoy boils.

Gauge If Randolph's can be run on the right-hand side, with the only way out via the cauldron, the level will be low to medium. If after running Randolph's you can exit by the right-hand shoot thereby avoiding the cauldron, the river is medium to high. At this level the water through the gorge is quite powerful with eddies full of boils; a swim could be long and uncomfortable. 0.2 on the SEPA gauge should be considered a minimum flow.

Access Turn off the A940 onto the B9007. A lay-by serving the viewpoint for Randolph's Leap provides car parking. A network

of footpaths on the opposite side of the road leads you down to various access points along the river. If you wish to paddle the leap, take a set of steps off the road opposite the south end of the lay-by giving you access to the large eddy above the narrow entrance into the lead-in to Randolph's. To avoid this fairly serious start, take the gate access opposite the north end of the lay-by and follow the path down to the river. When you come to the top of the bank turn right and follow the path until you come to a steep path down to the river. A strand of wire has been fixed to give support on this descent.

Description   Randolph's Leap is a grade 5 rapid with some scary rock formations. It can be anything from straightforward to testing depending on water levels. After Randolph's, the river runs up to grade 3 for about 1½kms until it passes Logie Estate Farm and House located on the right bank. It now enters the gorge with the pace picking up and the difficulty gradually increasing. Shortly after a heavier rapid which runs round a right-hand bend you encounter the first grade 4, Triple Steps. The second of these steps is normally run on the left as there have been a number of pinnings on the right drop. In big water the stopper formed at the bottom of the third drop becomes quite serious and will recirculate a swimmer. After a short breather and one further drop comes Corkscrew, which can be inspected from a small beach on river right. The slab formation in the centre of the river on the first drop forms a horizontal corkscrew effect at certain levels, hence the name. The next rapid of note is about $1/2$km further on and drops into a short narrow gorge section with a fairly heavy stopper to catch the unwary. This brings you quickly to The Slot, found to the left of a large rock that splits the river. Normally portaged, the drop is still occasionally paddled, but may result in paddler, boat and all being sucked under the undercut rock on river right, to be exited some distance below. It is almost impossible to tell if there is any debris in this undercut, so the general advice is to portage. This rapid should not be underrated. At high levels the drop to the left can be run. This is the end of the serious rapids and the fun time begins. There are a number of good playspots, it's up to you to find them! The take-out is on river right, next to some obvious sandstone cliffs, about 300m below the last rapid. You can just spot the footpath meandering up the steep slope that takes you to the Mains of Sluie Farm.

Other important points Please park at the Sluie Walk car park on the west side of the A940. The little cottages at the Mains of Sluie have been converted to a cottage and bunkhouse. The occupants are definitely paddler friendly but take care to change discreetly out of view from the cottage. At present (Aug 2004) there is no problem with driving down the track to collect boats, but please drive carefully as walkers and other vehicles including tractors all use this road.

Contributor:
Jim Gibson

Divie 135

Introduction Flowing from the Dava Moors, the Divie joins the lower section of the Findhorn. A cracking spate paddle, giving continuous interest with twisting rapids and mini-gorges, it is often paddled in conjunction with the Findhorn Gorge for a full day out.

Grade	**4(5)**
Length	**4km**
OS sheet	**27**

Water Level Very wet. The river only has a small catchment, so it needs to have been raining hard.

Gauge Follow the road just below the Randolph's Leap section to the bridge crossing the Divie. The rapid just upstream needs to be well covered, with the water a good peaty colour.

Access Follow the A940 from Dava to the village of Edinhillie. Take the minor road running upstream alongside the river. The road passes a 7 arch stone viaduct (constructed in 1863 as part of the original main Highland Railway line). Put in at a small lay-by near the river. The trip finishes at the bridge just before the confluence with the Findhorn, downstream of Randolph's Leap. Cars can be left at the put-in for the Findhorn Gorge, or if you fancy a longer paddle, at the take-out by the Mains of Sluie.

Description An easy introduction leads to a fence crossing the river - either portage or limbo your way round. The river is continuous with a series of small technical grade 3 drops, as you pass the village. The next section flows into a mini-gorge, giving a variety of rapids and small drops, at times hidden round the next bend. The gradient eases as you approach the large estate house, which soon indicates the start of the Falls of Feakirk. Take out on river left and follow the footpath round to a good inspection platform. This section is a series of falls, each 3-4m in height. The final one is technical, and requires the right water level.

Contributors:
Chris Forrest and
Andy England

Below the Falls, the river eases until the road bridge, just before the confluence with the Findhorn.

Other important points Careful inspection and safety cover is recommended for the Falls.

136 Dorback Burn

Grade	**5**
Length	**1km**
OS sheet	**27**

Description A tight and exciting tributary of the Divie, to which it provides an alternative start, the Dorback can only really be run at very high water levels. You should note that you miss out the first rapid on the Divie by starting here.

Contributor: Andy England

137 Spey

Grade	**1/2**
Length	**8km**
OS sheet	**27**

Introduction The Spey rises on the west of Scotland, running almost the whole width of the country on a level with Aviemore before emptying into the North Sea. A major river system which provides year round interest for the canoeist, the Spey is one of Britain's most beautiful rivers. The river is navigable for most of its length (some 120km), although the access situation is delicate. It is best to contact the SCA office or website for up to date information if you are planning to do the whole trip. The biggest hazard is the Spey Dam, just above Laggan Bridge, and many touring canoeists choose to start further downstream at Newtonmore, where the flow is more reliable. The most popular stretch on the river, described below, has two main grade 2 rapids. It runs from Ballindalloch down to the Tandhu Distillery and will take 3-4 hours to paddle with a novice group in normal flows.

Water Level The Spey can be paddled in almost all conditions.

Gauge The A95/A941 runs along the Spey between Elgin and Speybridge, with many opportunities to assess the amount of water in the river.

Access To reach Ballindalloch from Grantown-on-Spey, drive north-east on the A95, turn off at Marypark crossing the river at Blacksboat Bridge. Turn left onto the B9102 and drive upstream for 3 miles to the point where the river comes to within 15m of the road (158 369). This put-in can be a particularly busy area with fishermen and paddlers looking to park. Please use the lay-bys furthest

'downstream' and be considerate. Alternatively, put in on the right
bank by a railway bridge (168 368). The disused railway line is now
part of the Speyside Way long distance footpath. It can be reached
by turning off the A95 at Bridge of Avon and driving to the end
of the minor road. The take-out is at the Tamdhu distillery. Drive
North on the B9102 turning off right to the distillery at Knockando.
There is ample parking close to the old railway line, but please do
not obstruct the footpath and be discreet about where you change.

Description From the put-in at Ballindalloch, the river strolls down
at a leisurely pace to the old railway bridge, past a left-hand bend
and on to the confluence with the Avon (arn). Here a short rapid
forms round the right-hand bend. This is followed by another
straightforward rapid with a wave in the centre, which makes a
good spot to learn to surf. The river bends left as it approaches
Blacks Boat Rapid (Gd 2). This is a long ramp of fast water, followed
by a wave train. For the next 3km the river eases with many short
rapids and waves. Continue until the river bends to the right and
the Tamdhu Distillery comes into view. This signals the approach to
Knockando, (Gd 2). The rapid provides interest in most conditions,
although it can become a little 'washed out' when the river is high.
The take-out is immediately below the rapid on the left bank, with a
steep path leading up to the old disused railway platform.

Other important points In recent years substantial bridges have
been built through constructive communication between paddlers
and anglers. Workable local agreements have been formulated
between angling interests and the main user groups in an effort to
reduce the pressure on this busy river. The main user groups have
agreed to limit their canoeing between Dellefure Burn (085 316)
and Aberlour to Tuesdays, Thursdays, Fridays and Sundays during
the fishing season (llth Feb - 30th Sep). Although other paddlers
are not covered by this arrangement it would be helpful if other
large groups can also focus their activity on the above days. If this
is not possible please contact the estate on 01340 810 343/810 278
to discuss the best time to paddle on any particular day. As part of
the above arrangement Knockando access point and rapid has been
designated a 'white water training area', including the provision
of a toilet and changing facility for paddlers. The training site is
available every day between 10am and 10pm. Please stay between
the white posts (i.e. don't play in the pools above and below the
rapids) and portage up along the right-hand bank. Thanks!

Contributor:
David Craig

138 River Avon

Grade   **3(5)**
Length   **22km**
OS sheet **28**

Introduction Set at the northern foot of the Cairngorm Mountains in Moray, the river can be paddled from just east of Tomintoul to the River Spey at Ballindalloch. The Avon is a spate run through shingle banks with occasional smooth rocky rapids, surrounded by open wooded banks and fields. Although the full trip is very long, it can be broken down to shorter lengths using various lay-bys and access at bridges along the route.

Water Level Wet/Very wet. The river has to be high to make this trip worthwhile: the higher the better. The river level drops very quickly, almost overnight. After prolonged rain or snow melt it rises quickly and flash floods have been witnessed. Rescue can be difficult due to lack of good eddies and a swim may be a long one.

Gauge The river level can be checked and viewed from various points along the A939 Bridge of Avon to Tomintoul road, or the B9136 Bridge of Avon to Ballindalloch road. When no bedrock is showing through the rapids, the level will be at least medium.

Access The river can be accessed from the various road bridges. To the east of Tomintoul on the minor road to Delnabo Estate, parking is available at the Queen's View. From here it is a short walk down to the river at the road bridge. The next bridge is close to the junction of the A939 and B9136 at Bridge of Avon. Park in the lay-by on the north side of the A939 on the south side of the river. From this point it is possible to take access or egress immediately after the biggest rapid on the river, Distillery Falls. Take out on river right just below Ballindalloch Bridge on the A95. There is generally limited parking close by at the war memorial. Alternatively you can continue on down to join the River Spey with possible egress at Knockando Rapid, (see River Spey description).

Description For much of its length, the Avon flows over open shingle and boulder banks. At high flows these give play-ful wave trains and some stoppers that you may think twice before exploring. At dry low levels the river becomes bumpy and scrapey and it is best to retain your plastic for another day. Distillery Falls is the main event of the river. The buildings of the Distillery come into view on river right and serve as a warning of the rapid approaching. This two-tier drop is normally taken on the right. Just below this rapid is a footbridge; you can take out on river left and walk over the bridge and up a footpath taking you onto the B9136. There is a lay-by, which parks a maximum of two cars, on the north side of the road to the west of the Distillery. Although fishermen use this lay-by, it is unlikely to be in use by them at the level that you are paddling the river. Continuing on downstream, there is a minor road bridge and some parking on river left about 2km below here. The trip meanders on to the take out at Ballindalloch.

Other important points The Upper Avon has been paddled from its source at Loch Avon, by walking in over Cairn Gorm mountain.

Contributor:
Jim Gibson

Dulnain 139

Grade	3
Length	3km
OS sheet	36

Introduction The Dulnain flows into the Spey upstream of Grantown on Spey. Most of the Dulnain has a gentle gradient which offers little in the way of white water. However, two short sections do provide some pleasant grade 3, the lower section rising to grade 4 in big spate conditions. These sections are good for intermediate paddlers when the river is just high enough to be worth paddling and advanced paddlers will enjoy it as a quick blast in spate.

Water Level Wet / Very wet - just don't bother in low water.

Gauge If the river is brown and fast at Dulnain Bridge, it's runnable. If the rocks underneath the old bridge in Carrbridge are all covered it is in spate.

Access For the upper section you can get on at the A9 road bridge at (897 225) through a red gate on the southbound side, and take out at Carrbridge (906 229). The lower section is best started at Balnaan (977 247) with a choice of egress at Dulnain Bridge (997 248) the new A95 road bridge or on the Spey.

Description The upper section is a gentle grade 1/2 and is fairly shallow and braided until Carrbridge where there is a picturesque rapid (Gd 3) under the old packhorse bridge. It is an easy but short section for teaching white water skills and the final rapid

makes a nice end to a short trip. If you are going to paddle the lower section after the upper it is best to arrange transport as the 8km in between are very, very flat. Starting the lower section at Balnaan provides a short warm-up before the gradient steepens and the fun begins. This section is not desperately difficult, and a big man-made wall on river right heralds the first and biggest drop on the river which is usually run just left of centre. After this is a long boulder garden with plenty of small eddies, little waves and playful pour-overs - it's quality fun at the grade (3). An eddy on the upstream right of the bridge in Dulnain Bridge village should not be missed if you want to stop and play.

The small stopper above the bridge is ideal for teaching basic freestyle moves but it is too small, shallow and flushy even for experts to throw lots of vertical ends here. Take out 50m below the bridge on the left to follow a footpath and steps up to the road and ample car parking in the old garage forecourt. You can continue downstream for a little more grade 2 action and egress at the new A95 road bridge or on to the Spey; however, the Dulnain Bridge take-out is the easiest. The lower section can be done as a 'park and play' trip as it is only a few hundred yards to carry up from the car park at the old garage to the first significant drop.

Contributor:
Dave Aldritt

140 Cas Burn / Allt Mor

Grade **4/5**
Length **1km**
OS sheet **27**

Introduction This burn flows beside the Cairngorm ski area near Aviemore. It's a rather bizarre concept going to a ski centre for a paddle. This is a small continuous spate burn, in which the fun never lets up. It makes a good alternative to skiing or winter climbing when conditions are adverse.

Water Level The river needs to be absolutely going off. It requires really heavy rain plus snow melt in order to bring it up to, and past bank full. Late winter is often a good time to try and catch this river.

Gauge Follow the road uphill from Glenmore village. After about a mile you reach a road bridge over a braided stretch of river. This needs to be well covered with enough water to float over the boulders. The rest of the river is more channelled.

Access From the A9, turn off towards Aviemore. Follow the signs to Glenmore then continue for a further mile to the second road bridge (see above). The egress point is 250m downstream, at the footbridge. If the level is right, follow the road up to Cairngorm Ski Centre and park in the lowest of the car parks. The put-in is only a few metres away.

Description The burn is continually very tight, steep and exciting. There are no eddies and the only way to stop is to hang onto a lump of turf, which usually results in spinning round and running the burn backwards until you can turn back round - even more wicked fun. As the gradient steepens the action heats up to give continuous drops into shallow pools. All too soon, the burns spills into the Allt Mor. From here the run is steady at first. However, you soon pass the footbridge by the reindeer compound, below which the river splits. Check your choice of channel, then take a deep breath. The pace picks up here with steep continuous boulder rapids. Keep an eye out for fallen trees. Once past the road bridge, the burn eases as you approach the take-out. It is possible to continue for an extra kilometre, but the rest of the run is a bit of an anticlimax, with little technical interest and plenty of tree problems.

Other important points If you enjoyed this run and don't mind some walking, it is possible to boat from Coire an t -Sneachda. For this follow the climbers' path round for as long as it seems possible to paddle. Elbow pads are useful, more to save your cag than your elbows. Be warned - this river has been variously described as grade 3 or grade 5, depending on who you talk to. Keep an open mind and make your own decision.

Contributors:
Roland Bone
and Chris Forrest

Eidart / Top Feshie 141

Introduction The Eidart and Top Feshie is a mega wilderness adventure. We ended up doing it as a multi-day trip and with 13 hours of paddling. There's a lot of really good white water on this trip, but beware, it has the potential to be a major epic.

Water Level If it's not wet, don't go. You'll need it to be raining consistently for the two hours before you paddle. It took us many attempts to get enough water and then, when we did, we had a little too much!

Grade	**5**
Length	**22km**
OS sheet	**43**

Access Park in Achlean car park as per the normal Feshie run. It took us 5 hours in windy conditions to carry the boats the 8km to the put-in and no less than six attempts to get the required flow. It may be best to take the boats in beforehand, or know someone with a helicopter to drop them off… we didn't. Following the Carn Ban Mor track from Achlean, you gain a height of 1030m on the walk in.

Description Given the adventurous nature of this paddle, if you need a blow-by-blow description don't go there. We decided the first 500m were too out of control given the water level, remoteness and our small party of two. Hurt yourself here and you're a long way from anywhere, especially in the weather you're likely to be here. The first 500m would offer serious sliding fun and, if it wasn't so remote, would be a classic in its own right. We put in just before the confluence of the other major Eidart tributary at (917 946). Frequent grade 4 drops break up the slightly bony run down to the Eidart gorges. Watch out for these gorges, which contain grade 6 portages. The final gorge finishes in the biggest waterfall on the Eidart, just after a footbridge 500m before the Feshie. Although it was August, we ran out of daylight by this point. We found the remains of a hut and slept on upturned kayaks covered with heather, as flashes of lightning lit the sky. The next day we paddled the Top Feshie, which has lots of good grade 4 and 5 white water - we paddled some and walked some. The exciting paddling continued for about 4 km with a class 6 drop marking the end of this section. 11km of grade 2/3 float and scrape, with stunning scenery, leads to the take-out at Achlean car park. This is the put-in for the regular Upper Feshie. We talked about carrying on, but didn't have it in us.

Contributor:
John Mason

Other important points Note the approach to this river requires a map and compass and the knowledge to use them. It is a seriously remote mountain paddle. For a bigger scale map use OS 'Outdoor leisure 3' 1:25000 'The Cairngorms, Aviemore & Glen Avon'.

142 Feshie

Grade **3(3+)**
Length **7km**
OS sheet **35**

Introduction The Feshie is a major tributary of the Spey, which drains the western fringe of the Cairngorm Mountains. It joins the River Spey at the small village of Kincraig, halfway between Aviemore and Kingussie. In its upper reaches the river is generally straightforward with shingle rapids. A short lower gorge provides the best of the white water, making a good intermediate trip with a couple of usable playspots in high water.

Water Level Moderately wet / Very wet. With even a little water the last gorge can be entertaining. Higher flows are required to avoid a bump and a scrape in the upper section.

Gauge Check the flow at Feshiebridge on the B970, near the take-out. If all the rocks are covered in the last rapid the river is at a good level. If some rocks are still showing the upper stretch could be a bit 'scrapey'.

Access The put-in for this upper stretch is at Achlean Farm. Vehicles should be parked at the roadside on the high ground before reaching the croft. To get to the river without causing conflict, follow the path upstream, above and away from the croft. Please do not cut through the steading or cross the moorland immediately below or downstream of the croft. To access the upper rapids if you don't have a shuttle, it is possible to park by the cattle grid before the woods (after Glen Feshie Hostel), and walk down to the river on forestry land (before the cattle grid / fence). Walking upstream for 150m gives access to some nice rapids. For those more interested in paddling the gorge, it is possible to drop off boats at Feshie Bridge and walk up the 'right of way' on river left, for around 400m. Take out at the car park 100m downstream of Feshiebridge. Please use this car park to keep the road and Glen Tilt track free.

Description The first rapid below Achlean is some 200m long with one small shoot. This is followed by a series of fast but flat stretches of water interspersed with a series of small interesting falls requiring some judgement. Below Tolvah, the river becomes grade 2 with shingle rapids as the river becomes braided and shallow for a couple of miles. Throughout this section, watch out for damaged fencing which may hang in or above the river. After this quiet stretch the left bank becomes steeper and the gorge begins. Just upstream of Lagganlia Centre on a left-hand bend a small stream, the Allt Mharcaidh enters from the right. The river is about grade 2 at this point. The stretch from here to Feshiebridge provides some interesting grade 3+ paddling in good conditions. The grade can go up considerably in high

water. It is possible to view the lower part of this stretch from the Feshie Bridge.

Contributors:
David Craig and
Roland Bone

Other important points Look out for fences in the upper stretch and fallen trees, which may become lodged in the gorge. Lagganlia Centre has accomodation for paddlers and runs canoe/kayak courses. Residents have unlimited access to the Feshie through their grounds.

143 Tromie

Grade	3(5)
Length	4km
OS sheet	35

Introduction The Tromie is a tributary of the Spey that runs roughly parallel with the Feshie, its eastern neighbour. The Tromie, and most particularly the one major rapid above and below the B970 bridge, is a river which should be treated with respect. Above this rapid lies plenty of fast grade 2/3, but even this is not really a place for novices. In essence, this is a short 300m 'park and blast' for competent paddlers.

Water Level Rain overnight or all morning is essential.

Gauge Look upstream from the B970 bridge - what you see is what you get!

Access As you are driving up the glen you can choose any suitable spot near to the river. The road does eventually cross the river (779 969), but here (and elsewhere) avoid parking too close to the few houses in the area. Take out on river left (789 996) after the B970 bridge. There is a path back to the bridge where you can park easily enough.

Description The Tromie is by no means a classic Scottish run, but it is good sport at high flows, and the final rapid on the section described here is more dangerous than it might first appear. The gradient from the top of the single-track road is fairly even and thus offers a steady and continuous grade 3 ride in spate conditions. It is not technically difficult but eddies are hard to find because the river is often in amongst the trees or nudging ever-higher over the shallow banks. The occasional stopper forms over larger boulders, but most of the river bed is shingle until you reach the harder rocks which form the rapids before the take-out. Although the final rapid has no big, scary waterfall or elbow-bashing constriction it does have some retentive holes which you don't want to play with. A swim here would hurt more than your pride, and you need to be on the right line from top to bottom to avoid trouble. Hit the right lines and it runs very sweetly indeed, grade 4 at its lowest runnable level and worth a 5 in spate. Note that less than 200m downstream of this rapid is a shallow weir which forms a very even and holding stopper at some levels, so your safety and rescue plans should consider this feature accordingly.

Other important points There is a lot of other short and exciting stuff nearby (Calder, Feshie, Cas, Falls of Truim) and if the Tromie is up, these are also likely to be flowing well.

Contributor:
Dave Aldritt

Calder 144

Grade	**4**
Length	**2km**
OS sheet	**35**

○○○

Introduction On the western edge of the Cairngorms, the River Calder crosses the A86 at Newtonmore, and is a small tributary of the Spey. A nice little spate river, it is navigable from quite far up the glen, although the best of the paddling is generally considered to be found in the lower gorge. The run consists of a shallow lead in, followed by a small bedrock gorge, which is fun with the right amount of water. At very high flows, this run should be considered grade 5.

Water Level Wet/Very wet. A good amount of water is required to make this a sporting run.

Gauge To judge the level of the river, take a look from the road-bridge on the A86 - if it looks shallow but easily paddleable at this point then upstream will be fine. If it looks like a bump and scrape here, it will be even shallower above the gorge and probably not worth the effort.

Access The road bridge just west of Newtonmore on the road to Spean Bridge (A86) makes a suitable take-out. It is easily found and there is room to park upstream of the bridge on the river left. Finding the put-in is equally straightforward. Turn north in the town up the 'Old Glen Road' and into the valley. The single-track

road winds its way to a small car parking area close to a small bridge over an even smaller burn. Paddling down the burn offers a good alternative to walking down to the Calder. If the burn is too dry, it is likely that the Calder also needs more water. The river has been paddled from higher up, and this could be considered if you fancy a longer run. If you only have one car this is a great short run. Try dropping off your boats at the steep bank below the second cattle grid, parking at the A86 take-out, and then walking back up the path - this lets you inspect the gorge as well. Follow the bobcat signposts after walking past the cemetery.

Description Initially the river just splashes its way over shingle beds. Dodging the odd boulder whilst struggling to find the line with the most water is the biggest challenge. As you get warmed up so does the river, then the gorge begins. The change in character is fairly sudden as the river narrows into a channel cut through the banks of solid rock. The scale of things is still pretty small, as are the eddies, but you need a long neck to see around the corners and over the drops. At high water you may prefer to inspect the whole gorge from the bank beforehand. However, once you enter the gorge you are not irreversibly committed as inspection or portaging remains possible all the way through. There is one corner, which is just a little nastier than the rest. It has an undercut on the left, which could be problematic if you don't have the right line. The little gorge ends almost as suddenly as it began and in no time at all you are at the main road bridge. There is little to be found in the way of playholes on the river, as it is just too shallow for most of its length.

Other important points There are a number of other small burns in the area, which also run when the Calder is up. Try the Feith Talagain Burn and the Rough Burn: creek boats and elbow pads are recommended.

Contributor:
Dave Aldritt

Truim 145

Introduction The Truim flows north from Dalwhinnie to join the Spey by Newtonmore. A short distraction worth combining with a trip to the Pattack or the Calder, the Falls of Truim provide what is probably the only real white water interest on the river.

Grade	**4**
Length	**100m**
OS sheet	**35**

Water Level Wet. It's a bit of a lottery getting the right level.

Gauge Peek over the bridge and eye up the falls. They will be better with a decent flow.

Access To get there, take the second right travelling south on the A9 from Newtonmore. There is a car park on the left just after turning off the A9. Park here and walk back towards the A9, taking the small road on the left down to the falls. Get on just above the minor road bridge, river left.

Contributor:
John Mason

Description At a low level, the falls could be best summarised as, 'short, scenic and silly', best left to the salmon who can apparently be seen jumping there in the summer. At a higher water level they would be good for a short blast. Probably along the lines of, 'short, scenic and sexy', especially if a slap around the face from a wet salmon turns you on.

Other important points Please don't disrupt the otherwise peaceful lives of the residents who live in the house that overlooks the falls.

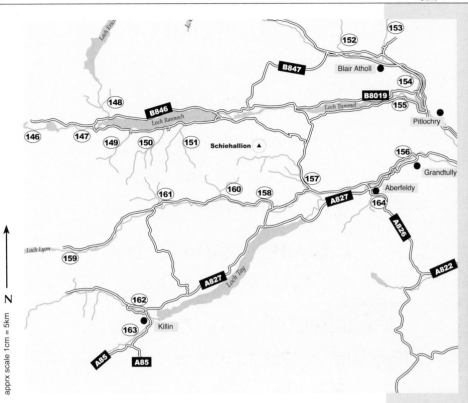

apprx scale 1cm = 5km

N

Tay & Tribs

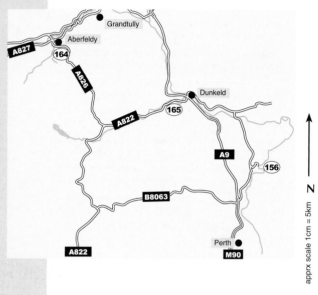

N

apprx scale 1cm = 5km

Tay & Tribs Continued

Tay & Tribs

The River Tay drains a vast chunk of Scotland from Ben Lui in the west to Forfar in the east and from as far north as Glenshee, with its waters eventually reaching the sea at Dundee. It is a fine river for touring and from source to sea it must make a fantastic journey. The two main white water sections can be found at Grandtully and Stanley and these sections are of interest to slalom paddlers, rafters and playboaters alike. It is, however, the Tay's many tributaries that offer most to the white water paddler. This section is focused on those rivers that join the Tay in its western and central reaches. The runs in the extreme east of the catchment area can be found in the Up fae Dundee section of the guide. Those looking for the hardest runs should make for the Keltney Burn, Bruar or Dall Burn. Great grade 4 boating can be found across the region from the Lochay in the west to the Tilt and Braan in the east. Grade 3/4 runs such as the Gaur, Lyon and Tummel round off a superb area.

Garbh Ghaoir 146

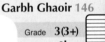

Grade	**3 (3+)**
Length	**6km**
OS sheet	**51**

◯◯◯

Introduction The Garbh Ghaoir lies at the eastern edge of Rannoch Moor, at the end of one of Scotland's longest cul-de-sacs: a wild and beautiful location. Garbh means rough and this describes both the rapids and the granite boulders that characterize this little gem. The relative remoteness of the Garbh Ghaoir provides a feeling of exploration.

Water Level Very wet. The Garbh Ghaoir needs water primarily because, to make this trip worthwhile, the Gaur needs to be running.

Gauge If the Gaur is running, the Garbh Ghaoir will be a good paddle. If water is flowing over the Gaur dam, it will be in excellent condition.

Access Follow the B846 (forever) until the road ends at Rannoch Station, where ample parking is available. A careful crossing of the railway gives access to the Dubh Lochan and then Loch Laidon and the Garbh Ghaoir. The most practical egress

is at the Gaur dam. Paddle the length of Loch Eighneach and portage the dam on the right-hand side by the access road.

Description The paddle across the spectacular Loch Laidon and the search for the Garbh Ghaoir can be entertaining in itself. Initially the river calmly meanders until a sudden drop off signals the start of 2 long boulder rapids, the second under a railway bridge. The river narrows and steepens again by a forest plantation. In high water the line on this drop is not obvious. More boulder rapids lead to a bouncy exit into Loch Eighneach.

Contributor:
Peter Crane

147 Gaur

Grade   **3(4)**
Length   **4km**
OS sheet   **51**

Introduction The Gaur makes up part of the Rannoch/Tummel hydro system. It flows in an easterly direction, into Loch Rannoch. When combined with the Garbh Ghaoir, this paddle makes a fine mini-expedition through a beautiful open glen.

Water Level Very wet weather is needed to ensure that the power station is running, or better still, the Gaur dam is overflowing.

Gauge The first rapid on the Gaur runs next to the road about 1km before the dam. If rocks are visible but there is a clean line, the river is at a good height. If no rocks are showing, the river is running high and the stoppers will be big.

Access Park either off the road opposite the power station alongside the river, or better still, continue to Rannoch station, and paddle the Garbh Ghaoir. Take out at Bridge of Gaur, on the left-hand side. Limited discreet parking is available on the south side of the bridge.

Description The steep bouldery section directly below the dam is generally a good grade 4 when the dam is overflowing. However, it can become scarily big and has been run away from in very high water! The normal trip starts at the power station. After about 1km, the river narrows and flows alongside the road. A rounded boulder on the right signals the start of the first rapid. At grade 4, this is the hardest rapid on the section. Below this, the river calms until it reaches a large island. From here to the finish, there is a series of continuous boulder rapids. In high water, large stoppers form in this section.

Contributor:
Peter Crane

Ericht 148

Grade	**4/5**
Length	**7km**
OS sheet	**42**

Introduction The Ericht has a huge catchment, gathering water from the hills surrounding Loch Ericht and draining down into Loch Rannoch and the Tummel river system. Sadly most of the water that should flow down the Ericht is diverted by a hydro scheme. At first the river is open and very bouldery at low flows. The main gorge, which starts just after a small dam, is steeper and more serious. Bedrock is the scene from here on. The gorge itself is beautiful, but watch out for fences in the upper stretch.

Water Level Very wet. The Ericht can only be paddled when water is being released from the dam at Loch Ericht.

Gauge The size of the plume expelled from the valve at the dam gives an indication of the flow. If this looks massive, the river will be high.

Access Turn off the A9 just north of Pitlochry, heading towards Kinloch Rannoch. Follow the north shore for nearly 30 miles through Tummel Bridge and Kinloch Rannoch. At Bridge of Ericht turn off the main road towards Loch Ericht. A key can sometimes be arranged from Rannoch Power Station. Otherwise it's a full on 8km walk to the put-in. Park after the dam, at an old shed. Shuttle vehicles are best left before the power station on Loch Rannoch, where there is a lay-by on the left.

Description Initially the river is grade 2, but watch out for 3 fences, which need to be portaged. After about a kilometre, a small dam appears which should be portaged on the left. Immediately after this is a grade 5 rapid. This may be shallow and should be boofed on the right. The river continues then splits around an island. Take the left-hand channel, since the right goes over a nasty grade 6 drop. The left-hand side has a series of nice grade 3-5 rapids. The weir-like drop should be run down the middle (Gd 4+). Small rapids continue to the loch. Turn right and paddle down to the car.

Contributor:
Johnny McLaren

149 Allt Camghouran

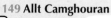

Grade **4(5)**
Length **1km**
OS sheet **42**

Description This is the furthest west of 3 burns that flow into the south side of Loch Rannoch. On a wet day, why not run all 3 – you'll have a blast. Walk up the track on river left for a short spate run with some big holes to avoid.

Contributor: Andy Jackson

150 Dall Burn

Grade **4/5**
Length **2½km**
OS sheet **42**

Introduction The Dall Burn begins life on the high ground to the north of Glen Lyon. It flows through Rannoch Forest and is the best of the three small rivers running into the south side of Loch Rannoch. This is a small river with an unrelenting gradient in a beautiful forest setting, which provides some big pushy water with plenty of dubious looking falls. At the right flow it is a very fast and action packed trip.

Water Level Very wet. Heavy rain on the day will be required. Perhaps the same weather that would bring the Upper Keltney Burn into nick.

Gauge Check the flow at the road bridge at the bottom of the river, just before it joins Loch Rannoch. At the right level this section will look full and certainly not a bump and scrape. This is definitely one to keep for a wet day.

Access From Kinloch Rannoch, take the road that leads along the south side of Loch Rannoch. You come to the Dall Burn a little under ½ a mile beyond the entrance to Rannoch School. This is the take-out. You need to leave your vehicle here and take your boat for a scenic wander on foot through the forest to find the put-in. A track leads upstream on river left past some houses and outbuildings of the school to a bridge over the river. 200m beyond here you should branch left off the track and continue on river left via a path. Put in at the forest road bridge, 1½km further upstream.

Description The action starts straightaway with good read and run water. As the gradient picks up you will want to scout the first large set of falls you come to. There are several drops in this

Findhorn - Dulsie Gorge - Strathspey - www.beyondadventure.co.uk

North Esk - Up fae Dundee - Chris Dickinson

North Esk - Fish Ladder Falls - Up fae Dundee - Chris Dickinson

Falls of Tummel - Tay and Tribs - www.liquidlife.co.uk

Gaur - Tay and Tribs - www.beyondadventure.co.uk

section and the overall impression at a high flow is that of big holes and shallow landings. In a couple of places there are staircase rapids of shallow angled slabs lying close together. It is generally easy to pick and choose which drops you want to run and those you'd rather not. After the bridge the gradient eases and it's fast grade 3 water to the loch.

Other important points The Dall Burn is the water supply for Rannoch School so please take care not to be the source of any pollution. The track to the put-in involves trekking past several of the buildings and houses associated with the school, so the run is probably best avoided by large noisy groups.

❝ On the first and only time I have paddled the Dall Burn it was a wintry day with 6" of snow lying on the ground. Despite or perhaps because of the freezing temperatures we were keen to put on and get paddling as quickly as possible. As we flushed down the early rapids the trip was going well and we were getting in tune with the river. As we approached the first steepening I opted to run a small slab to gain an eddy which would give me a good view of the cascade below. Failing to punch the hole at the base of the slab, I had a short but frantic fight with the tow back before being drawn back into the hole. A solid drilling in the hole followed. As I was surfed I could feel that the situation was beginning to get a bit out of control. Despite my best efforts I was unable to escape the clutches of the stopper and each time I rolled up I was treated to a great view of the grade 5 falls which lay immediately below and which I was now resigned to swimming over. At some point I lost grip of my paddle and it wasn't much longer before I opted to swim. Chris Forrest like all good paddling buddies had by now made the bank and was watching my trashing, throw-bag in hand. As I re-circed briefly in the hole he was able to bag me and drag my cold and shaken body to the side. The humiliation didn't stop there as with no sign of my paddles I had to resort to dragging my boat back down through the forest. As I staggered through the snow drifts I had plenty of time in which to contemplate my mistake as I watched Chris run the classy stretch of water. My description of the burn is based on the memory of this cold and hazy experience so best treat it as the uncontrolled ramblings of a deranged survivor. It could have been worse, at least I found my paddles in the loch! **❞**

Contributor:
Andy Jackson

151 Allt Carie

Grade **4/5**
Length **1km**
OS sheet **42**

Contributor:
Andy Jackson

Access The Carrie Burn is the next river east of the Dall Burn. It flows into Loch Rannoch beside a Forestry Commission car park and picnic site. To reach the put-in, walk up the track behind the campsite.

Description This run has some good action at the start then one notable drop and slide below the footbridge just downstream of the campsite.

152 Bruar

Grade **4/5**
Length **½km**
OS sheet **43**

Introduction The Bruar flows into the Perthshire Garry, 9 miles north of Pitlochry. This is a short but sweet run with beautiful river features in a steep sided wooded gorge. The small drops are separated by tight sections, which in high water become challenging in themselves.

Water Level Wet. You need a fair amount of rain to make this run worthwhile. Get it too high and there would be little space for scouting, too low and you would struggle to get through the tighter drops. The burn rises very quickly once the ground is wet.

Gauge Go to the signpost on the path at the House of Bruar and look upstream. There should be enough water for you to scrape/float out. If it looks fast and brown then the river is scarily high.

Access The run is accessed from the Falls of Bruar Walk. Turn off the A9, some 9 miles north of Pitlochry, following signs for the Falls of Bruar. Head towards the House of Bruar Visitor Centre and park up. This is the take-out. To get to the put-in, it's boats on shoulders time. Walk up the Falls of Bruar path, under the railway bridge and up, always up! The path is on river right. Follow this all the way to an arched stone bridge over the river. It is possible to scout the river on the way up by peering into the gorge. The usual put-in is on river right, downstream of the bridge and below the fall. A slightly used path has been formed down the steep banking, which is likely to be slippy when the rain is coming down (the time you are most likely to be on the river).

Description There are a number of falls above the usual put-in, which the adventurous may wish to explore. The uppermost falls are some 20m high and will probably hurt - decide for yourself! The drop just above the bridge may go, with a good bit of protection and the right water levels (has anyone run these monsters yet?). From below the bridge and natural rock arch the short section is classic pool-drop, with smooth slabby bedrock falls into what are, on the whole, clean pools. The falls directly under the bridge are a no go, with a shallow rocky pool. From the usual put-in pool, there are six drops in total, which are all fairly easy to scout from the river. The first drop is round a left-hand bend. From there you're into the gorge proper and get a good view down into the depths as the sides close in. The rest of the trip is read and run, except at one narrower drop which is generally paddled on the right. Carry on until you get to the signpost that you walked past on the way up. At time of writing there are a couple of trees in the river. The second rapid is blocked at the exit, you can portage river right, it's slippy! The final fall has a tree 25m below the base of the fall. You can still run the drop but you have to clean it and go hard left to get past the tree.

Other important points There have never been any access problems here to my knowledge. However, the House of Bruar Visitor Centre is quite a classy place and I don't think they would be too keen on a bunch of paddlers dropping their pants in the car park. Please be discreet, or better still get changed before you get here. The usual rules apply with walking up the path, closing gates etc.

Contributor:
Cam Allan

Tilt 153

Grade	**4(5)**
Length	**6km**
OS sheet	**43**

Introduction The Tilt is a classic north Perthshire river, which runs close to the A9 at the village of Blair Atholl. It is a major tributary of the River Garry. This is a spectacular trip through one of Scotland's most beautiful glens. The river is continually 'busy', spending most of its time in a steep gorge. Unusual rock formations sloping down into the water with a number of rock shelves make up the best of the rapids. A really excellent trip, that is always worth the walk-in.

Water Level Moderately wet / Very wet. The lower 3km of the river, from the first bridge reached travelling up Glen Tilt, can be scraped most of year. The main run, from above Gilbert's Bridge, is best at a higher flow. This can often be found in the winter and particularly during the spring run off. The upper 10km run, from the third bridge at Marble Lodge, requires very high flows.

Gauge Judge the flow from the road bridge in Blair Atholl. The river flows through a wide rocky river bed. If all rocks are covered the river is high. When the river is flowing in a third of the width of the river bed, it can be considered to be at a low level.

Access To reach the river, turn off the A9 towards Blair Atholl, and follow the signs for the castle. Take the minor road opposite the Bridge of Tilt Hotel. Turn left after about ½ a mile and cross the Old Bridge. There is a large car park here with a map showing the track up the glen. Currently there is no vehicular access permitted up Glen Tilt (Blair Atholl Estates). The track makes for an easy walk alongside the river to the put-ins. The 3km lower section starts from the first bridge. If water levels allow it is definitely worth the effort to carry on to the second bridge (Gilbert's) which gives a 6km run. Real hard cases carry on up to the third bridge at Marble Lodge for a 10km trip. Take out just above the Blair Atholl road bridge. Either walk up river right to the car park or take out on river left at a lay-by close to the Bridge of Tilt Hotel.

Description Above Gilbert's Bridge the glen is open, but below it soon narrows to a steep gorge with a number of fairly straightforward ledges, and one memorable twisting constriction. At really high flows this initial gorge becomes one long grade 5 rapid. From the lower put-in (at the first bridge) the river enters a second wider gorge. Often this section is a bit shallow. Take care as a large tree blockage is found just round a left-hand corner. One or more large trees block the main passage. Chain Bridge Fall (Gd 5), lies just beyond. Inspect, chicken-chute or portage on river left. A great fast section continues through the last narrow bedrock gorge. A final narrow undercut slot (Gd 4+) can be found just before Blair Atholl.

Contributor:
Paul Stone

Other important points The access arrangements, although restrictive, apply to all glen users and not just to paddlers.

154 Garry

Grade **2/3(5)**
Length **2km**
OS sheet **43**

Introduction The Perthshire Garry flows alongside the A9 from Drumochter summit. The section described is at Killiecrankie between Pitlochry and Blair Atholl. This river makes a pleasant trip through a scenic gorge with three harder sections, where the river becomes narrow and technical.

Water Level Moderately wet/Very wet. At lower flows the river is generally grade 1/2 with a couple of grade 3s and a portage. At high flows the speed of the river increases dramatically with violent boils coming off the sides of the gorge, making the trip at least a grade harder.

Gauge The best place to gauge the flow is at the put-in. If the upstream rapid looks more than grade 3 the river is high.

Access To reach the put-in from the north, turn off the A9 south of Blair Atholl and take the B8079 towards Killiecrankie. After about 2 miles, a small road crosses the river. Park here, taking care not to block access along this narrow road. Walk upstream on river left, past a dog-leg in the river. The put-in is 100m above this. To get to the take-out, carry on down the B8079. Turn right on the B8019 at Garry bridge. There is ample parking in the council car park immediately after the bridge on the right-hand side. From the south, take the B8079 turning off the A9 just after Pitlochry. Continue until you reach the junction with the B8019 and the take-out.

Description The first rapid above the bridge can be inspected from the bank as you approach the put-in. This is followed by Dog Leg Falls, some 50m below the bridge, which can also be inspected before getting in. Although grade 3 at lower flows, this fall becomes quite chunky at high flows with a challenging approach, and warrants a grade of 4+. Below this fall, the river flattens but is still fast flowing as it leads down to the main constriction at Soldier's Leap, some ½km below the bridge. It's well worth checking this one out before getting on, particularly if you don't know the river, as the drop is hard to spot from river level, and there are no eddies close above it. The constriction has been run, but at low flows the lead in is technical and several boats have become wrapped above the gap. At high flows, the Leap begins to open up and is less technical, (Gd 4+). Below the Leap, the gorge is a scenic grade 1/2 paddle. A metal footbridge crosses the river, about 200m above the take-out on river right, just before the Garry road bridge. A short steep walk up the bank brings you to the car park. Do not continue past the road bridge as there is a nasty weir.

Other important points There is a riverside path all the way along the run. It is on river left at the put-in, and crosses the

Contributor:
Rod Webster

river at the small iron bridge mentioned above, coming out at the take-out on river right. This is a popular tourist walk and there is a well laid out Visitor's Centre beside the path near the put-in. Beware of trees after high winds or floods.

155 Tummel (Upper)

Grade **2/3 (4+)**
Length   **5km**
OS sheet   **42**

○○○

Water Level There is usually some compensation flow coming from the dam, which will give enough water to paddle this section at grade 2/3.

Access Turn off the A9 towards Kinloch Rannoch. From Tummel Bridge continue up river left on the B846, for about 3 miles until you see the large dam (722 592). There is limited parking here beside the road. Scramble down the steep bank and then follow the track to put in immediately below the dam. The main drop (732 592) can be inspected from the road, river left, on the way to the put-in, but you are on rocks approx 10m above river level. To find the take-out, drive back down the road until the river is once more close to the road (742 594). There is a grade 3 rapid here, which can be inspected, but very limited parking. Alternatively there is a convenient car park just upstream of Tummel Bridge (400m above the last rapid).

Description The first 1½km provides some pleasant pool drop rapids at around grade 3. As you pass a large gatehouse on river left, watch out for the main drop of the river. You will see a large rock outcrop - get out river right to inspect or portage. This long rapid has a gnarly lead-in to a double-tier drop of about 3m, and lands in a grippy looking stopper closed in on both sides. Safety cover/rescue would be very difficult from above, but it's possible to put a safety boat in below. The river continues below here at grade 2/3 until the road joins the river again. A last fun grade 3 shoot, river left, marks a possible take-out, or continue to Tummel Bridge on flat water for another 2km. There is a small grade 2+ rapid just above the bridge. Below Tummel Bridge the river is flat but the volume is increased from the hydro out-take. It's possible to continue into Loch Tummel and take out at several places onto the small road on the south side of the loch.

Contributor:
Dave Francis

Tummel Lower 155

Grade	**3(4)**
Length	**4km**
OS sheet	**52**

Introduction A major tributary of the Tay, (at least it was before the hydro board kidnapped all the water) the Tummel is crossed by the A9 near the picturesque town of Pitlochry. A nice short summer trip, it can be combined with a run on the Tay or rock climbing at nearby crags. During the summer months a regular dam release provides a runnable flow. The Tummel can also be run at other times of the year but like the Upper Spean can be hit or miss.

Water Level Summer dam releases or very wet weather are needed for this run. Higher flows can result in the grades of the main rapids increasing.

Gauge Look at the first rapid close to the road. If this can be run without scraping, then the level is fine. If the rapid is a 'white-wash' the river is high.

Access Driving north, take the right-hand turn off the A9 towards Foss (929 581). Follow this minor road and the river appears very soon, (signposted the Linn of Tummel). Drive up and put in below the dam. Limited parking is possible at a small lay-by at the entrance to the hydro-electric plant. Walk down through the hydro-electric works via a small path branching right and following the fish ladder down to the river. An excellent take-out is available at the picnic site next to the bottom power house, where the Tummel spills into Loch Faskally. You can't miss the turning down to the take-out, as the road passes through an enormous arch illustrating the size of the tunnel created to carry the water of this large river basin through the hydro works. The arch is a memorial to the workers who lost their lives during the building of the hydro system.

Description From the put-in, easy water for some distance brings you to the first steep grade 3 rapid. Below this the river becomes more interesting. A large flat pool leads down into the rapid that can be seen from the road. The entrance is through a small slot and round a couple of tight turns, classic technical grade 3 paddling. More small ledges follow, leading you to the playhole, good for 'new school' low volume boats. One more ledge then follows before the Linn of Tummel. At medium flows the Linn comprises of two small fun grade 4 drops. If the river is higher the Linn can reach grade 5 and have some meaty holes.

Before the creation of Loch Faskally, the Falls would have been much higher. They are now 'drowned' with only the top couple of metres remaining to be paddled. Even now, variations in the height of the loch will affect how sticky the final hole is.

Contributors:
Roland Bone
and Andy Jackson

Other important points Please don't overcrowd the parking at the put-in lay-by.

Tay

The main white water sections of the Tay are at Grandtully near Aberfeldy, and at Stanley just outside Perth. For touring or instructional purposes it is best to look at an OS map to sort out a put-in and take-out. The River Tay can be accessed easily for much of the way up the A9 and A827. The Tay offers plenty of river activity for a variety of users throughout the year, with playboating, competition, rafting and touring all occurring regularly. The river is one of the longest in Scotland and can be paddled all the way from source to estuary. For those who aren't into paddling too far, the playspots are easily accessed from the road.

156 Tay (Grandtully)

Grade **1/2(3)**
Length **7km**
OS sheet **52**

Introduction The section from Aberfeldy to the rapids at Grandtully makes a good trip with some surfable waves.

Water Level Dry/Very wet. The Tay can be paddled all year round. Some of the playspots require certain water levels to be working well.

Gauge The river is very much take it as you see it.

Access To reach the Grandtully rapid/slalom site, turn off the A9 at Ballinluig. Follow the A827 towards Aberfeldy, taking the right turn after you cross the river. About a mile after this bridge you reach Grandtully. There is a small charge for parking and/or camping in the Old Station Yard (with a discount for SCA members), reached by turning left opposite the riverside café. A path alongside the river takes you from the café, upstream to the put-in. This is the main white water section so just carry back up for another go. It is also possible to do the grade 1/2 trip down to Grandtully starting

in Aberfeldy or even Kenmore. To reach the put-in, continue along
the A827 until you get to Aberfeldy. Turn right in the village onto
the B846 signposted to Weem and put in where the road crosses
the river. Alternatively, for a shorter trip, there is a dedicated SCA
access point on the north bank of the river, a little over 2 miles
above Grandtully Rapid. Cross the bridge in Grandtully, turn left,
and drive along the back road towards Weem. The parking area is
reached after 2.3 miles at (883 516).

Description From Aberfeldy down, the Tay provides some grade
2 water, and some surfable waves. Grandtully offers slalom facilities over grade 3 water. There is a playhole that works at medium
levels to the left of the centre rock at the start of the first small fall
200m below the put-in for the slalom site. Below the bridge there
is a small surf wave above a largish hole. The hole is powerful but
allows blasts etc. Walk back up from here to the start again.

Contributor:
Roland Bone

Tay (Stanley) 156

Grade **1/2(3)**
Length **3km**
OS sheet **53**

Introduction The Stanley section is a good all-round site, catering
for beginners, raceheads and playboaters alike.

Water Level The river can be paddled all year round.

Access Driving north from Perth on the A9, take the first turning,
the B9099, signposted for Stanley. After about 2 miles, there is a
car park on your left. This is the take-out at Thistlebrig. To reach
the put-in, continue on into the village. Turn right after the village
green, then left at the T-junction. From here take the right turn
onto Linn Road, which leads down to the river. Parking is a real
problem, so where possible, please use the car park in the village
and sort a shuttle out from there.

Description Upstream from the put-in is Campsie Linn. The Linn
offers whirlpools and a large wave at certain heights, which starts
to tube over when the river is high. At this level the whirlpools
are powerful and can take boaters down for a whirley ride. Below
the Linn is the Wall – a well defined deep eddy line for cartwheel-
ing, cut-backs and other moves. 500m downstream is the weir.
The centre shoot is usually the best for playing. In high water, a
large stopper may form below the weir, which should be treated

with caution. At higher levels still, the whole weir is washed out, and a large green wave appears on the right. This wave has awesome potential for some great rides. From here you can paddle back upstream to the car park, or continue on to Thistlebrig. Below the weir is grade 1/2 water, with one or two more playspots. Good waves lie just above the obvious right-hand bend if the river is up. In high water, a good surf wave forms at the end of this bend. At most levels, you only get one shot here, although it is easy enough to carry back up (river left) for another go. After a further 2km, large cliffs on the right-hand side mark the approach of the last rapid at Thistlebrig (Gd 2). There is a good surf wave here at lower levels, but it is hard to stay on for long and the paddle back up the eddy is a slog. Take out below this and follow the track uphill to the lower car park, or if the water is high, check out Wee Eric, the friendly wave/hole 200m downstream, river right.

Other important points Stanley is possibly the most kayaked site in Scotland, particularly in the summer. Please be sensitive with access. Share shuttles with other boaters to avoid causing congestion. If there are any access problems, please contact the River Advisor or SCA office.

The weir is made out of concrete with metal spikes. It is slowly falling apart and metal spikes may protrude. Generally these do not cause a problem, but the odd injury has occurred in the past. At high levels, the whirlpools at Campsie Linn are very dangerous and should be treated with respect. This is not a good place for a swim.

Contributor:
Roland Bone

157 Keltney Burn (Upper)

Grade	**4(5)**
Length	**3km**
OS sheet	**52**

Introduction A tributary of the River Lyon, the Keltney Burn drains from the much-trampled hill, Schiehallion. This is a great run, well worth the long walk in. With full-on drops and ledges, padded out with fast and interesting rapids and all in the back of beyond, this is a real mountain river.

Water Level Very wet. It will need to be going some to get this section running. At really big flows the trip is at its best. At more moderate flows it can be a bit scrapey between the falls and you would be better running the lower stretch.

Gauge Check the level at the metal bridge by the Keltneyburn Hotel in Glen Lyon. The river bed should be fully covered, with no rocks showing below the bridge, if the upper stretch is to be runnable.

Access From the Keltneyburn Hotel, drive north up the B846. The lower section is close to the road at this point but is hidden in a deep gorge. After 2½ miles there is a deer park and caravan site on the left-hand side of the road. Just before this, and at the start of a straight in the road, there is space to park a vehicle or two by a forest gate. The river can be seen coming from the hills on the left. This is the take-out for the Upper Keltney, and also the put-in for the lower section. To get to the upper put-in continue on the B846, turning left at the minor road marked Schiehallion. After 2 miles the parking area used for access to Schiehallion is reached on the left. Try not to be put off by the strange looks from the hillwalkers as you unload the boats, several miles from the nearest body of water. Initially you follow the main Schiehallion path past the forest and onto the open moor. After ½km, turn left and follow the remains of the old track that contours around the hill. After 2km, the track peters out. Continue to contour round the hill, aiming for the flattening in the river at (739 533).

Description Fast and shallow rapids begin almost straight away. A 2m ledge, which requires a peak, comes up quickly and serves as a good warning for its bigger brother not far below. This 5m fall is just off vertical, and it's quite a challenge to make the boof and avoid the strong towback (Gd 5). If you choose to portage, this can be done at river level on the left, though you do have to fight your way round a rocky point and risk being sucked back into the hole you were trying to avoid! At high flows, the gorge after the fall is really good grade 4 fun. You now find yourself being flushed along more open water with several mini-gorges concealing grade 4/5 water. A straight stretch of grade 3/4 water tries to lure you into the lower gorge. Don't let it! As soon as you spot the river banks beginning to steepen, you should climb out on river left. Beyond here a couple more runnable drops and a fence blocking the river lead to a major cataract dividing the upper and lower sections. This is not going to be very nice at the kind of flows that make the upper river paddleable. You could continue to the lip of this monster, but it will be harder to get out of the gorge and the drops on the run in look hard to scout

from river level. It is a 1km walk on river left down the hill and through the deer park to the road.

Other important points You are way out there on this one, so take enough gear and some spare clothes/food. It might be worth taking a map and compass if the weather is really grotty. Please take care not to damage the fences at the deer park as you walk out.

Contributor:
Andy Jackson

157 Keltney Burn (Lower)

Grade	**4(5)**
Length	**3km**
OS sheet	**52**

Introduction A tributary of the River Lyon, the Keltney Burn runs in a deep gorge next to the B846, in the heart of Perthshire. It's steep and technical run in a narrow gorge requiring a portage round some high (unrunnable?) falls: a fun excursion, but not of the same quality as the upper section.

Water Level Wet. As the section runs in a narrow gorge, it comes into condition regularly and would probably be too exciting in full flood!

Gauge Check the level at the metal bridge by the Keltneyburn Hotel in Glen Lyon. The small fall immediately upstream of the bridge should look entertaining for the gorge to be worthwhile. If the river is covering all the rocks below the bridge the upper section would be a better bet.

Access The metal bridge by the Keltneyburn Hotel makes a good take-out. To find the put-in, follow the description to reach the take-out for the upper section.

Description Initially the river winds its way through the narrow gorge with the odd grade 4 ledge. Trees are likely to be a hazard on this section. Halfway through the run there is a twisting fall into a narrow and grippy hole (Gd 5). Easy water and a tree blockage signals the approach of the Falls of Keltney. The first of these high falls is easily runnable, but how to get out of the pothole before the next drop is less obvious. Portaging the falls on river right you can get to the car quickly by continuing on the forest road, but it's worth making the effort to lower back into the gorge below the Falls and complete the trip.

Contributor:
Andy Jackson

Lyon 158

Grade **3/4(5)**
Length **3km**
OS sheet **51**

Introduction The Lyon drains part of Rannoch Moor, between Loch Rannoch and Loch Tay. The large catchment area provides a good volume run that holds its water really well. This run is through a bizarre gorge full of weird features, with the forest occasionally providing a leafy canopy.

Water Level Medium wet/Wet. The Lyon is heavily affected by various dams in its upper reaches and you are normally left with a reliable but measly compensation flow.

Gauge The bridge at the take-out can be used to gauge the flow. If the water is covering the concrete, the river is running high. If the water is 6 inches below the concrete, the river is still OK.

Access From the A9 take the A827 to Aberfeldy. Turn right in the town onto the B846, cross the Tay and continue until you reach Keltneyburn. Take the left turn here, signposted to Glen Lyon. After about 3 miles, just after Fortingall (famous for its ancient yew tree), the road splits. The left fork leads down to a bridge over the Lyon - this is the take-out. To reach the put-in return to where the road forks. Turn left up the glen and continue for about 3 miles to where the river levels out again. At the time of writing, handy 'No Canoeing' signs in the lay-by marked the put-in nicely.

Description The first 2km are straightforward grade 3/4, with the river running through a variety of weird little gorges. The initial section has a couple of tight slots, which are passable with care, and one or two fun playspots. After about 1½km, the rapids get more continuous until you find a series of drops ending in a constriction. Although it does get run, at almost all levels this constriction merits a portage and is very dangerous. Make sure that you have noted a suitable eddy well above this spot before you get on the river. After this, the river eases off until one final 1m drop, which forms a large pour-over in high water; this is run down either edge.

Other important points Remember to smile at all times in case the fishermen are taking photos and do not get caught stealing 'No Canoeing' signs! Hill walkers and kayakers alike have had problems accessing the hills and rivers in Glen Lyon. The landowner's

Contributors:
Dave Kwant and
Alan Meikle

attitude has been quite obstructive in the past and you would be best to have your arguments well prepared. This is particularly the case in the lower part of the glen with the main white water run and the Invervar Burn being points of contention.

159 Lyon (Upper)

Grade	2-4
Length	4km
OS sheet	51

Contributor:
Alan Meikle

Access Follow the description for the Lyon, then drive further up the glen beside the river for nearly 20 miles to find Loch Lyon.

Description From the put-in at Loch Lyon, the first 1km has some good rapids ranging from grade 2-4. The rest of the way to the Stronuich Reservoir is flatter with a couple of nice grade 2s. Below the reservoir, there are a few nice rapids, although these are usually considered too spread out to make a worthwhile trip.

160 Invervar Burn

Grade	4/5
Length	1km
OS sheet	51

Contributor:
Dave Kwant

Access To find the river, drive up Glen Lyon. As you enter Invervar, there is a footpath clearly marked on your right, just before the bridge over the burn. Walk up until you get to a small man-made dam – get on below it.

Description This entertaining trip is true short boat territory. In its top half, the Invervar descends in a continuous series of little slabby drops into small pools, with the surrounding forest lending a certain air of mystique. The bottom half contains larger drops, which are best inspected on the walk up. This burn runs quite often, but would be full-on in high water.

161 Innerwick Burn

Grade	3/4(5)
Length	1km
OS sheet	51

Contributor:
Dave Kwant

Access To find the run, continue up Glen Lyon. As you go through Innerwick, look out for a dirt track leading up the side of the burn just before the bridge. Get on where the burn splits into three.

Description The burn at Innerwick is less steep than the Invervar and runs through a more open glen. The top half has a constant gradient providing grade 3/4 paddling. The river then drops into a gorge where it becomes a little more serious with small slabby falls. The crux is a logslide off a 2m ledge to avoid rocks.

Lochay 162

Grade	**4(5)**
Length	**8km**
OS sheet	**51**

Introduction The Lochay flows into the west end of Loch Tay, near the village of Killin. The River Lochay is a medium volume river in a quiet and unspoiled glen. It can be thought of as a mini River Orchy, with long flat stretches separated by bedrock rapids and falls.

Water Level Wet/Very wet. This river requires a fair amount of water to be worthwhile, especially in its upper reaches, which would feel bony in anything other than a reasonable flow.

Gauge To judge the flow, take a drive up the glen. The river is close to the road, and it should be easy to decide if this run is at the right level. Make sure that you check the level above the out-flow from the power station, about 2½ miles up the glen. Even if the river is a little bony to run the whole section, expert kayakers may derive some amusement by running the Falls of Lochay. For the whole trip to be on, as a rough guide 0.8 on the SEPA gauge for the Dochart could probably be considered a minimum flow.

Access From Killin, drive north on the A827. Take either of the two minor roads that lead up Glen Lochay. For the full trip, drive to the head of the glen and put in near Kenknock. The road bridge just downstream of the power station outflow makes a good take-out.

Description From the put-in, you are into good rapids straight away. A slightly shallow 3m fall gives the trip a kick start. After 1km or so, the rapids ease and there is a long stretch of flat water. The next set of rapids start way too far downstream, so be prepared for a long paddle or a quick shuttle by car. The river continues with more dead water and the odd entertaining grade 4 ledge. The best is saved till last in the form of the Falls of Lochay, which lie behind the power station. Best scouted from river right, these five drops form an impressive cascade, quite pushy in a high flow, (Gd 5).

Other important points At the right level, this is a good run that deserves to be more popular. It twins well with a trip to the Falls of Dochart, although both may not be up together on the same day.

Contributor:
Andy Jackson

163 Dochart

Grade	**4**
Length	**½km**
OS sheet	**51**

Introduction The River Dochart flows through the charming highland village of Killin, at the west end of Loch Tay. The Falls themselves flow right past the door of the Clachaig Hotel, a great place for a celebratory drink, or a stiff whisky to calm the nerves. This is touristville, so in the summer be prepared to boat with an audience. For the white water paddler, this truly is a one hit wonder, but if you're in the area with the right water level, its worth getting on.

Water Level Wet/Very wet. This stretch requires medium to high flows. Due to its long flat upper reaches, the river is slow to come up but holds its water well, and may be worth visiting even a day or two after heavy rain.

Gauge A quick look over the bridge in Killin will tell you all you need to know. 0.5 on the SEPA gauge should be considered a minimal level.

Access Either walk up the road with your boat and put in just upstream of Killin, or if you fancy a warm up, drive west on the A827 for about a mile. There is a 'lay-by' on the right-hand side, near where the river comes close to the road. Take out at the end of the white water on river right. A good path leads back upstream to the village. Do not be tempted to stray into Loch Tay, as reaching the next take-out involves about 1½km of flat-water paddling.

Description At medium/high flows, this is a great fun rapid. The usual line follows the main flow to the right of the top island and on through the left-hand bridge arch. This gives the crux of the run, and is best inspected before you get on. The menacing hole under the bridge is normally avoided on the left. Watch out for fishermen in the eddy on river left. The action doesn't end quite here, and the rapid continues below the bridge. There is a ledge some 200m downstream which can form a retentive hole. At high flows the whole stretch should probably be considered a grade 5, and a powerful one at that.

Contributors:
Andy Jackson
Alan Meikle and
Anna Gordon

Other important points Above the Falls, the Dochart has good potential for an easy touring trip. Keep an eye out for the Lix Toll rapids some 3km above Killin, which make a long grade 3 when there is enough water and don't forget to take out in good time before the Falls.

Urlar Burn (Moness Burn) 164

Grade	**4**
Length	**2km**
OS sheet	**52**

Introduction The Urlar Burn runs right through the Tayside village of Aberfeldy. The Urlar is a long roller coaster run, with very little chance to wave to the tourists in Aberfeldy as you pass. At a good level, it is just one long rapid.

Water Level Very wet. In fact almost unfeasibly wet!

Gauge Look over the bridge in Aberfeldy. If the river is flowing hard and all the rocks are covered, it should be a really good run.

Access Turn off the A9 at Ballinluig, and follow the A827 towards Aberfeldy. Park at the car park for the Falls of Moness, which you find by turning left (south) on to the A826 in Aberfeldy. Follow the riverside path upstream and put on where you feel comfortable. If you feel comfortable with the Falls of Moness you should go and see your doctor. Take out on the River Tay or upstream of the golf course in Aberfeldy, (856 490).

Description This river has excellent bouldery rapids with all the holes, rocks and pour-overs you'd expect. There are 3 good drops in the vicinity of the car park, which make the crux of the run and are probably worth a look.

Contributor:
Andy Burton

Other important points Watch out for the low bridge!

Braan (Top) 165

Grade	**4**
Length	**4km**
OS sheet	**52**

Introduction The Braan flows into the Tay near Dunkeld in central Perthshire. It has four distinct sections depending on the amount of rain around and how challenged you wish to feel. The top section can only be done in extreme flood and is only possible on a few days each year. It is similar to a higher Alpine river.

Access Turn off the A9 at Dunkeld and follow the A822. Park in the obvious lay-by on the right, about half a mile before the village of Amulree. It's a short walk over the field to the river. Take out at the bridge by Dullator Farm. There is some parking here, but be careful not to block the farm road.

Contributor:
Eddie Palmer

Description The run starts with 2km of good grade 4 bouldery rapids with large holes. As the river comes back to the road there is a 'ski-jump' rock, which can be nasty. At a house on the left bank, the river splits around an island and becomes grade 2-3 for a further 2km down to Dullator Farm and bridge.

165 Braan (Upper)

Grade	**2/3**
Length	**2km**
OS sheet	**52**

Description This stretch is good for white water novices, and also provides an easier alternative for the faint-hearted when the river is in flood. Putting on at the take-out for the top section gives 2km of grade 2/3 paddling down to Meikle Findowie Farm where a metal bridge crosses over the river. There is ample parking here and a friendly farmer. To find the metal bridge, turn off the A822 about a mile upstream of the point where the A822 crosses the river. In high water the trip can be extended by putting on higher up the Braan or at the small burn which flows under the A822, just east of the A822/A826 road junction.

Contributor: Eddie Palmer

165 Braan (Middle)

Grade	**3/4**
Length	**5km**
OS sheet	**52**

Introduction This is a fun trip which picks up pace as it goes, culminating in the awesome but unrunnable cascade at Rumbling Bridge.

Water Level Very wet. This is a river that rises and falls quickly and needs a good flow to be runnable.

Gauge There is a gauge in the Hermitage car park at the bottom of the gorge. For this stretch, 8 or above will give an exciting trip. 0.9 on the SEPA gauge should be considered a minimum flow.

Access Put in at the metal bridge described above or for a longer warm-up at the start of the upper section. Confident paddlers may prefer to start further down, just upstream of the A822 road bridge, parking in the lay-by past the farm. There is a convenient take-out at a stone bridge about a mile upstream of the Rumbling Falls, eminently suitable for intermediate groups, and another at a lay-by on the A822, around ½ mile above the falls. More experienced paddlers could take out above Rumbling Bridge, or portage round river right to continue down the gorge.

Description From the steel bridge 1km of easier water leads to the start of a little grade 3 gorge and the rapid under the A822, which can reach grade 4 in high water. The river then flattens out for ½km until a white house marks the start of a 200m long rapid, which can be powerful in high water. Below here the river eases to grade 1/2 and the first take-out is reached. Easy water and the second take-out follow before the approach to Rumbling Bridge. The first drop of the run-in goes on the left at grade 4+. However, a big hole can form at high water and this would be a very bad place to be out of control. There is little time from here to make the last take-out on river right.

Contributors:
Dave Kwant,
Ian Thom and
Alan Meikle

Other important points Try very hard not to get swept over Rumbling Bridge Falls!

Braan (Lower) 165

Introduction Just before joining the River Tay at Dunkeld, the River Braan cascades over the waterfall at Rumbling Bridge and drops into an impressive and scenic gorge. Christened the 'Mad Mile', the gorge section is fast, continuous and exciting when high. At a lower level the run is more bouldery and reaching the river may prove to be the biggest challenge.

Grade	4/5
Length	2km
OS sheet	52

Water Level Wet/Very wet. This river tends to go up and down very quickly, often within half a day. The gorge is at its best when high, giving a continuous and quite pushy run.

Gauge There is a gauge in the Hermitage car park. 7-10 is low/medium. 11+ is high.

Access To reach the put-in, turn off the A9 onto the A822 at Dunkeld. After 2 miles turn off right for Rumbling Bridge. There is a car park immediately on the right and it is a short walk to Rumbling Bridge. After gawking at the fall you can gain the river via an awkward muddy gully. This is about 20m below the bridge on river right, scramble down the 2nd gully, which has a tree across it. Take out at the Hermitage car park, signposted off the A9 just north of Dunkeld and the A822 turning. If you have only one car you may find it easiest to walk/run the shuttle via the

woodland path on river left. Alternatively it is possible to extend the trip by continuing down to the main A9 bridge or on into Dunkeld itself.

Description At a high flow the excitement starts immediately with continuous grade 4 for the first kilometre, a real cracking stretch. Rapids follow in quick succession; this is not a good place to swim, especially if the river is high. Towards the end of this section, a left-hand bend, a big eddy and a tree in the river mark the approach to Splitter (Gd 5). Best scouted from the left, this rapid is blocked by a huge central boulder. The left-hand channel has a nasty pothole, which is not recommended especially at low/ medium flows. Much of the best action is in this short top section and for those who've had enough excitement, it's possible to carry back up the left bank to the car. Below Splitter the river eases with a few small rapids. The next major rapid is The Coffin (Gd 5+), a river-wide ledge with a very nasty towback at high flows. From here there are a couple of grade 3/4 rapids before Hermitage Falls (Gd 6), which is portaged on the left. Easy water then leads down to the take-out at the Hermitage car park. The section from here to Dunkeld is grade 2/3 when the river is high. It includes a good site for slalom training behind the Forestry Commission Offices.

Contributors:
Dave Kwant
and Alan Meikle

Other important points Be sure to take out well above Hermitage Falls!

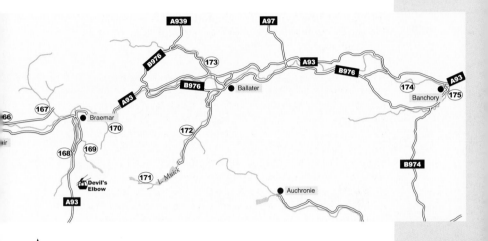

Up fae Dundee

N

approx. scale 1cm = 5km

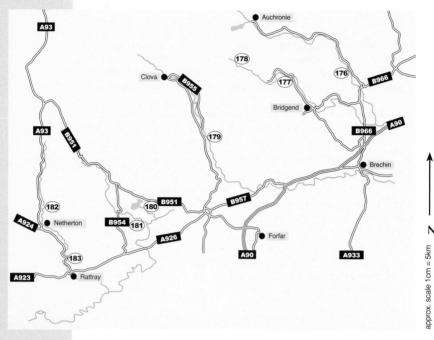

approx. scale 1cm = 5km

Up fae Dundee Continued

Up fae Dundee

Under this chapter we have included the rivers of the Angus
Glens as well as those runs which drain the eastern Cairngorms
and form the mighty River Dee. The former includes such classics
as the West Water and the North Esk, which provides high quality
and generally dependable grade 3 and 4 paddling for much of the
year. By contrast the creeks in the upper reaches of the Dee offer
challenging spate trips up to grade 5! The Lui, Quoich and Garbh
Allt compare favourably with many of the classic runs of the west.
As for the Melgan; well that's in a world of its own! Although this
area does not see as much rain as other parts of Scotland, its
rivers are generally longer with larger and easier angled catchment basins. As a result the rivers will often stay up for a day
or two after the run-off has finished on the west of the country.
Given the dominant weather pattern in Scotland, of unsettled
weather sweeping in from the south-west, you can use this to
your advantage. You can often enjoy the rivers on the west coast,
which see the rain first and are quick to rise on one day, and by a
short drive, catch the runs on the east the next.

Lui 166

Grade	**4/5**
Length	**1km**
OS sheet	**43**

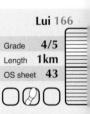

Introduction Part of the Mar Lodge estate owned by the
National Trust for Scotland, the Lui runs through an area of natural beauty, entering the River Dee near to the village of Braemar.
This is a short, slabby bedrock run with an inspiring cascade. It is
set in a beautiful and easily accessible, yet reasonably secluded,
part of a popular glen.

Water Level Wet. Not having a loch to feed it, and only being
small itself, the Lui takes its time to come up, but drops faster than
a stone. If the ground is wet, a couple of nights rain will bring the
river up to a paddleable if low level. Snow melt or heavy rain in
the eastern Cairngorms is needed to get it running well.

Gauge As a minimum, the slabs closest to the track end should
be reasonably well covered.

Access From Braemar, follow the Linn of Dee road. About 400m
past the Linn of Dee car park (063 898), the Lui appears. Park beside

the river, but be careful not to obstruct the locked gate on the left, which is used by the mountain rescue team and for access to Derry Lodge. This is the take-out. Walk up either side of the river for about a kilometre until an obvious flattening. If the road is busy or you have several vehicles, it's best to use the Linn of Dee / Cairngorm access car park. From this car park, follow the Derry Lodge track then cut down to the river and continue upstream.

Description There's fun to be had from the outset, with the Lui splitting around a small island and running over smooth pink slabs. This is followed by an excellent cascade falling about 5m over 30m, complete with obstacles, and ending in a freestyle-freefall drop into a hole. The chances are you'll almost have recovered by the time you reach the next highlight, but you can always get your breath back as you check it for wood. This is a must, as the situation changes often - at the time of writing both channels were totally blocked. If there's no wood, a great line exists river left, down a slab into a slot and, quite often, around and around in the slot. At medium to low levels you can stand close enough to the hole to catch your saucer-eyed pals as they return for the rinse cycle! An Aberdeen Uni Magic Bat once spent two weeks in there, somewhere. The rest of the run to the road bridge is made up of easy angled fun slabs. For those who want to go further there is one more small rapid before the river bumbles into the Dee.

Other important points This area is popular with a range of outdoor types, but particularly walkers and nature lovers. The importance of keeping the gate clear can't be over-estimated.

Contributors:
Andy England
and Alastair Collis

167 Quoich

Grade **4/5(5+)**
Length **2km**
OS sheet **43**

Introduction The Quoich is located in the Cairngorms close to Braemar, but on the opposite side of the Dee. The Quoich is a short, scary-fun run in a beautiful place. It is all bedrock pool-drop, characterised by unusual narrow slots. Rapids can be inspected and protected from the safety of the bank or easily walked around.

Water Level This run needs substantial snow melt or heavy rain in the eastern Cairngorms to bring it into condition. It has similar requirements to the Lui, but is better with a drop more water.

Gauge As you set out from Braemar on the minor road, look for the Quoich across the glen on your right, recognizable by a low metal bridge and braided course on the Dee's floodplain. It's hard to get a real feel for the Quoich at this point, but it will be obvious whether the river is in spate. The river should be at least bump-scrape floatable all the way to the car park by the Linn of Quoich. For more assurances check the first rapid (a few hundred metres upstream). There should be enough water to be able to paddle over the ledge on river right (although this is usually a portage at such levels). More water makes the river harder. Less water makes one rapid harder but the rest a scrape. The Quoich has no loch but a good catchment and drops quite rapidly.

Access To get to the put-in from Braemar, drive towards and past the Linn of Dee. At the end of the minor road there is a car park close to the Linn of Quoich, (118 912). From here you've got two choices, but either way's a hike. You can follow the track which starts just before the road bridge all the way to the put-in or, if you want to see what you're letting yourself in for, follow the riverside footpath from the car park. Cross the bridge over the Linn and follow the main track until it reaches a floodplain. This is your start point.

Description It's worth walking as far as a small rapid about 100m upstream of the obvious first fall, as this is your only warm up. The fall itself is a 3-4m drop into a deep slot and fluffy hole - a great swimming pool if the river's too low to paddle and you need cooling off! Check for wood. Downstream lies a beautiful ledge drop into what can be, at high levels, a really sticky hole. A two-man team once had a scary 'this is how not to do it' time on this drop. Al Collis took the fall and went deep, with safety from the bank. The bank, though, is very slippy and the nearest anchor a very baby tree. You get the picture. While Al retends, throws ends, doesn't breathe, recircs … his safety is too busy trying not to fall in to help! After all the excitement there's still the Punch Bowl and the Linn, probably the most serious rapid on the Quoich. The Punch Bowl is a textbook pothole, set in smooth slabs on river right, and nicely away from the line, whereas the Linn is an amazing slot less than a metre wide at the upstream entrance, and not much wider where it spits you out 15m downstream. The tempting wee gorge that follows contains a well hidden undercut and probable portage. You'll see a drop with

wood left and a slab right. What you won't see unless you get out river right and scramble round to look, is the undercut just downstream, which most of the river goes under. Dave Kwant once spent between 20 and 30 seconds checking out the underside of the cliff, before finally managing to pull himself out. The boat stayed there another two days. You have been warned! Depending on the water level this undercut may be passable, but please take care to check it out or just get off after the Linn and carry (river left) round the last gorge. After the gorge opens up, it's an easy bimble back to the car park.

Contributors:
Andy England
and Alastair Collis

Other important points The river is part of the Mar Lodge Estate owned by the National Trust for Scotland. The water is used as a supply for the nearby house, so please make relevant considerations. There is great wild camping in the area, but it is quite a popular spot with walkers and picnickers.

168 Clunie

Grade **4**
Length **200m**
OS sheet **43**

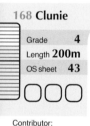

Contributor:
Andy England

Description The action on the Clunie can be seen from the road bridge in Braemar, or closer up by scrambling down the path beside the hotel. The latter option puts you in a great position to see your mate's face as they swim out of the bottom hole! Some steps on river right bring you to a path that takes you back up to the road.

169 Callater

Grade **4**
Length **2km**
OS sheet **43**

Introduction Funnily enough the Callater is in Glen Callater, which joins the A93 (Glen Shee road) about 2 miles south of Braemar. The Callater Burn is a big-spate classic. It's got the characteristic of Scotch Broth, albeit in quite a small bowl! Open moorland, wide boulder bounces and bedrock drops, slots and slabs, and a stunning wee gorge to leave a sweet taste.

Water Level Wet/Very wet. Definitely a spate run - lots of rain or major snow melt is needed. It runs high as you like, but not low (the river bed is used for gorge walking most of the year!). Loch-fed, it doesn't rise or fall as quickly as some of the other rivers in the area.

Gauge From the lay-by, look at the last eddy before the deer fence (under the bridge). Is there any shingle showing? Can you see any rocks in the last corner of the gorge? If the answer to either of these is yes, it's too low. If the river's churning brown and you're unsure whether you'll make it to the bank before the deer fence, then the level's right. You can gauge the level for yourself as you walk up the burn. If you're thinking of travelling a distance, it's worth phoning Braemar Mountain Sports (013397 41242) to get an idea of levels.

Access The take-out is found about 2 miles south of Braemar on the A93 (Glen Shee road). There are no obvious signs, but look for a small road bridge (157 882) and lay-by on the opposite side of the road to a house (Auchallater), that the burn passes beside. You can almost see the bottom of the gorge from your car. This is a popular spot with walkers - the other way to Lochnagar - so there may be a few cars. Nearly all of the river can be seen whilst walking in. Carry up the track from the lay-by for about 2km. When your body feels like giving up, you're almost halfway! The easiest gauge is to look for the footbridge; there's nothing great upstream of here. The Callater is a water supply for Auchallater House, so please take relevant care - the track is also important for ghillies and mountain rescue, so leave room in the lay-by for their landrovers. If you wish to extend the trip as far as Braemar (see below) there are obvious shuttle implications and concerns about getting round the deer fence under the bridge. Sometimes it is possible to get around it, but please take great care to do no damage. The alternatives all involve fences, so check out your options and be aware of the residents of Auchallater House.

Description Depending on your group, and the water level, the Callater is all read and run. There are no big waterfalls or nasty surprises, just great quality rapids. However, the eddies are small and chase boating is frantic. The hardest rapid, with a greedy hole, is a few hundred metres upstream of the gorge - worth protecting as a swim from here could be long and bumpy. The entrance to the gorge is a classic roller coaster run, while the gorge itself is surprisingly straightforward. Complacency though, is often rewarded by a scramble for the last eddy above the deer fence, as your group gets spat out of the gorge just metres upstream of the take-out bridge.

Contributor:
Andy England

170 Garbh Allt (Glenbeg Burn)

Grade   **4/5**
Length   **1km**
OS sheet   **43**

Introduction A classic Deeside burn, the Garbh Allt flows into the Dee some 4 miles east of Braemar. This is a short but intense run with beautiful river features - most notably smooth pink granite slabs. The slabby sections are separated by bouldery bits, which in high water, become challenging in themselves. You never stop feeling like you're going downhill until you reach your car. The Falls of Garbh Allt themselves were reputedly Queen Victoria's favourite waterfall; a cast iron bridge was erected to give her a better view of this eye-pleasing cascade. With its setting in an old pine forest, this small mountain burn is today still as eye catching as ever.

Water Level Wet. Serious rain or lots of snow melt from Lochnagar is needed for this one. Get it too high and it's scary, with a probable portage - too low and you could scrape down the slabs but not paddle between them. The burn rises very quickly once the ground is wet.

Gauge Cross the suspension bridge over the River Dee and follow the track. Look upstream at the first bridge (with a deer fence under it). The shingle on the river right fork should be covered well enough to scrape/float out, and there should be water coming in from a fork on river left - it probably won't look like enough water, but that's okay.

Access The run is accessed from North Deeside road, about 4 miles east of Braemar and 1 mile east of the obvious Invercauld Bridge. It is hard to see the river from the road, so look out for a white suspension footbridge with a very small area to pull in, (197 908). This is the take-out. To reach the put-in, carry over the footbridge or paddle over the Dee underneath it, then turn right along a landrover track. Follow this over a low track bridge and take a left. Keep going uphill (always a good sign!) ignoring rights and lefts until you see a small footbridge high above a rapid. Cross the bridge and follow the path even further uphill to a cast iron bridge over some enticing granite slabs. Put in just upstream, or carry a bit further and do the slabs you can see (the ones that end in the perfect hole above waterfalls!).

Description Some of the classiest action is metres from the put-in, with smooth bedrock slabs into a great deep plunge pool. This is the highest fall on the run, which leaves no time for a warm-up or psyche-up. It is, though, fluffier than it looks - and with such a scenic back-drop you'll need to do it twice for the cameras! Once you leave the comfort of the pool, you're into the run proper and need to be alert. Boulders feed quickly into slabs with only tiny eddies for inspecting and, depending on the water height, some pretty chunky holes craftily scattered. Everything is generally read and run, but it's worth checking the rapid you walked over on the way up, under the footbridge. In the centre is a well-shaped broaching rock, and at very high levels a hole that you'll be glad to swim out of! Once through, it's back to read and run until you see the shingle beds and the bridge carrying the landrover track near the take-out. Remember there's a deer fence under the bridge, and the gathering eddy is quite small.

Other important points Although on the Balmoral Estate and as such part of the royal backyard, access has never been a problem. Don't be insulted if men with dark glasses and Inspector Gadget coats ask what you're up to when the Queen's in residence.

Contributors:
Andy England
and Alastair Collis

Allt an Dubh Loch 171

Access Drive up past the put-in for the Muick, to the Spittal of Glenmuick car park, and then walk to the edge of Loch Muick. It's a 4km paddle across to the far end of the loch, followed by a short 3km stroll up the track. Put in just below the Dubh Loch and make sure you have a camera.

Grade	5
Length	**3km**
OS sheet	**44**

Description For those masochists who enjoy remote and challenging runs, the Allt an Dubh Loch may provide an entertaining outing. This small burn flows over some classy slabs and drops on its short journey from the Dubh Loch into Loch Muick.

Contributor:
Andy Jackson

172 Muick

Grade **3+(5)**
Length **5km**
OS sheet **44**

Introduction Situated in Royal Deeside close to the famous crags of Lochnagar, the Muick drains into the Dee near Ballater. This fast bouncy grade 3 boulder trip is divided into 2 sections by the impressive Linn of Muick. This fall can only be paddled at low flows, when the rest of the river would not be worth contemplating.

Water Level Extremely wet.

Gauge All the rivers in the area need to be brown and churning, or this river will feel like a rocky ditch.

Access Take the B976 from Ballater towards Braemar. After less then a mile, at Bridge of Muick, turn off onto a minor road leading up the glen to the car park for Lochnagar. After about 1½ miles, a road leads down to a bridge over the river. This is the take-out. To reach the put-in, return to the road up the glen, and continue on for another 3 miles to the next bridge. Find a lay-by in the section above the bridge and carry down to the river. It's probably worth stopping on the way up for a look at the Linn and to scout for eddies to stop in.

Description The river starts off fairly open. As it flows under the first bridge the gradient increases slightly, giving fast continuous grade 3+ water with the odd good 'catch it if you can' wave. The river is a mass of boulders making it impossible to try and follow a given route. This is read and run territory, crashing through waves and avoiding small pour-overs, making up the line as you go. The Linn of Muick comes up less than a kilometre after the bridge. Make sure you take out in plenty of time! This 10m 2-stage fall would not be a good one to do by accident! Below the falls, there is more of the same, although the features are slightly more broken with fewer surfable waves. Take out at the next road bridge.

Contributors:
Bridget Thomas
and Andy Jackson

173 Gairn

Grade   **3/4**
Length   **1km**
OS sheet **37**

Access The Gairn lies directly across the valley from Glen Muick and is easily accessed from the A939.

Description This is a reasonably large river and relatively straightforward for much of its length. There is some white water in the last kilometre at Bridge of Gairn, before the confluence with the Dee. At high flows this is grade 3/4.

Contributor:
Andy Jackson

Dee (Top) 174

Grade	1/3
Length	14km
OS sht.	37/44

Introduction The Dee is the main river basin draining the southern Cairngorms. It flows eastwards, entering the North Sea in Aberdeen. The Dee can be paddled from the Linn of Dee, near Breamar, to the boat club in Aberdeen. Most of the way the water is grade 1, although there are occasional entertaining rapids. The two most frequently paddled white water sections are described here. Both have some play potential at most levels.

Water Level Moderately wet/Very wet. You can nearly always get down the Dee, so it's a good summer river when there's nothing else, but the different rapids all come into condition at different levels. The top section is most fun at very high flows and is a good alternative in spate conditions when the other Deeside burns have become too scary.

Gauge The river flows parallel to the A93 for most of its length, making it easy to get an idea of the flow.

Access For the top section head out of Braemar on the Linn of Dee road. The take-out at Victoria Bridge is reached after about 3 miles. To get to the put-in continue up the road and park by the bridge over the Linn of Dee. If there is not much space here, you can unload the boats and then continue on to the nearby Forestry Commission car park. Walk down to the river and put in below the Linn.

Description At very high water the section from below the Linn of Dee has some good potential. The rapids are straightforward but powerful, flushing together in the upper reaches. In these conditions, there are some large relatively friendly stoppers behind the Youth Hostel, which provide an entertaining finish to the trip. At lower flows there is more time to collect the pieces between the rapids.

Other important points This is one of Scotland's prime salmon fishing rivers. Local Access Agreements exist for some parts of the river, and relationships with the fishermen are generally excellent,

so please contact the River Adviser, through the SCA office or website, to check the access situation. From source to sea, this is a fine touring river with good interest and scenery throughout. Access points are available at regular intervals along the river - again talk to the SCA for details. The rapid above Dinnet Bridge can reach grade 3 at high levels. There is a stopper upstream of the bridge, which can be more meaty than expected, and may catch the unwary tourer.

Contributors:
Bridget Thomas
and Zosia Patterson

174 Dee (Lower)

Grade	**2(3)**
Length	**11km**
OS sheet	**38**

Access Head out of Aberdeen on the A93. The put-in is beside the obvious bridge in Potarch. To reach the take-out, return on the A93 towards Aberdeen. Turn right at the traffic lights in Banchory and park in the large public car park. For those who like to park and play you can access the river at Invercannie waterworks. Please contact a local club or the River Advisor to get information on the current access situation at Invercannie.

Description The section from Potarch to Banchory is regularly paddled and gives continuous grade 2 water. The main rapids are at Cairnton, where there are some good surf waves at high flows, and Invercannie. In some conditions, these may be considered grade 3. At a medium flow, there is a fun but steep surf wave at Invercannie. This gets washed out at high flows and is best without too much water. However, when the river is very high, there is a great wave to surf downstream of here. One of the most memorable on the river, it's unfortunately hard to get back to once you've blown it.

Contributors:
Bridget Thomas
and Zosia Patterson

175 Water of Feugh

Grade	**4+**
Length	**200m**
OS sheet	**38**

Access From Banchory, take the B976 heading south over the River Dee (past the take-out for the Lower Dee section). After a few hundred yards a minor road branches off to the left, crossing the Water of Feugh.

Description This is a bit of a one-hit wonder, but it's fairly entertaining on a wet day. The Falls of Feugh are just upstream of the bridge and are a popular tourist attraction, particularly in late summer when the salmon are leaping.

Contributor:
Bridget Thomas

Nevis - Boulder Blast - Ryan Clements

Etive - Glen Etive & Glen Coe - Neil Farmer

Lugar - Burns Country - Douglas Wilcox

Carrick Lane - Burns Country - Douglas Wilcox

Cree - Burns Country - Neil Farmer

Carrick Lane - Burns Country - Douglas Wilcox

North Esk

The North Esk runs through Angus, halfway between Aberdeen and Dundee. It is in an attractive area, much loved and visited by Queen Victoria. The river itself is one of many that drain eastwards from the great Mounth plateau of the South-East Grampians. It starts life at the bottom of Glen Mark and weaves its way through the rounded foothills of the Angus Glens before heading across the Vale of Strathmore to Montrose Bay. The North Esk runs through a glen that is quiet and sleepy, except on rainy Wednesdays when the local universities invade! It is possible to navigate the river from its source in Loch Lee all the way to the sea, however after Gannocky Bridge the river is flat with some grade 2 and the occasional weir. As such it offers little for the white water boater. There are two main white water sections. The popular lower gorge is a real classic that deserves its reputation. It's a fun paddle at most levels, but becomes more pushy at high flows. The bouldery upper section requires lots of water, but is well worth visiting if the conditions are right. The North Esk is also a popular salmon river where other people get their enjoyment from fishing. At the moment the relationship with the fishermen is good, due to local boaters being friendly and considerate. The only other moving hazard here is the odd tree that becomes stuck, usually in the worst place possible.

North Esk (Upper) 176

Introduction This is the section at the head of the glen, starting from the put-in at Loch Lee car park. The enthusiastic can walk up to the loch from here. This section is a must in high water, and a good place to go if the lower section is too high. It is a boulder run with a couple of bedrock drops. The river is broad and open and has no constrictions on it.

Grade **4/4+**
Length **3½km**
OS sheet **44**

Water Level Very wet / Flood.

Gauge Looking upstream from Gannochy Bridge, the take-out for the lower section, the river has to be peaty brown and should appear to be in flood. The only true gauge is to drive to the top and check out the last rapid under Dalbrack Bridge, as this is the hardest obstacle. 1.0 on the SEPA gauge should be considered a minimum flow.

Access Driving north from Edzell on the B966, cross the river at Gannochy Bridge and turn left into Glen Esk. Access to this section is from the car park at the top of the glen close to Loch Lee. Egress is at Dalbrack Bridge, which is signposted off the main glen road. There is parking to be found just before the bridge.

Description Almost immediately the river starts to pick up in gradient and soon you are reading and running grade 3+ water. Watch out for a couple of tricky rapids that lurk for the unwary, (Gd 4+). The first major rapid is next to the road and can have a very tricky hole in the middle. The river now runs away round a corner and into a second rapid. The next two rapids are somewhat harder and are both carved from the bedrock, the rapid at Dalbrack having a particularly tricky slot to negotiate. The take-out is just around the corner from here on the left at a sandy beach.

Contributor:
Mark Sherriff

176 North Esk (Middle)

Grade **2(3+)**
Length **17km**
OS sheet **44**

Access The put-in is below Dalbrack Bridge on river left. Take out at the footbridge by the Scout Camp. There is a lay-by on the right side of the road; parking here is sensitive, so please take care.

Description The middle section consists of open grade 2 boulder fields, with little to keep up the enthusiasm. Half a dozen bedrock rapids exist, notably the one above Dalhastnie Bridge, which reaches grade 3/3+.

Contributor:
Mark Sherriff

176 North Esk (Lower)

Grade **3(4)**
Length **5km**
OS sheet **43**

Introduction The lower section ends at Gannochy Bridge near the village of Edzell. This section starts as a flat pebbly run, becoming steeper and gathering pace as it enters the Gannochy Gorge. The gorge is shallow at first, gradually cutting deeper into the bedrock to give deep pools intermixed with short technical rapids at regular intervals. Lower down the rock type changes, as does the character of the river, making it a varied and interesting paddle with a few surprises!

Water Level As most of this section is in a gorge, it can still be paddled in relatively dry conditions. However, the first kilometre down to the gorge becomes very shallow, deterring most people from paddling. Generally the river takes 3 or 4 days to drain from a high flow, but will remain navigable for some weeks after this. At very high flows the gorge becomes very boily and much more serious. The upper section may be a good option in these conditions.

Gauge The level can be easily inspected by looking upstream from the take-out at Gannochy Bridge. At low flows the river runs through a narrow channel about 2m wide at its narrowest point. Slabs of rock should be exposed to the right of this, leading up to the vegetated gorge wall. At these levels the top section may be too shallow and further inspection at the put-in is necessary. If the river is seen to be wider than 2m, and the rock slabs are covered to any extent, the whole section should be easily navigable. The two distinct large shelves of brickwork on the downstream side of the bridge are also a useful gauge. If the water level is above the bedrock, onto the first shelf, the river is navigable. If it rises to the next shelf, some six blocks higher, the river is running very high. At the put-in there are some concrete blocks in the channel beneath the footbridge. If these are not showing, then the river is reaching high flow and should be treated with caution. During spate conditions trees often become pinned across the river. 0.6 on the SEPA gauge should be considered a minimum flow.

Access From the A90, Dundee to Aberdeen road, turn off just north of Brechin signposted for Fettercairn / Edzel. The take-out is encountered first and is located at Gannochy Bridge, a little under 2 miles past Edzel. Cars can be parked in a lay-by on the left, just the other side of the bridge. On busy days, there is alternative parking on the Glen Esk road, found 100m past the bridge on the left. On no account should the grass in front of the house be used, as the landowner, a thoroughly reasonable chap, becomes somewhat unfriendly when his newly mown lawn acquires deep tyre tracks due to inconsiderate parking. To locate the put-in, take the Glen Esk / Invermark turn-off described above. 3 miles up this road parking can be found on the grass next to the 2nd entrance to Haughend Cottage. The first entrance is signed on the left-hand side. Care must be taken not to block the access track with vehicles. Further parking can be found on the verge, 100m down the road on the same side. Footpaths lead from both parking areas to the put-in by a metal footbridge.

Description For the first kilometre the river offers a good grade 1 paddle. A sharp right-angle bend and obvious rock walls signify the start of the gorge section. The gradient becomes slightly steeper with many enjoyable grade 3 rapids. A deep pool and horizon line signifies the first more difficult grade 3/4 rapid. Inspection, protection or portage is best made on the right-hand side. At lower levels this rapid is a sinuous channel, which, at higher flows becomes very boily with a nasty stopper forming on the bottom left-hand side. Below here, a good splat wall followed by a mini surf wave form at the right flows. A couple of straightforward rapids follow before the gorge walls become steeper, the channel narrows, and a horizon line is reached. Here the river drops through a narrow slot into a large cauldron. The powerful jet makes a good ender/cartwheel spot, although the pool is quite shallow in places. In very high water, the usual line becomes 'interesting' and a safer alternative opens up to the left of the rock shelf that forms the drop. The river now eases off and begins to open out until it once again plunges into a short narrow gorge (Gd 4). The entrance rapid, Double Drop, is a steep triplet of stoppers that tend to wash out in high flows. This is followed by a short gorge that constricts into a very narrow channel. Although this is a likely pinning spot at low flows, the entire rapid can be easily protected, inspected or portaged on the left-hand side. Easing off again the river returns to a pleasant grade 2/3 eventually widening, with the rock type changing to pebbly red sandstone. This marks the lead-in to the final rapid worthy of note, Fish Ladder Falls (Gd 4). A series of shallow stoppers well spaced over 200m, ends with an intimidating drop into a boily gorge, beneath the rotting skeleton of a high metal bridge. This is normally run just to the right of a fish ladder, keeping well away from undercuts on the far right-hand side. Inspection can be easily made on the left; however the final drop is very difficult to protect. A series of grade 2/3 rapids with the odd entertaining playspot leads to the take-out. Egress is possible on the left, some 20m before Gannochy Bridge. Steps are cut in the gorge wall, from where a footpath leads through a gate in the wall to the lay-by.

Contributors:
Robin Lofthouse
and Iain McKendry

Other important points On busy days please take note about the parking congestion at the take-out. Make the effort of leaving vehicles round the corner on the road up the glen and whatever you do don't park on the grass! Thanks.

West Water 177

Grade	**3/4(5)**
Length	**1km**
OS sheet	**44**

◯◯◯

Introduction The West Water flows through Glen Lethnot into open pasture to join the North Esk. A good grade 3/4 journey but seldom paddled, it is a spate run.

Water Level Wet/Very wet. As the river has a continuous gradient in upper Glen Lethnot, it runs off quickly and is only feasible after prolonged heavy rain or snow melt. The top section is best in huge flood. The lower section ending at The Loops requires less water and can be inspected from the picnic site.

Gauge Coming from the south, the South Esk bridge at Finavon is a useful area to gauge the water levels of the rivers of the Angus Glens. Under the bridge at Bridgend, there is a large flat rock. If this is covered there is probably sufficient water. When the water is just lapping over the rock the Water of Saughs is on (see below).

Access Most paddlers approach this river from the village of Edzell and the nearby North Esk. Driving north through Edzell, take the left turn at the end of the village towards Bridgend. Where the road first comes close to the river, a picnic site below the Purner's footbridge gives parking and a good take-out. To find the road up the glen, continue to Bridgend and after crossing the river, turn right up the minor road. Several put-ins make themselves easily available. The next bridge upstream of Bridgend is Stonyford Bridge. Access can be made anywhere above Stonyford Bridge (505 726) because the river passes close to the road.

Description The West Water has the appearance of a moorland river dropping through large boulders and ledges, but without the confinement of a gorge. This section gives continuous grade 3/4 paddling, when the river is high enough. Above Purner's Bridge lies The Loops, a left-twisting two-step grade 5 fall. These can be shallow on the left but to prevent poachers working from the narrow ledges, the falls have repeatedly been altered by the use of explosives. Nets and sniggers, thick poaching lines with large treble hooks have been found tangled in the gorge, so it's worth close inspection. The pools below The Loops are hot spots for anglers and care should be taken as the river is narrow at this point.

Contributor:
Stefan Janik

178 Water of Saughs

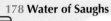

Grade **4/5+**
Length **4km**
OS sheet **44**

Access Continue on past the put-in for the West Water until the public road ends at a car park. Carry your boat up the road and then up the zigzag path at the head of the glen. Put in where the path is once again near the river.

Description This is a great run, which is well worth the effort. The hard white water is tucked away in the loop which flows away from the path, and may be worth inspecting before you commit to the carry. A series of slabby drops gives fun but serious white water. This is followed by easier water leading back to the car, or on down the West Water.

Contributor:
Stefan Janik

Other important points The West Water will need to be huge for this one. With less water the run should still go, and might be a little less serious.

179 South Esk

Grade **1/3**
Length **10km**
OS sheet **44**

Introduction The River South Esk flows from Glen Clova to Montrose Basin through a mixture of mountainous landscape, forested estates and open pasture. The greatest interest to kayakers lies along the geological fault, which separates red sandstone from Highland igneous rock. This fault provides the steepest paddling in the neighbouring rivers, the Blackwater and North Esk. The South Esk is bouldery with a mini-gorge above Cortachy Castle.

Water Level A quick way to assess the level without committing to a long drive up Glen Clova is from the A90 past Forfar at the Finavon Diner. Looking downstream from the bridge, a boulder weir/salmon pool has been constructed. If this is covered then the river is reasonable. If covered enough to form an easy play hole, then the river will be good. If the river is too low, surfing at Lunan Bay is an option or cave exploring on the Angus coast.

Access Driving up Glen Clova from Kirriemuir, the picnic site at Gella Bridge is reached after 8 miles. Despite the 'No canoeing sign' few problems have been reported at this put-in. In the past Cortachy Estate have been helpful but if contacted, the factor will only allow Sunday paddling during the salmon fishing season. It is therefore advisable to do the longer trip and not leave any vehicles at Cortachy, as there has been recent conflict with damage to fences and gates from the general public. Parking by the road is available a few hundred metres north of Cortachy as the Estate has recently put low barricades by the bridge to prevent the grass verges from being damaged. Longer touring trips can be made and the public park in Brechin makes a handy take-out. The owners below Finavon and Kinnaird Mill have been problematic in the past, but these beats are very short and can be paddled through very quickly.

Description The upper reaches contain two good grade 3 rapids. The first is a left-hand corner ledge situated 1½km from Gella Bridge. The outside of the corner has a narrow constriction, which is often choked by trees and rubbish and is best avoided. Sometimes called The Wall of Death it hardly merits the title. From there on grade 2 water leads into the gorge, which has some nice ledges and a final drop barred by two boulders/ledges giving left, right and middle shoots to choose from. In very high water the gorge can be grade 4. Below Cortachy bouncy grade 2s are found at regular intervals all the way to the sea. A number of steep weirs also provide sport, the most serious being below Brechin at Kinnairds Mill. It's quite long, with a steep salmon ladder that forms a set of powerful closed-ended stoppers. Recent improvements for salmon fishing have created pools and ledges providing playspots on the lower reaches.

Contributor:
Stefan Janik

Melgan 180

Introduction Tucked in the hills of Angus, the Melgan flows from Lintrathen Reservoir, joining the River Isla and flowing into the Tay near the famous beech hedge at Meiklelour. The Melgan starts as a rocky ditch that runs through farmland. Open to begin with, it drops into a shallow gorge that becomes deeper. The rapids are all hard and often committing. Their rough-hewn nature leads to the possibility of major damage to both kayak and paddler. Probably one of the more demanding/rewarding runs of the East.

Grade	5
Length	5km
OS sheet	53

Water Level Wet/Very wet. Lots water is needed to fill the reservoir, then more for the overflow.

Gauge With dam releases rare (it provides the main drinking water reservoir for the good people of Dundee and Perth) it is hard

to determine when the river will be running. The best time of year to check it out is October to April, as outside these times the water level in the loch shrinks rapidly due to demand. Allow several days of rain to fall before checking it out. Do not be alarmed by the lack of water coming down the dam outflow; this is not the Spean. As long as the right side of the top of the first drop looks runnable then there are high jinks to be had further down the river.

Access Head north out of Dundee on the A90. Turn off onto the A926 towards Kirriemuir. Go through Kirriemuir and take the B951 towards Glenshee. After about 8 miles there will be a left turn sign posted to Bridgend of Lintrathen. Follow the road to the village and park at the earth dam wall. Downstream is the top of the first drop. Go through the gate above the bridge and down to the channel below the dam wall. To find the take-out, follow the road on river right. Egress is from the second small bridge downstream approximately 2 miles along the minor road. Alternatively continue down the Isla to the bridge on the Alyth road.

Description The first drop is a two-stage fall, which gives you a flavour of the trip to come. If it looks too hard and you are going to walk it, put your boat back on the roof and move on. If the first drop looks too easy, be warned - it has kept a boat pinned for 36 hours. After this drop the river is flat for about 1km with the local 'friendly' farmer putting fences across it in a couple of places making carrying your boat around a nuisance but necessary. Two large 'gnarly falls' bring you to the main gorge section. This is made up of an 'interesting' series of drops, which have rearranged the front end of many a Topo and resulted in the loss of sanity of several paddlers (sadly not always temporarily). Trees can be quite a problem.

Contributor:
Alastair Collis

181 Isla

Grade	**2(6)**
Length	**6km**
OS sheet	**53**

Description The River Isla makes a dubious trip in a deep gorge from Reekie Linn, just below the B954 at Bridge of Craigisla, to the bridge on the Alyth road (see Melgan description). There are several awkward portages and few runnable rapids. In fact this trip is really just canyoning with a boat. Perhaps if you make the first descent of 'the Linn' you may be the kind of paddler who will find this stretch worthwhile. Having said that, this trip gets a surprising number of repeat descents, even if just for the novelty of leading others down to the ledge in the depths of the gorge with no apparent portage. Definitely stay away at high flows!

Contributor:
Bridget Thomas

Blackwater 182

Grade	**4**
Length	**5km**
OS sheet	**53**

Introduction The Blackwater drains the Cairngorms from Glenshee to the south. It runs parallel to the A93 (Blairgowrie to Braemar) until its confluence with the Ardle at Bridge of Cally. From here the river is known as the Ericht, flowing through Blairgowrie to meet the Isla and eventually the Tay. After the fun of Milton Falls, the Blackwater becomes a relatively quiet stretch of water flowing through lush Perthshire countryside. This all changes at Ashmore Gorge. Here you will find twisting rapids and drops, entertaining places to play and a few easily avoided undercuts. At the time of writing a tree in the river at Netherton is a significant hazard.

Water Level Moderately wet conditions are required for this section to run. With more water it becomes increasingly entertaining. At very high flows it is a serious run, which is a grade harder and demands a good deal more respect. As the Blackwater drains the Cairngorms, high flows are more frequent during spring snow melt.

Gauge Looking upstream over Netherton Bridge, two rocks are evident side by side in the middle of the stream. If they are showing well above the water, the river is too low to navigate. If they are nearly or completely covered, the river is running at a good level. If they are nowhere to be seen, then the Netherton rapid (upstream) should indicate what the high water conditions will involve. 0.8 on the SEPA gauge should be considered a minimum flow.

Access To reach the take-out, turn off the A93 Blairgowrie to Braemar road, about ¼ mile past Bridge of Cally. Follow the winding road to a bridge over the river. The SCA egress point is about 100m downstream of Netherton Bridge on river left (143 521). To reach the put-in, drive back to the A93 and continue up towards Braemar for 3 miles. The minor road to Blackhall Farm crosses the river at this point. Park in the lay-by next to the bridge and walk up the right bank. The put-in is immediately upstream of the Milton Falls, which can be seen from the bridge (138 569).

Description Putting in directly above Milton Falls doesn't leave much time to warm up. Many ice-cream heads have been experienced here, normally by those wiping the sleep from their eyes in the spring snow melt. The final drop is split, most paddlers opting for the right chute, as the left-hand chute has been known to pin boats. After the falls, the river eases off until Ashmore Gorge. This is marked by steeply rising walls and a right-hand bend guarded by a large truck sized boulder. Care should be taken here, as trees often block the river immediately upstream of the trickiest piece of the gorge. Inspection of the following rapid is advised on the left bank. If the start of the rapid has a drop exceeding 1m, then the river is at low-medium flow. A route down the right is best to avoid a sharply undercut rock on the left. If the rapid is a series of holes, with no obvious drop, then the river is high. Whatever route is taken, it is sure to be an entertaining ride. Rapids continue to be frequent and fun with the odd place to play. A short quiet section signifies the end of Ashmore Gorge. The Netherton rapid follows, which unless in spate, winds from right to left and back, with a good playhole for those with a quick roll. Beyond this, the river drops past a small rock face, and rounds a corner to the bridge, giving a nice rapid, Slide over Darling, (Gd 3). Continue on downstream for about 100m to reach the take-out on river left. A steep climb and short walk bring you back to a gate beside the bridge.

Other important points The egress point has been negotiated with the locals to avoid damage to trees and the river banks. If adhered to, relations with the residents should remain friendly. Care should be taken to avoid causing difficulties for lorries crossing the narrow bridge - try leaving your car further up the road, opposite the church. Please also be discreet about changing. When the river is low, the section between Milton Falls and Ashmore Gorge becomes very shallow, and the North Esk is probably a better bet.

Contributors:
Iain McKendry
Robin Lofthouse
and Paul Jackson

183 Ericht

Grade **2/3(5)**
Length **5km**
OS sheet **53**

Introduction The Ericht runs from its formation at the confluence of the Ardle and Blackwater at Bridge of Cally, alongside the A93 into Blairgowrie, and then on to join the Isla before passing Coupar Angus. The section of the Ericht above Blairgowrie is relatively open with a variety of rapids, and a few interesting playspots when the river is high. It offers a mellow alternative for those unwilling to tackle its close neighbour, the Blackwater. At 'normal' heights, it is a gem among grade 2/3 rivers affording constant and testing fun in an ever changing but always beautiful setting.

Water Level Moderately wet/Very wet. The Ericht can be paddled in moderately wet conditions, but really only shows its true potential in very wet conditions. Spring snow melt can also quickly aid the water levels, due to close proximity to Glenshee and beyond.

Gauge Look upstream over the bridge in Blairgowrie. If there are few or no rocks showing above the small weir, the river can be regarded as runnable. Seeing more rocks indicates that the run will be a 'bump and scrape'. 0.9 on the SEPA gauge should be considered a minimum flow.

Access The usual put-in point is opposite and immediately below Craighall House, which is reached by parking in a small lay-by around 100m north of the metal bridge on the A93 (Braemar) road, some 2 miles north of Blairgowrie. The approach to the river is interesting in itself. Cross the road and scramble down the steep wooded bank until a path is reached which, followed north, will take the now muddied paddler to an eddy under the cliffs supporting Craighall House. The first egress is immediately downstream of a weir (457 179), at the small bridge by Keithbank Mill, using the car parking offered by the Mill's visitor centre. Alternatively, the paddler can re-enter the river after Cargill's Leap, and paddle down to above the bridge in Blairgowrie, using the parking facilities on the right bank immediately upstream of the bridge.

Description From the put-in below Craighall House, the river offers some small surf spots, and is generally simple. The first kilometre through secluded, mixed woodland provides opportunity for an energetic workout between sharp eddy lines and enjoyable surf waves. Passing under the road bridge over the A93 after around 1½km, you enter the once thriving and now beautifully overgrown mill country, where more distinct rapids are to be found. A broken down weir offers little hazard if taken carefully, and the paddler soon passes the confluence of

the Lornty Burn on the right. From here paddle under a pipe and around either side of an island, ready to break out to portage the weir. The 2m high weir (457 179) should be portaged as, at most levels it has a significant towback. It can be portaged left, and the 'lade' (millstream) used to reach the path at Keithbank Mill, for easy egress there, or portaged right, and the river paddled for the remaining 200m to the footbridge above the next portage or egress point at Cargill's Leap (455 180). The Leap, even at levels when it appears simple, hides large undercuts and caverns. You may decide to run Cargill's through the narrow, back-looping, head-grinding chicken chute on river right but beware of the easy looking left-hand run. The aerated water conceals a shelf which, they say, can take your boat and half of your body. This is followed by a seemingly simple corner that, as indicated by the boily water downstream, hides a sump-like feature, which is best avoided. Re-entering the river after the Leap offers a few hundred metres of light paddling to the car park, river right, above the partially broken weir at the bridge in Blairgowrie.

Other important points   From Bridge of Cally, the river runs through the scenic, tempting, but dangerous Craighall Gorge, (scene of TV rescue shows). This deep canyon has at its crux a nasty tree choked and undercut passage. At the best of times this will be difficult and dangerous to portage and we suspect it will often be impossible to get round. Other than this nastiness there is no white water of note in this gorge and it is definitely not recommended!

Contributors:
Dave Lee
Iain McKendry

On Sunday 27th February 2000, Donald Bryce drowned in the turbulent waters downstream of Cargill's Leap while helping with a high water kayak inspection for this guide. He had just turned 21. Donald was a very popular mountain and river enthusiast, and a great role model, who lived life to the full. It is speculated that a popped spraydeck caused his tragic swim as he was a fluent roller.

These pages are written in his memory and dedicated to his loving and supportive family. He will be forever missed by his many companions.

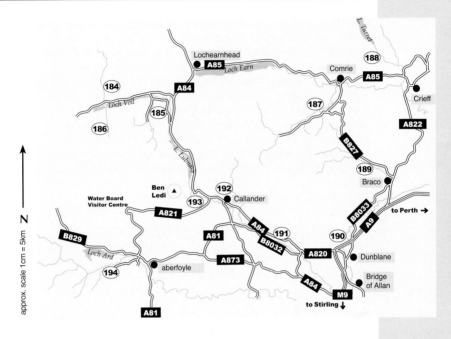

Central

Central

Under this heading we have include those rivers from Stirling to the Trossachs. The Leny is the best known of these runs and has the added advantage that it holds its water well and can be worth visiting even several days after the last rains. In wet conditions why not explore some of the smaller creeks such as the Calair Burn or the Knaik? Alternatively, the Teith and Allan Water offer slightly easier runs when there is a bit of water around. If the rivers are high, then both the Turret and the Duchray Water offer fine adventures easily accessed from the Central Belt.

184 Monachyle Burn

Grade   **4/5**
Length **3½km**
OS sheet   **57**

Introduction The Monachyle is on the north side of Loch Voil near Balquhidder. It is 20 minutes drive north west of the River Leny, in between Callander and Killin. Next time you're visiting Rob Roy's grave near Balquhidder, the rivers are all huge, it's still raining, and you happen to have your Topo on the roof, go and give the Monachyle Burn a shot. Small eddies, constant boulders, a couple of trees, and 2 portages, this run never gets really steep but it keeps on going.

Water Level Wet / Very wet. In fact as much as possible. Just make sure you can get back along the road if the loch's rising.

Gauge From where the road crosses the burn, look below and above the falls (second portage). If there ain't much water - don't do it. If the river is really surging along - get on quick before it goes down again.

Access From Callander, drive north on the A84 past the River Leny, Loch Lubnaig, and the River Balvag (you'll get a good feel for how much water there is as you drive). Turn off right to Balquhidder (the road loops back under the main road) and carry on along the north side of the loch for about 5 miles. If you get to the Monachyle Hotel, you've just driven over the Monachyle Burn. Go back and decide if there is enough water, before driving another ½ mile to find a forest track on the right. From here walk up the track till it stops 3km further up and get in.

Description Put in where the track ends and seal launch down the track. Watch out for the weir after 5 minutes - eddy right. The top section is small, tight, rocky and fun until another burn comes in from the right. The river picks up here, crashing through some nice boulders before a scenic breather section where the river flows under the track. You could get in here if you've walked far enough on the way up - or equally get out here if you're scared on the way down! From here the burn rounds a corner into the forest and steepens up. Probably the best set of rapids is coming up. Keep a look out for trees, a couple of slightly harder sections and the first portage - keep eddy-hopping. The portage has a bumpy line on the left, a sieved pothole on the right and a nice easy walk round the bank on the left. Get in again and paddle through a few nice features to the top of the 2nd portage where you can get out and have a pint in the hotel.

Other important information This trip twins well with a visit to the Calair Burn. Alternatively, take a polo ball and play on the rugby pitch below the take-out. Something to do on a rare occasion when there is too much water!

Contributor:
Kenny Biggin

Calair Burn 185

Introduction The Calair Burn is a small river running north towards Balquhidder, on the edge of the Trossachs. A short stretch with some great grade 4 boating, this is a good run to squeeze in at the end of the day.

Grade	**4**
Length	**1km**
OS sheet	**57**

○ ○ ○

Water Level Wet/Very wet. Definitely a spate run.

Gauge You should be able to get a good feel for the level from the rapid at the take-out bridge. If it is only 'passable' the run will be a bit bumpy. If this rapid looks fast and fun, the run will be quite hectic!

Access Find Balquhidder by turning off the A84 via the underpass at the Kingshouse Hotel. Turn left in Balquhidder and left again at the 4-way junction in 700m. The bridge over the river at this point makes a suitable take-out. To reach the put-in, return to the 4-way junction, turn left and follow the road up the glen. You will find a suitable spot to get on after a mile or so, just beyond the edge of the forest.

Contributors:
Andy Jackson
and Roland Bone

Description Flat initially, the lower river soon enters its steep final kilometre, which contains the best of the action. Generally the rapids are grade 4, though it could be harder at a really big flow. A nice 3m ledge is followed by a fast and twisting slide. The run-in to the ledge is quite full-on, with only a few small eddies. If you find yourself unexpectedly on the lip just boof in the middle! This little section is really full-on in high water, definitely 4+ with two crucial moves in order to avoid a spanking. Unfortunately the end comes all too soon and the fun is over till another day.

185 Calair (Upper)

Grade	**4(5)**
Length	**1km**
OS sheet	**57**

Gauge If the river is churning brown and really stonking, this trip will be on.

Access Drive up the road as far as is possible beyond the normal put-in for the Calair and park in the hillwalkers' lay-by. This is the take-out. Walk upstream as far as you wish.

Contributor:
Roland Bone

Description The boating in this top section is very continuous grade 3/4 with few eddies. One particularly meaty fall appears near a deer fence, and may merit some protection. Below this, the river carries on much the same with one or two holes that have a punchy feel.

186 Inverlochlarig Burn

Grade	**3-5**
Length	**500m**
OS sheet	**57**

Description The Inverlochlarig Burn, west of the Calair Burn, is worth a paddle if the Calair is up. A short, steep section with some tricky spots, we only paddled about 500m. Above this was some continuous grade 4+/5. It was a 500m walk from the end of the section back to the car park.

Contributor: Ian Thom

187 Water of Ruchill

Grade	**3+(5)**
Length	**12km**
OS sheet	**57**

Introduction This Perthshire river runs from the top of Glen Artney into the town of Comrie. The Ruchill is a bouldery river with a continuous drop. Apart from the difficult rapids in the middle which definitely require inspection and perhaps portaging, it's a get on and go river. At the level where all the boulders are covered, expect one or two meaty stoppers on the way down. The river is brilliant in full spate, but is best avoided at this level unless you know the river, or are a very experienced group.

Water Level Wet/Very wet. This run is only suitable after prolonged heavy rain. The catchment is Glen Artney. There are many feeder burns but it is a small glen, so the river rises and falls very quickly.

Gauge You can get an indication of water levels from the Earn at Comrie. As you drive up the glen all the side streams should be flowing well for this trip to be on. It is only worth paddling if all the rocks at the access point are covered.

Access Glen Artney is definitely a 'sporting' glen, i.e. fishing and shooting. At the levels we require for paddling there is unlikely to be any conflict with fishermen. There is a single-track road that runs beside the river to the top of the glen. 1 mile from the end of the road at Glen Artney Lodge there is a picnic spot/car park. Please only use this public access point. The take-out is on the left bank below the main road bridge in Comrie, after the confluence with the River Earn. Car parking is easily found close to the river, but please be considerate.

Description From the start, you are into continuous bouldery rapids. After around 2½km, these lead to a major rapid at Eas nan Luib, (marked as Sput a Chleibh on the OS map, 734 178). This long rapid can be broken into three sections with little respite in between. It is best to consider it as a single rapid, since once started, you are committed to the rest. Although considered grade 4 at low flows, this rapid is a challenging grade 5 when the rest of the run is in condition. A long ramp leads to a twisting, boily rapid and finally a steep, difficult drop with a tight exit that cannot be protected. Halfway between Eas nan Luib and Comrie there is another rapid near Cultybraggan Camp, which is grade 4 in higher water. You may wish to inspect. From here, easier water leads down to the confluence with the Earn just above Comrie.

Contributors: Dave Walsh and Drew Milroy

Other important points If the Knaik is running, this river probably will be too.

188 Turret

Grade **4(5)**
Length **4km**
OS sheet **52**

Introduction The Turret joins the River Earn at Crieff, giving a fun but somewhat rocky trip. An open upper section with some bedrock falls is followed by a lower gorge.

Water Level Very wet. This trip would have run more often before the water was stolen by the creation of Loch Turret reservoir. It needs a prolonged period of wet weather to bring the level up enough to overflow the dam. The run is more likely to be going towards the end of the winter than after the drier summer period.

Gauge Driving up the glen, it is possible to peer into the gorge from the water works building at the side of the road. You will however get a truer picture of the flow as you drive to the reservoir. It should be obvious whether there is sufficient water for the run.

Access Driving west from Crieff on the A85, you cross the river as you leave town. Turn right after the bridge. Cross the next bridge over the river by the distillery and take the first left. The best take-out is just before the road crosses the Barvick Burn where the road climbs away from the river. Put in at the top of the glen, after the nasty weir below the dam spillway.

Description The upper stretch is mainly an open boulder run with a couple of classy falls. Highlights include a 4m fall (which we suspect is shallow) and another sizeable fall around large boulders, both grade 5. As the river continues to the bridge halfway through the run it gets rather blocked and there are several trees growing in unhelpful places. Below this bridge lies the Falls of Turret. This is a two-stage drop, the first half of which is very marginal and almost certainly a portage. You could probably walk the first drop and have the option of putting in for the lower one via a small path on river left. Below here the river continues in a narrow gorge. This has been paddled at lower flows aided by the water exiting from the pipe at the water works. It is described as grade 3, and although it is probably better at higher flows, you would then need to be very careful about trees.

Other important points If the river is high, it would probably be wise to scout the lower gorge before putting on to assess how feasible it is. This would give the option of taking out at the bridge above the falls if you don't like what you see.

Contributors:
Andy Jackson
and Dave Kwant

Knaik 189

Introduction The Knaik is a small Perthshire run near Braco. This is a nice and easy spate run with some drops and a large ramp/slide. Fast and fun, it can feel rather tight at times.

Grade **2/3(4)**
Length **4½km**
OS sheet **57**

Water Level Very wet.

Gauge At the bridge over the Knaik the river should look brown and churning - this is the ideal height. The river is very 'flashy', it can be up and down in a matter of hours. The ideal time to paddle it is immediately after a heavy thunderstorm.

Access To reach the take-out, drive up the A9 and take the turn off for Braco (A822). Drive through Braco and park at the bridge on the left. Please change and sort the shuttle out here. To get to the put-in, drive out of Braco and take the first left turning up the glen, (the B827 towards Comrie). You can see the river as you drive up. Depending on the amount of water you can start as high up the glen as is possible.

Description The river starts narrow and straightforward, with shallow grade 2 water. There are a few blind corners and over-hanging trees keep the paddler alert. Soon a breakout is required on the right to portage a fence that spans the width of the river. The eddies are small, so keep well spaced. Below this the river carries on at the same pace. Turning a few corners a horizon line appears, marking the start of 4 drops. At high flows, these have large stoppers on the first two. The fourth is perhaps the best - comprising a 5-6m slide into a hole (Gd 4). The acceleration on this is tremendous, and the hole pushes through nicely! Below this the river is good continuous fun, with some great surf waves on the way to the road bridge at Braco. Take out on the left bank shortly after the bridge and walk over to the car park.

Other important points Keep your eyes peeled for debris/fallen trees etc. Take out in plenty of time to portage the fence over the river.

Contributor:
Roland Bone

190 Allan Water

Grade	**3/4**
Length	**7km**
OS sheet	**57**

Introduction A Stirlingshire river fed from the Ochils and Coire Odhar, the Allan is easily accessible from the A9. It is a highly enjoyable and continuous spate run. Long rapids, formed by bedrock and boulder combinations provide good surf waves, eddy lines and pour-overs. For first timers the river should be flavoured high, when it gives an excellent and continuous run with seemingly endless brown waves and playspots! For those who know the river, and therefore won't be reading this guide, there are playspots in lower water, but the rest of the river is a scrape.

Water Levels Very wet. The Allan has a small catchment, and relies on run-off from the small burns feeding it. It peaks after 12 or more hours of heavy rain. Once it stops raining, the river drains very quickly.

Gauge The park in Bridge of Allan is the usual place to check the flow. The water should ideally be well over the weir and chocolate brown, with an intimidating stopper forming under the bridge. If the river is spilling into the park, expect an outstanding and eventful trip. 0.9 on the SEPA gauge should be considered a minimum level.

Access Park by the bridge, and take out either on the right above the weir in Bridge of Allan or on the left below it. Parking at the put-in is limited so it is best to sort out your shuttle to take as few cars as possible to the top. Drive up the A9 until the turn off for Kinbuck, turn right and then left down the road signposted to Ashfield. As you approach the village you drive over a railway bridge. Access to the river on foot is from the track on the right.

Description At high flows this river is impressive right from the start. The rapids blur into one continuous stretch of waves, providing constant entertainment. It is however, easy to get complacent and end up in one of the Allan's many innocuous looking holes. If you have never paddled the river before, particularly in spate, it would be prudent to inspect at the major rapids. The first of these, Ashfield Weir and Mill Falls (Gd 4), are found just after the put-in. Inspection is easiest from river right. After some good paddling, an obvious stone railway bridge on the right warns of the next major rapid, Cathedral Weir in Dunblane. This weir has a nasty towback and is generally inspected or portaged on river right. It can be shot close to the right bank. The shoot at the side is very boily and boats have been known to pin across the exit. Below Dunblane, a scenic grade 3 stretch leads to the Wall of Death, a grade 4 fall, which is difficult to inspect, but has several possible lines. The final weir under the bridge at Bridge of Allan is renowned for its holding power and is not a place for the faint-hearted. Inspect or finish on the right above the weir.

Other important points This is a spate run, so keep your eyes open for tree blockages and other debris; expect to be surfing waves with large tree stumps! Although technically easy, in high flows the continuous nature, overhanging branches and lack of eddies make this river a serious undertaking for those who aren't confident or can't reliably roll on big water.

Contributors:
Roland Bone
Dave Walsh and
Drew Milroy

Teith 191

Grade	2
Length	12km
OS sheet	57

Introduction Fed from Loch Lubnaig by the River Leny and Loch Venachar (which is dam controlled), the Teith flows through Callander and on to Stirling. In flood, the Teith makes a good trip even for more experienced paddlers, but it is not then recommended for novices due to overhanging trees and the lack of eddies.

Water Level The river can be paddled at most water levels, but is best avoided when low. The water board only releases water when Loch Venachar is too high. They try to avoid peak spates on the Leny to prevent flooding in Callander. This sometimes leads to a situation where the water is still high in the Teith when it is dropping on the Leny.

Gauge The water level is best viewed from the Meadows car park in Callander. If the car park is flooded, then the river is in full spate. It will be a big bouncy grade 2, with small holes and surf waves on which to play. It is worth considering paddling down to Deanston at this level.

Access Driving north along the A84 from Stirling, just before you cross the Teith Bridge at Doune, there is a minor road on the left which leads to the egress at Deanston. Further up the A84, the

usual egress below the Torrie Rapid is from a lay-by on the right at Drumvaich. Put in from the Meadows car park, adjacent to the river at the north end of Callander.

Description The main rapid at Torrie is usually shot down a chute on the left. In high water there are big holes on the right and big waves below Torrie. The usual egress is 800m below Torrie on the left bank. It is difficult to see but there is a gauge post and an indistinct path at a small eddy. It is possible to continue down to Deanston. There is a large weir above Deanston, which should be inspected due to the metal rails in the salmon run. These have damaged kayaks in the past. There is an extremely large and intimidating hole at the bottom of the weir in high water. Shoot the weir just left of a salmon run to take the tail through the bottom hole. Get the line wrong and you're mincemeat! Take out immediately below the treatment plant at Deanston on the river right, or continue to the bridge to savour the playwaves opposite Deanston distillery.

Other important points The river is heavily fished during the season and should be avoided in low water. It is better to paddle on a Sunday, when the river is full, or out of season to avoid those folk waving about long stick like things in the middle of the river. The trip can be further extended from Deanston down to Stirling at grade 1.

Contributors:
Dave Walsh
and Drew Milroy

192 Keltie

Grade	**4(5)**
Length	**5km**
OS sheet	**57**

Introduction The Keltie flows into the Teith above Callander. A dream river that I've talked about and looked at a lot more than I've actually done. The whole river is an excellent run, broken up by Bracklin Falls, which are unlike any others. There aren't many places in Scotland that have slab formations quite like this. The main rapids on the river are bedrock interspersed with boulder gardens and a couple of shingle beaches thrown in for good measure.

Water Level Wet / Very wet. One of those rivers that, for the stretches in between the falls, the more water the better. However, some of the falls get kinda scary when it's really wet so a compromise needs to be reached. It certainly needs saturated ground and a fair quantity of rain the night before to bring it into condition.

Gauge From the bridge at the take-out, you can get a pretty good idea of the level. If it's really rocky, it's too low; not rocky at all, it may be too high! For a much better idea, look at the top falls. Try and get a balance between: a) the hole at the bottom of the first 3-tier fall being a muncher; and, b) the slab lead-in to Kerplunk having enough water to paddle rather than scrape. Be wary of getting on if you're not sure, since it rises quickly, and you may change your mind when you get to Bracklin. The section between Kerplunk and Bracklin is an absolute nightmare if it's too low - trust me!

Access On the Stirling road the take-out is about a mile from Callander where the river runs under the road opposite a campsite. Bracklin Falls are signed (small sign) up a road on the right just as you enter Callander from the south - opposite the 'Roman Camp'. Make sure you keep on this road instead of going into the Golf Club. The road goes steeply up and you come to a car park on the right. There is a sign here telling you about the Falls. The 15-minute walk in or out from here is a good alternative put-in or take-out point, and also a good place for shuttle-bunnies and tourists to walk in to take photos. To reach the upper put-in, instead of stopping at the car park, keep going up the road (through the gate) for another couple of miles. There is a slip road off to the right with a locked gate. Park here and walk down to see the upper falls and put-in. If you don't want to do these, you probably won't want to do Bracklin.

Description Put in above the bridge and negotiate the first 3-tier drop as best you can. Don't get stuck in the hole, then continue on through the gorge leading up to Kerplunk - watch out for the flat rock at the bottom. A couple of kilometres of fairly constant though easyish rapids follows (don't do this section unless the river is pumping) before Bracklin Falls are reached. Make sure you eddy out before them, since the top two falls are of 'iffy' run-nability. Get in immediately below the 2nd drop, down through the grippy hole and over the 3m ledge. Eddy-out above the bridge to regroup, before bashing down under the bridge through The Gates of Shangri-La. Eddy-out left behind the huge boulder (you'll have to trust me here), and then get as good a boof as you can off Haggis Trap - the next (7m+) vertical slab. If you're well and truly trashed by this point, then hard luck 'cos there's one more to go, Trouble or Quits - a 3m drop onto rock, or a slippy seal-launch off the rock on the left. Then walk back up and do it

Contributor:
Kenny Biggin

again! After Bracklin there is little to speak of although it's nice to float down reminiscing about the falls. There are several grade 3+ rapids and a couple of small holes/waves to play in depending on the level. If the river is low, it might be worth walking out from the falls rather than scraping down the rest.

193 Leny

Grade **3/4(5)**
Length **3km**
OS sheet **57**

Introduction The river is fed from Loch Lubnaig and runs into the Teith at Callander. The Leny is one of those rivers that you will never get bored of. In high water it is a continuous run, with the Falls becoming a challenge demanding respect from the most experienced paddlers. Although very short, it can be paddled in as little as 20 minutes, most will want to play and enjoy the run.

Water Level Medium/Wet. Although the river comes up slowly and needs a prolonged period of rain to get to a recommended height, it does hold its level well once the loch is high, and may still be good a few days after rain. Because the river is fed from the loch, even when it is really high the water is often clear.

Gauge The river needs to look high to be good. Check the level at the Falls of Leny, these are safest at a medium level, i.e. most of the rocks will be covered. The gauge on the upstream side of the road bridge at the Lade Inn take-out is best viewed on river right.

6″ and the top section is low, the Falls not really possible, but bottom section has play potential.

1′ the Falls can be paddled both sides but are scrapey and hold pinning potential.

4′+ now serious - the Falls and gorge below are grade 5. The breakout above the Falls (last gasp eddy) will be very tight.

0.7 on the SEPA gauge should be considered a minimum flow.

Access From Callander drive north on the A84. Park in the lay-by next to the river (587 095), just past the turn-off for the Ben Ledi car park. Alternatively cross the river and park in the Ben Ledi car park. To find the take-out, drive back towards Callander and turn off towards the Lade Inn. Drive over the river to the public car park. Please do not park at the Lade Inn car park unless you intend to have a drink there afterwards. If you want to inspect the Falls, there is a car park on the right travelling north, signposted to the Falls of Leny. Access on foot gives a view of the Falls and the rapids below. The police are concerned about people parking their cars on the grass verges. Please use the designated car parks/lay-by.

Description The first section starts off with easy rapids, but soon gains momentum. There are some good playspots including one good playhole at higher flows and an excellent bouncy grade 3 rapid above the Falls. It's only a short distance from the start to the Falls, with very small eddies in high water. Look for the eddy on the right at the remains of the second old railway bridge. There are 2 eddies immediately above the Falls. Choose either the right or left, depending on which side you want to paddle/portage. If all else fails, Last Gasp Eddy is immediately above the Falls on the left. Miss it and you paddle the Falls backwards! The portage on the right bank is the easiest; the Falls themselves are more usually tackled on the left. The exit and gorge below should be inspected in very high water as a huge hole forms. Below the Falls the river continues to be interesting with 2 notable grade 3/4 rapids: Wee Stinker which comes after a right-hand bend, is followed by a bouncy stretch leading to the S-Bends. These offset stoppers get nasty at high flows.
Below here some good eddy lines and a nice playhole break up the journey to the take-out.

Other important points Although the river is regularly paddled, the Falls should be treated with respect. The whole river has been paddled in an open canoe, but for the less experienced it would be more appropriate to put in at the Lade Inn and extend your trip down the Teith. Although the bottom section of the Leny is easy, a trip through the 'everglades' is not recommended for novices due to overhanging trees.

Contributors:
Dave Walsh
and Drew Milroy

194 Duchray Water

Grade **3/4(5)**
Length **9km**
OS sheet **57**

Contributor:
Dave Walsh

Introduction The Duchray Water runs through Loch Ard Forest to Aberfoyle in the Trossachs. Draining the slopes of Ben Lomond via many small burns, the river rises and falls very quickly. It is a continuous run lined by trees and with few eddies when in spate. With a number of potentially dangerous rapids, not obvious once on the river, it is important to pre-scout the 2 major drops. The rest of the river is not technically difficult, but every corner seems to hide an impossible fall, which never materializes. There is a very high fall near the end, bringing relief from the apprehension.

Water Level Wet/Very wet. A spate river only, this one needs to be at the top of its banks, or better still starting to flood in Aberfoyle.

Gauge At the put-in, all the boulders should be covered to ensure a good flow. You can get a feel from all the surrounding burns, which need to be high.

Access The put-in at Loch Dubh is accessed via a forestry road, from the end of the public road at Loch Dhu. If you want to take a car to the put-in, you will need permission from Forest Enterprise at Aberfoyle. They can generally help, but please phone them on 01877 382 258, as access may depend on tree felling activity. An OS map is also worth having. The take-out is at the car park next to the river in Aberfoyle.

Description Small rapids soon lead to a grade 4 section and fall. Do not mistake this for the grade 5 Linn that lies below. The approach to the Linn of Blairvaich (453 997), a 10m waterfall, is marked by a forest road bridge. The section immediately below the bridge can be tricky with few eddies before the waterfall, which hides round a corner. You may want to portage the whole section. This can be done with difficulty on the left. The fall which has a large pool at its base has been run, but it feels a long way down! The river now gives a lovely bouncy continuous run for over 5km before the next major drop, which is a grade 5. This can be inspected by taking the forest track at Milton to the campsites and is just beyond a house (490 002).

Other important points If you are in the area when everything is flooding this one is worth a look.

The South

The South

Urban Delights

Burns Country

Borders

Take care when parking and changing!

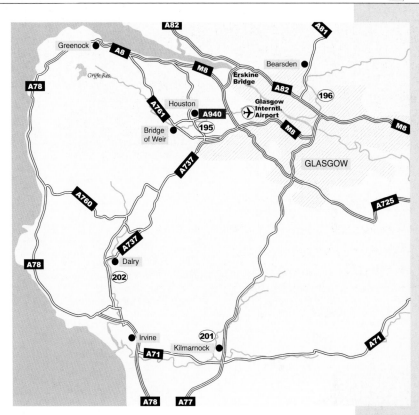

Urban Delights

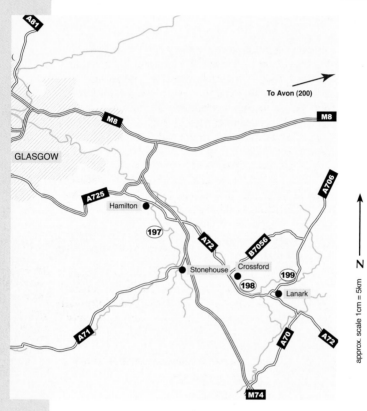

Urban Delights Continued

Urban Delights

Although not renowned for amazing scenery and pristine rivers, the Central Belt should not be written off as a white water venue. Much favoured by city dwellers catching an evening paddle, and offering an option for students and others who always have limited petrol in the car, these rivers feature some nice paddling. Often you will have to compete with shopping trollies and abandoned washing machines for space in the eddy and the colour of the water may prove a tad worrying, but for the dedicated enthusiast armed with their nose clips, a lot of fun can be had! In wet conditions, the Clyde and Kelvin offer some 'interesting' playboating and on both the Gryfe and Mousewater there is a drop or two that will give you something to think about.

Gryfe 195

Introduction The River Gryfe lies just west of Glasgow close to the airport. The only white water of note lies between the villages of Bridge of Weir and Houston. The Gryfe offers a straightforward trip with the exception of a couple of weirs and one surprisingly powerful drop.

Grade	**3(4+)**
Length	**4km**
OS sheet	**63**

Water Level Wet / Very wet. A good amount of rain is required but the river holds its water reasonably well.

Gauge It is easy to check the level where the river flows under the A761 in Bridge of Weir. The river should appear bank full and flowing well. If it is a bit bony you could consider doing just the first kilometre including the main fall. 0.4 on the SEPA gauge should be considered a minimum flow.

Access From the bridge in Bridge of Weir, drive south and take the first right leading under the railway and upstream. After half a mile carry down through the fields to get on where the river is flat. To find the take-out, return to Bridge of Weir. Recross the river and take the first right towards Houston. At the roundabout, take the first exit and then after half a mile, turn right into the Craigend Housing Scheme. You come to the river on your right, where it flattens under a metal bridge.

Description Take care at the first weir as it can have a nasty hole. Good playful water continues through Bridge of Weir until a horizon line signals the main event. This is normally taken by a double step on the right, jumping the powerful pour-over. Fast shallow grade 3 water lasts for less than a kilometre before the river eases to flat. At Houston the gradient picks up again starting with another terminal looking weir. Portage or inspect from the left. The final few hundred metres are hidden in a leafy tunnel where lack of headroom is the main obstacle.

Contributor:
Andy Jackson

196 Kelvin

Grade	3/4
Length	5km
OS sheet	64

Introduction The Kelvin runs through the West End of Glasgow. Despite its urban setting, this can be a surprisingly good trip, parts of which become quite serious at high flows. The main features are old weirs - the two unbroken ones at Kelvindale and the Botanic Gardens should be approached with care. For those with a good immune system (water quality can be particularly poor), the Kelvin offers some great playing at the right levels.

Water Level Wet.

Gauge 1 on the gauge below Great Western Road is a good level. To judge the play level, look upstream from Gibson Street. There is a 2 foot, round opening in the wall on river left. Half the pipe is about optimum.

Access Maryhill Road (the A81) crosses the Kelvin just before Bearsden. Turning right at the traffic lights, the river can be accessed by the entrance to the golf course. Alternatively, it is possible to put in below the nasty weir, just above Kelvindale Road. The river is accessed through the housing scheme on Grantully Drive. If you just want to play, put in just above Kelvin Bridge on Great Western Road and take out behind Kelvingrove Art Gallery. It is possible to continue down to the Clyde. This involves a long walk back to your car on the left bank at the river mouth, past a lorry park by a roundabout on the Clydeside Expressway.

Description The top section is grade 2, and offers a good novice section, but be sure to get novices out well before the big V-shaped Kelvindale Weir as this can get very nasty at high flows. From

Kelvindale Weir down to the River Clyde is grade 3/4. The ledge weir just after Queen Margaret Drive also demands care in higher flows, as it can be grippy and difficult to paddle through. There is a fun wave under Great Western Road, a good taily/whirly spot outside The Big Blue (pub), and a great playspot at medium flows at the broken weir, just outside Kelvingrove Art Gallery. Those who avoid flat water at all costs can access the river right here, however note that this is not a nice place to swim due to the city water and concrete weir just round the corner. The main interest on the lower stretch down to the Clyde is Kelvin Falls, just beside the transport museum. If the river is high, these Falls can be quite serious and worth a look if only to make sure there is enough headroom to get under the bridge.

Contributors:
Robin Cole and
Kenny Biggin

Avon (Glasgow) 197

Introduction The Avon is about 40 minutes drive to the south of Glasgow near Larkhall. The lower section passes through the spectacular Chatelherault Park and joins the River Clyde at Strathclyde Park. The river flows through steep wooded gorges, made up of sedimentary rocks. This means that there are few obvious narrows and the river is semi-continuous, particularly in the lower section.

Grade **3(4)**
Length **11km**
OS sheet **64**

Water Level Wet. There needs to have been a wet spell and preferably rain the night before paddling this one. The upper stretch is narrower and may still be OK when the lower section is 'scrapey'.

Gauge The best gauge is at Larkhall. If there is enough water running down the river left of the big weir to avoid scraping your boat too much, the upper section will be quite good. 0.8 on the SEPA gauge should be considered a minimum flow for the upper section, whilst 0.6 is the minimum for the lower. If the short half-width concrete weir just below the put-in is covered, the lower section is worth doing. If the island is covered, the river is in spate.

Access To find the upper put-in, take Junction 7 off the M74 and turn onto the A71 signed to Larkhall. Go straight on at the roundabout and then turn off the A71 into Stonehouse. Turn right (north) onto Argyll Street in the centre of the village (opposite 'The Cross' bus stop). Pass a church on the right, and drive down

the hill, under the bypass to the bridge over the Avon. To find the take-out, and the start of the lower section, take the Larkhall turn off the M74. Go straight through the village and down a steep hill to Millheugh. Park by the mini-roundabout, below a large weir. Egress either at Strathclyde Park, or drive through Hamilton on the B7078 and turn right just before the bridge over the Avon.

Description After putting on at Stonehouse, the river gradually builds up to give two fun grade 4 rapids: the aptly named Boulderfield is followed by a 3m chute, The Big Lynn. The 5m high weir at Millheugh (Larkhall) at the end of the grade 4 section is best taken down the vertical right-hand side. This gives a safe but unusual and exciting finish to the upper section. From Larkhall, the lower section builds up to give continuous grade 3 paddling. At the entrance to the gorge, the river takes a right-hand bend. 200m below this, there is a straightforward rapid with a tricky full width stopper hidden at the bottom. The best rapids are those near the end, directly below the high road bridge at Chatelherault. The final weir at Hamilton can be shot hard right.

Other important points If levels are very high, the Cander Water may make a more exciting start to this section - have a look at it from the long, high bridge just before you turn off the A71 into Stonehouse and decide for yourself. Information is very scanty on this run, has anyone paddled it yet? The Cander joins the Avon above the main rapids on its upper section, leaving about 2km before you reach Millheugh weir in Larkhall.

Contributor:
Robin Cole and
Kenny Biggin

198 Clyde

Grade	2/3
Length	5km
OS sheet	71

Introduction Ah, the bonnie Clyde - the heart of the city and in its day one of the greatest shipbuilding rivers in the world. The best of the paddling on the Clyde lies upstream of Glasgow, close to Lanark. The main section below Stoneybyres is grade 2/3, and makes a good intermediate trip.

Water Level Medium/Very wet. This large river is generally paddleable, except after prolonged dry spells of a week or more.

Gauge 0.5 on the SEPA gauge should be considered a minimum flow.

Access Although the Clyde may be paddled from New Lanark to Strathclyde Park, the most paddled section is from Stoneybyres to Crossford. The put-in is ¼ mile below Stoneybyres Power Station on the south bank. A footpath goes down to the river from the A72 about 150m south of the junction with the A744 Kirkmuirhill Road. Park on the opposite side of the road in the lay-by/slip road. Egress is below Crossford Bridge, on the A72. Heading north, pass the Crossford Inn on your right, and take the first right. This road turns sharp left. Go down the drive on your right to the river. If in doubt, get out above Crossford Bridge on river right.

Description The main features are the obvious rapids at Hazelbank and the excellent waves/stoppers below Crossford Bridge.

Other important points For the inquisitive test piece seeker, or the timid sightseer, the Falls of Clyde are well worth a look. This is one of the most impressive big volume gorges in Scotland, which would be one of the classic test pieces of Scottish paddling if only it was just slightly more do-able! The gorge itself has its water diverted through Stoneybyres Power Station, but there is usually more than enough water anyway. In addition, there are several official release days each year – one being on Easter Sunday. To find the usual viewpoint, drive to Lanark and then continue on through New Lanark until you reach the Clyde. For a closer look at the best line, try the nature trails on river left. The falls themselves consist of Bonnighton Linn and Corra Linn with Stoneybyres Falls some 4km downstream. Bonnighton Linn looks possible down a 3-tier 'chicken-chute' on the far left. The ½km section below this may have been run and looks to be around grade 4, getting harder if the river is releasing. The gorge ends with Corra Linn, which is split into two big falls. The first might just about work via a fast and scary blast route extreme right. However, the second fall has rocks and ledges throughout and is also enormous! But don't let me put you off – so long as I get to see the photos when it gets done.

Contributor:
Robin Cole and
Kenny Biggin

198 Clyde (Garrion Weir)

Playspot

OS sheet **33**

Gauge The river should be considered high when water is going over the lip of the weir.

Access Coming from Glasgow, turn off the M74 to Lanark. If you get to the big roundabout that's formed by two bridges over the Clyde you've gone too far, but you can see the weir just upstream. So, head back the way you've come and turn right downhill (to a nursery / garden centre). Follow that road all the way back to a dead end next to the roundabout. Carry your boat across the roundabout and then 20m or so up the road to Lanark. There's a track down to the river (please don't park here). The best way to get up to the weir is to cross the river and walk up the bank on the east side. This takes you right up to the playspot.

Description This is an OK playspot close to Glasgow with easy access. The river flow is directed down the right, forming quite a good stopper. The pool is deep, but shallows quickly so it's quite a safe place to swim. At low and medium flows, cartwheels, pop-outs, and back loops are all possible. The stopper is not too difficult to get out of and you always seems to wash out when upside down. At higher flows a big hole forms WHICH IS AS YET UNTRIED. However it could be a grand place to play...

Contributor:
Robin Cole

199 Mousewater

Grade **3(4)**

Length **3½km**

OS sheet **72**

Introduction The Mousewater flows into the Clyde near the Falls of Clyde. It is in Lanarkshire, about an hour's drive south-east of Glasgow. A nice run, just far enough out of the Central Belt to be semi-hygienic, yet close enough to Glasgow and Edinburgh for the students and fat cats. The Mousewater runs through a combination of flat farmland and steep-sided wooded gorge. It could be classed as a 2-hit wonder but in reasonable flows the section in-between is quick and enjoyable enough, and the 2 hits good enough, to make the whole run worth doing. A new hydro scheme is to be built at the falls at the start of the run. The water will be returned to the river at the foot of the falls so only the falls themselves will be affected. At time of writing it is unclear whether the new weir to be built across the lip of the falls will make the drop harder or not.

Water Levels Wet/Very wet. As with most hereabouts, this river definitely needs rainfall. Wait until it has rained for a week in Glasgow to saturate the ground and then rained some more the night before you go. This is a hard one to catch really high but it is fairly good if you can. Because of the flattish farmland above it, the Mousewater also tends to stay at a reasonable level for a couple of days after rain.

Gauge When you look from the put-in bridge at the pool way below, you'll get a pretty good feel for whether its high or not. If the falls here are obviously separate tiers with plenty of rocks showing, but you can still see a line worth running, then it's probably just about worth doing - though the sections in-between the 2 main falls will be 'scrapey' and boring. If, on the other hand, the falls are one seething mass of water with a few munchy stoppers and it doesn't look like you'll be scraping anything except luck on the way down, then why are you sitting in the car reading this - get changed and get a photo! Once the hydro scheme is in place, look at the volume of water being returned to the river and the rapids immediately downstream to decide if there's enough flow.

Access From Lanark, take the A706 (signed Whitburn and Linlithgow). Keep going for a couple of miles past a couple of churches and the fire station until you reach some traffic lights. Turn right up the hill. Stop on the verge beside the old gate or on the other side of the bridge if it's busy. Walk back down to the traffic lights and take a deep breath before looking off the bridge. This is the put-in. From here, go back into Lanark, turn right onto the main street and then turn left onto Mouse Bank Road. Keep going until you twist down a narrow hedged hill to a bridge over the river. This is the first take-out. You can paddle on from here down to the confluence with the Clyde, adding another kilometre or so of gorge, but this is only worth it if the river is high - the take-out is at the caravan site at the confluence with the Clyde.

Description The first falls are the best and hardest. They are right at the put-in, so are easy to look at and to walk round if you want to. I always come away from the Mousewater wanting to do the first falls again - it's a shame they're at the start instead of the end! There follows a nice twisting gorge with nothing too hard. With a lot of

water the gorge is good fun and makes the river worth doing for folk who don't fancy the first drop. The second notable set of rapids is about halfway down after several twisty gorge sections with plenty of tree jam possibilities. To scout the falls, eddy out right opposite a large rock wall on the left - clamber steeply up the right bank beside a tiny stream and onto the path from where you can walk along and have a look. The section down to the lower take-out is in a spectacular wooded gorge and is pretty good if there is loads of water. There is nothing too serious but it does let you finish on a few rapids rather than the flat that leads up to the first take-out.

Contributor:
Kenny Biggin

200 Avon (Edinburgh)

Grade	**2/3**
Length	**6km**
OS sheet	**65**

Introduction Flowing through Linlithgow this grade 2/3 run is worth a go for anyone in the Central Belt area. Considering its location, the water is quite clean and the river surrounded by pleasant forest, with a nice nature walk beside the river.

Water Level Very wet. If it chucks it down in the Edinburgh area for a few days, then this one should be running.

Access Put in at the bridge where the A801 crosses the Avon. Safe parking can be found by turning left directly after the bridge (coming from the north) and driving a short distance along the road. It is also possible to put in higher up. Take out in Linlithgow just after the bridge. Below the weir is the best take-out as the river is very canalised in the short section actually in Linlithgow.

Description The river consists of mainly grade 2 and 3 rapids and gets better further down in a sort of half gorge section. The only major hazard is a bizarre little weir that drops straight into a grade 2 rapid. The river gets more powerful with a lot of water.

Contributor:
Douglas Rae

Other important points Close to this is the River Almond. I've not paddled this yet but it looks quite good and may be around a grade harder than the Avon.

Fenwick 201

Introduction This section of the Fenwick flows into Kilmarnock. This is a little gem, which needs heavy rain to bring it up.

Grade	**3/4**
Length	**4km**
OS sheet	**70**

Water Level Very wet.

Gauge Take a look at the flow over Beansburn Ford, about halfway down the run between the B7038 and B7082. If you can paddle over this ford there should be enough water for the trip.

Contributors:
Neil Farmer
and Greg McColm

Access To reach the put-in, turn off the A77 onto the B7038 just north of Kilmarnock. At the first mini-roundabout follow the signs to Kilmarnock. Take the first left down a country lane to a small stone bridge across the Fenwick. To reach the take-out, continue on the B7038 into Kilmarnock. Follow the one-way system until the road is close to the river. Downstream is a railway bridge and the last fall can be seen upstream. Get out 100m above the bridge.

Description Starting flat, the river gradually steepens. There is some good paddling to be had, but also a few obstacles to be aware of. The first appears quickly, marked by a factory high on the right bank. Get out here and portage left: the river swings round a left-hand bend and through a barbed wire fence. The drop in Dean Park can be interesting. Here the river constricts to around 3m and drops over a ledge. Boof on the left into a nasty slot/hole (not recommended) or run down the rapid on the right. About 400m after, is the ford. Remember your green cross code and watch out for the weir immediately downstream. The last fall in Kilmarnock is worth a look. This is a good take-out, since the weir under the high railway bridge in Kilmarnock is dangerous and should not be run.

Garnock 202

Introduction The Garnock flows into the Firth of Clyde at Irvine Bay. The section from Dalry to Dalgarven Mill makes an ideal trip for beginners consisting mainly of drops and pools created by anglers.

Grade	**2(3)**
Length	**4km**
OS sheet	**63**

Water Level Wet/Very wet. This river requires prolonged heavy rain and is only really viable for 6 hours after the rain stops.

Gauge The river should look full.

Access Driving into Dalry from the north, turn left off the A737 into the car park behind a disused mill (297 494). Put in from the car park on the west bank of the river. Take out on the east bank at Dalgarven Mill (296 458). Use the pebble pad on river left after the bridge.

Description A very small play weir marks the start of the run, just downstream from a railway bridge. From here the river is generally uniform, with a constant gradient the whole way, relieved by periodic artificial small weirs. Although some of these are broken and should be treated with caution, they do create a few waves, V-rapids, eddy lines and one or two playholes.

Contributors:
Graeme Bruce
and Andy Watt

Other important points There are a few small gabion basket weirs, but most of the man-made drops require caution as they have been formed by inserting steel pins into the river bed and then using timber, brick or anything else possible to hold back the water. There are also some trapped branches, wires and other obstacles in places.

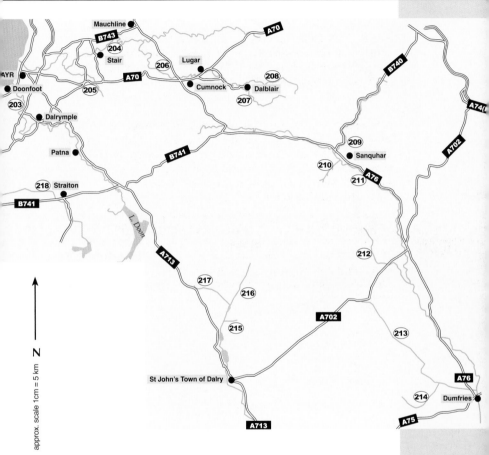

approx. scale 1cm = 5 km   N

Burns Country

Burns Country Continued

Burns Country

This area is popular with paddlers from the Central Belt, though perhaps unfairly it is often considered to play 'second fiddle' to a trip into the Highlands. Easily accessible from Carlisle and the M6, it is also a popular destination for those visiting from across the border. The rivers described here are in many ways the local paddlers' pick of the bunch. Many other great runs exist and it's rumoured that a dedicated guide will be produced for this area. Playboaters will find something of value on the Nith at almost all levels but for most other runs you will need to wait for rain.

Doon (Ness Glen) 203

Grade	3
Length	5km
OS sheet	77

Introduction This river flows from Loch Doon near Dalmellington, in a north-westerly direction, to join the Firth of Clyde near Ayr. The Ness Glen section runs from the dam at Loch Doon to the bridge under the B741.

Water Level The dam at Loch Doon releases a constant compensation flow of 2.6 cumecs, which gives enough water to paddle the Ness Glen section throughout the year. This stretch is not recommended when there is a lot of water around due to the serious tree hazard.

Access Drive south along the A713, through Dalmellington. After the town, take the second right, signposted to Loch Doon. Drive over the dam and park on the left. Follow the path on the river left. To get to the egress, drive back through Dalmellington and follow the B741 to Straiton, where the road crosses the River Doon.

Description The run starts below the dam. The weir 40m downstream is often run in the middle, but has seriously damaged a boat! (Portage right if you wish). What follows is tight, steep and enjoyable. All of the rapids are grade 3 and can be inspected, but be very careful of tree blockages. Care should be taken and paddlers should be confident of making breakouts. After approx 2km, the river flattens out, paddle over Bogran Loch and to the car.

Contributor:
Neil Farmer

203 Doon (Middle)

Grade **2/3**
Length **10km**
OS sheet **76**

Introduction The Doon is particularly attractive; a pleasant bouncy paddle in this middle section, more gentle in the lower reaches. It is however a prime salmon river, which is heavily fished between April and October. For a mellow trip, consider paddling on Sundays or out-with the fishing season.

Water Level The dam at Loch Doon impounds the headwaters of the river. Because of this, the river rises only slowly after rain, and soon drops off again. The middle section is best in spate conditions, during or immediately after very heavy rain.

Gauge The river has to look high to be runnable.

Access Driving south-east from Ayr on the A713, the put-in is at the road bridge in the village of Patna. For the take-out in Dalrymple, drive back towards Ayr. Turn left on the B7034 and drive in to the village. Turn left onto the B742, and park by the bridge. For a shorter trip there is good parking and access to the river on the left-hand bank at Skeldon Bridge, (turn left off the B7034 onto a minor road approximately 1 mile before Dalrymple).

Description Too shallow to paddle except after heavy rain, the section from Patna to Dalrymple is generally grade 3/3+ in spate conditions. The first real hazard on this stretch is the low footbridge at Carnochan Farm, some 3km below the put-in. This can be run at some flows or portaged on the right. After a further kilometre, the river narrows through Boreland Glen. Following this is Skeldon Mill and the access point, river left, at Skeldon Bridge. Three further weirs bring you to Dalrymple fish farm. The river splits round an island below here. Keep to the right hand channel, since a barbed wire fence blocks the left. From here it's not far to the take-out, river right below the bridge in Dalrymple.

Contributor:
David Wilbraham

203 Doon (Lower)

Grade **2**
Length **5km**
OS sheet **70**

Introduction The section from Auchendrane to Doonfoot can be paddled in lower water than the middle section and is generally grade 2.

Access Put in south of Ayr, where the A77 crosses the river at Auchendrane. Parking is limited, so please be considerate. Access is on the left bank. To reach the take-out, drive back towards Ayr for a couple of miles. Take the minor road to Doonfoot, where there is a handy public car park.

Description Numerous small weirs and fishing pools have been constructed during the last few years. Watch out for barbed wire fencing which extends into the edge of the river from the right bank below the first bend. Nether Auchendrane rapids appear after 1½km, followed by four weirs. The last, below the A719 bridge at Doonfoot, is schedule for reconstruction and its new characteristics are unknown.

Contributor:
David Wilbraham

Ayr 204

Introduction The Ayr winds through central Ayrshire. A pleasant paddle through spectacular sandstone gorges, the Ayr is a good, safe beginners' river, similar in difficulty to the Teith, near Callander.

Grade **2/3(4)**
Length **30km**
OS sheet **70**

Water Level Moderately wet / Very wet. Although this large river holds its water for several days after rain, it can be a bit of a scrape when low. In general, the more water the better.

Gauge There is no obvious gauge. If there are lots of rocks showing, the river is too low.

Access The river can be accessed at numerous points including Sorn, Catrine, Mauchline, Failford, Stair, Auchincruive and Ayr. The best white water sections are Mauchline to Stair and Stair to Achincruvie. To get to the put-in, turn right (west) in the village of Mauchline, 100m before the A76 (Kilmarnock to Dumfries road), crosses the River Ayr. Follow this to an old bridge over the river where there is parking and access. Take out at the obvious bridge in Stair or continue to Achincruvie.

Description The rapids on the Ayr are generally straightforward. When the river is high a great surf wave forms below the small weir in Stair (Gd 2). At monster flows, this wave is truly superb... a river-wide, glassy wave of 1.5m, with a breaking top and

Contributors:
Robin Cole and
Max Twomey

friendly eddy. If you are paddling any of the other sections, watch out for the following features:

- Double weir at Catrine (Gd 4)
- Small rapid/fall at Auchincruive (Gd 3)
- Weir by university in Ayr - very serious when the river is high.

205 Water of Coyle

Grade **1/2(4)**
Length **6km**
OS sheet **70**

Description The Water of Coyle can be paddled from the A70 to its confluence with the Ayr. This section is mainly grade 1/2, shallow and polluted by farm run-off, but if you are desperate for some action, there is a 4m, grade 4 fall at Sundrum Castle.

Contributor: Max Twomey and Brian Taggart

206 Lugar

Grade **2/3**
Length **19km**
OS sheet **70**

Introduction The Lugar flows into the River Ayr. An enjoyable and scenic spate river, the Lugar divides into three sections, offering both impressive sandstone gorges and an open, meandering river.

Water Level This river needs rain to make it worthwhile, and generally the more the better. If it looks runnable at your put-in, it should be OK for the rest of the trip.

Access The river splits neatly into 3 runs from Lugar (A70) near Cumnock to Mauchline (A76). The best access points are as follows.
- Put-in: small bridge in Lugar (594 214).
- Put-in/take-out: public park in Cumnock (565 203).
- Put-in/take-out: road bridge, Ochiltree (511 213), parking on far side of weir.
- Take-out: Barskimming Bridge, Mauchline (492 253).

Description The first section has an interesting rapid under the first road bridge then goes through a short but interesting gorge above Cumnock. From Cumnock the river flattens off though a few good surf waves can be found. After Ochiltree the river once again enters a gorge, never too difficult but with some good water. The scenery here is impressive, so too are some of the caves which have been cut from the rock including Peden's Cave, a Covenanter meeting place. The run ends just after the confluence with the Ayr.

Contributor:
Max Twomey

Glenmuir Water 207

Grade	4
Length	3km
OS sheet	71

Introduction The Glenmuir Water flows into the Gass Water, which is itself a tributary of the Ayr. The 'Cubes' section lies close to the confluence with the Gass Water near Lugar. The scenic gorge near the start makes a wonderful steep and narrow run, the grade of which varies greatly with water level.

Water Level Little more than a burn, this run needs lots of rain to make it paddleable. It rises and falls quickly, and is hard to catch at a good level. At lower levels the run can be quite rocky and is therefore best run in someone else's boat!

Gauge A message on the bridge at the put-in proclaims 'Low water mark' with an arrow and water level indicator below. It was probably put there by the anglers but serves well for paddlers also - any lower than the mark and it'll be too rocky. From the put-in bridge almost all of the rocks upstream need to be covered. If the burn is obviously in spate it's a full on grade 5.

Access From Cumnock, take the A70 for Muirkirk. ½ mile after Lugar, take a right turn up Glen Muir. After about 2 miles turn right down to a bridge and the put-in (613 203). Take out at the footbridge in Lugar (594 214), after the confluence with Bellow Water. You can park opposite the football field.

Description The run starts very gently until a sharp left-hand bend heralds the start of the gorge. After the first few drops the gorge turns sharp right - this is the S-bend. It contains a siphon and is worth inspecting. If you miss the breakout, keep right! As the gorge walls fall away you'll find what is possibly the best bit of the river, a long twisting rapid ending with a tasty couple of stoppers. In bigger water the run is fairly continuous, but at lower levels it's more pool/drop in nature. It may be worth checking the gorge for trees before entering.

Other important points Just above the take-out is a series of fast playwaves. Look to the right bank and you may spot the cave where William Murdoch first discovered how to obtain town gas from coal, an important step in the industrial revolution. This led on to developments such as motorised transport for all and polyethylene kayaks, though seemingly some North Ayrshire paddlers still prefer to construct their own from sticks and animal skins!

Contributors:
Neil Farmer
Greg McColm
and Max Twomey

208 Bellow Water (Gass Water)

Grade	**5**
Length	**200m**
OS sheet	**71**

Description The Bellow Water (or Gass Water) has been run from the road bridge near the confluence with the Glenmuir Water, including the impressive fall at the end. Lots of water is needed so that you can make the left-hand line on the falls.

Contributors: Neil Farmer, Greg McColm and Max Twomey

209 Crawick Water

Grade	**3**
Length	**2km**
OS sheet	**71**

Introduction The Crawick (croik) is a small tributary that joins the Nith just before Sanquhar. The river drops into a narrow, steep sided and very pleasant gorge before emerging to join the Nith.

Water Level Wet / Very wet. The Crawick holds its level well for a couple of days after heavy rain.

Gauge There is a footbridge just above the A76 road bridge at the traffic lights on the north side of Sanquhar. Looking upstream from here, if the burn looks just full enough to float a boat then the gorge should be grade 3. When the burn here is full, the gorge can be grade 4 or 5.

Access The take-out for this run is at the bridge described above. To reach the put-in, head north on the A76, then turn off up the B740, towards Crawfordjohn. Continue along the road until the river joins the road and there is a handy lay-by.

Description The river starts with a series of shallow shingle banks. After about ½km, the fun starts as the river drops into the

gorge. This gives continuous grade 3 water with a tricky drop
into the cauldron (Gd 4 in higher water) and an interesting final
drop. Here the river flows either side of a central rock. The safest
line is from left to right.

Contributors:
Dave Kwant and
Max Twomey

Other important points Combined with a run on the Nith, this
section makes a good day out.

Eucan 210

Introduction The Eucan, which joins the Nith at Sanquhar, is a
steep and technical run with two steep gorges and a portage or two.

Grade	**4/5**
Length	**5km**
OS sheet	**71**

Water Level Moderately wet/Wet. This burn needs some rain to
make it runnable but not too much. If other rivers in the area are
at a good level then this one might be a bit too full. The level can
rise and fall very quickly so take care.

Gauge From the road bridge at the end of the run, there should
be a few rocks showing above the water. If everything is covered
then the top gorge will be very continuous and the lower one
mostly unrunnable.

Access Sanquhar is on the A76 between Dumfries and Kilmarnock. Entering the village from the north, take the first minor
road on the right to cross the Nith by a bridge next to a small
picnic site. Turn right after this to reach the egress bridge in half
a mile. Going straight on after crossing the Nith brings you up
Glen Eucan. The most difficult section is just below Eucan Cottage and may be worth inspecting in advance. Continue up the
glen to the old waterworks. The put-in is anywhere above this, or
if the river's high enough, try driving to Glenglass and carrying a
further 2km for a steep, bolder run.

Description From the waterworks the river drops steeply
through the first gorge until a wooden bridge at Glenmaddie is
reached (possible egress). Look out for an overhead water pipe
½km after the waterworks and inspect/portage the fall which
lies a little further downstream. Easier water for 2km leads to the
main gorge which starts with read'n'run drops and gets progressively harder - inspect/portage the last falls. The only remaining

Contributor:
Max Twomey

obstacle is Eucan Fall (Gd 5) which is smaller than previous drops but may hold a powerful stopper.

Other important points In higher water both gorges become very continuous and some of the stoppers and tighter sections become very serious.

211 Nith

Grade **3/4**
Length **7km**
OS sheet **71**

Introduction The Nith works its way down from the South Ayrshire hills through Dumfries and on into the Solway Firth. The section described flows beside the A76 in a shallow wooded gorge, offering good grade 3 paddling with plenty of playspots.

Water Level Medium wet/Wet. The river comes up quite fast and holds its water for a day or two.

Gauge The level can be gauged at Drumlanrig Bridge. 1.5-2.5 is low, 2.5-3.0 is an ideal level (medium), 3+ is high. 0.4 on the SEPA gauge should be considered a minimum flow.

Access The most popular access is at Glen Airlie picnic site on the A76 near Mennock. Starting at Mennock bridge gives an extra couple of nice grade 3 rapids. To extend the trip even further, put in at the small picnic site in Sanquhar where the road heading up Euchan Glen crosses the river (alternative take-out for the Crawick). The small village of Enterkinfoot has a lay-by at its southern end offering another possible access/egress point or park'n'play for the lower playspot. For the normal take-out, turn off the A76 towards Drumlanrig Castle (worth visiting for the scones alone). Park at Drumlanrig Bridge.

Description The first 4km offers some nice grade 3 paddling. When high, the river gets very boily and can be a handful for the inexperienced. Two great playholes at Enterkinfoot and a few more rapids are followed by 1½km of flat water. Below this is a grade 4 gorge. In high water, this section is very boily and quite full on. You can inspect the first set of drops from the left. With less water it drops a grade but is still worth paddling at surprisingly low flows.

Contributor:
Dave Kwant and
Max Twomey

Other important points Watch out for the tree lodged in the gorge.

Scar Water (Scaur Water) 212

Grade	**4(5)**
Length	**8km**
OS sheet	**78**

Introduction The Scar runs through a pleasant wooded glen towards the village of Penpont and eventually joins the Nith below Thornhill. It has plenty of grade 3 water with a couple of 4's and one grade 5/portage.

Water Level Wet. A good amount of rain is needed, although the river holds its water well and can remain at a good runnable level for a couple of days after heavy rainfall.

Gauge Looking over the bridge at the take-out, if most of the rocks are covered then it should be a good run. Obviously at very high levels things get more serious. There is an automatic gauge just above the take-out, but unfortunately it's not (yet) on the SEPA website.

Access To find the take-out from Penpont, take the minor road south from the village to the bridge just on the outskirts. The best place to take out is river right on the downstream side. For the put-in, follow the A702 west towards Moniaive. Just outside the village a bridge crosses the Scar again. Take the next road on the right up Glen Scar. On the way you may wish to inspect the approach to the grade 5 section. This is at a popular picnic spot and so should not be too difficult to find. The put-in is where the road next crosses the river, just beyond Knockelly. It is possible to park one car a little further on and carry across a field.

Description The river starts off gently and builds to some fun sections of grade 3. A little under 1km beyond a small footbridge is the first grade 4, a twisting, boily rapid ending with a drop and stopper. Look out for a grassy left-hand bank before a left bend in the river. If you miss this you should get a breakout on the left immediately above the rapid. When the river is high, it's quite common for parties to miss the breakout completely and run this one blind. More grade 3 follows, before a rock barrier and the sound of crashing water signals the start of the grade 5 section, sometimes called Glenmalin Falls. These falls are long, difficult and committing with a tricky lead-in. Swimming at the top has been described as unpleasant. The last significant rapid is shortly after the A720 road bridge on a left bend. At normal levels it's read'n'run, but it's worth looking at if the river's high, particularly as tree blockages may occur after heavy spates.

Other important points There was a tree blocking the exit from the gorge at the time of writing (March 2004). It could be paddled past with care, but rescue would be tricky to set up. The section above the put-in may be worth exploring when the river is high enough.

Contributors:
Max Twomey and
Neil Farmer

213 Cairn Water

Grade   **2-4**
Length **20km**
OS sht.**78/84**

Description The Cairn Water joins the Nith just above Dumfries giving a grade 2/3 run from Dunscore, and a 3/4 section for the last 4km which includes Cluden Leap.

Contributor: Max Twomey

214 Old Water

Grade   **5**
Length **200m**
OS sheet   **84**

Introduction A tributary of the Cairn Water, the Old Water flows from a reservoir above Shawhead. The short section described runs under the minor road between Newbridge and Dunscore in a series of slides and falls ending in a deep gorge.

Water Level Local water levels need to be at medium level.

Gauge The main fall and indeed most of the section can be viewed from the Routin Brig. Use your own judgement as to whether it is runnable. At high levels the section is one scary mass of white water and escape from the plunge pool would be improbable. At too low a level, it will not be possible to float down the lead-in rapid.

Access Follow the A76 for about 3 miles heading north out of Dumfries. At Newbridge follow a minor road left towards Dunscore with the Cairn Water on your right. Continue for about 3 miles. The Old Water is crossed by a narrow bridge, the Routin Brig, at a T-junction. The section described is above and under the bridge. Put in as far above the Routin Brig falls as you wish, depending on water levels. Take out after the bridge, as there is not much of interest after the falls.

Description The short, fun lead-in section consists of a small drop followed by a steep narrow slot and slide into a tight S-bend. This is followed by another tight turn and the lead into the main fall, a 4m drop and 90° turn into a confined deep gorge. The plunge pool is deep but small - the correct line over the fall is critical to avoid a rocky landing and/or a difficult exit from behind the fall. A line slightly left of centre with that essential 90° turn at the top seems to work! The small plunge pool leads directly to the final drop under the bridge. This is a very tight 2m drop into a confined frothy pool that has rocks at the base, giving the potential for a heavy impact and vertical pin.

Contributor:
Bob Evans

Other important points This run is probably best treated as a stunt by those looking for some excitement.

Black Water 215

Introduction A short section and a bit of a two hit wonder, the entry drop is well worthwhile and the final drop is a challenge too.

Grade **4/5**
Length **800m**
OS sheet **84**

Gauge If water is flowing over the middle of the grade 5 rapid downstream of the bridge, the level is high.

Access From Castle Douglas drive up the A713 to St John's Town of Dalry. Take the first right, then carry straight on at the crossroads and follow the road (B7000) for 4½ miles until you get to the Youth Hostel. Carry the boat upstream for 800m along the public footpath to the waterfall. Put in on the flat section just upstream (263 588). The river eventually flattens out into a loch, so the take-out just after the road bridge is obvious.

Description The lead-in rapids provide a good warm up. They look innocent but I nearly winded myself on one of them! Once at the waterfall, there are two rocks forming rooster tails blocking the entrance. You'll need a manoeuvrable boat to zigzag through them. The waterfall is around 6m high and can be easily inspected. Setting up safety cover will be tricky though, since the fall is immediately followed by another smaller shoot. In low water the weir can be shot, but in high water, I'm told it gets quite serious. Before the loch there is one more rapid of note. In high water conditions it can be shot over the middle, but in low condi-

Contributor:
Jay Sigbrandt

tions the water flows river right over a fall whose exit is partly blocked by a submerged rock. Make your own mind up about this one, but safety cover is a good idea.

216 Water of Ken

Grade **2(3)**
Length **12km**
OS sheet **77**

Introduction This upper stretch of the Water of Ken has been paddled since the early seventies and was written up in Issue 77 of Canoeist. It needs a lot of water but gives a good paddle in a remote setting and you are likely to have it to yourself.

Water Level A typical Galloway spate burn, it needs to be very wet.

Gauge The water flowing under the High Bridge of Ken should look very scary… but don't worry, this is below the take-out. At the put-in, the river should be bank full.

Access From the A713 Ayr to Castle Douglas road, take the B729 at Carsphairn, turn right onto the B7000 and park on the verge just before the High Bridge of Ken (619 902). The take-out is river right 50m upstream. Observe it well, then just for fun, inspect the serious slots and drops beneath the bridge. It is not known if anyone has tried and survived these! To reach the put-in, return to the junction with the B729 and continue on it by turning right. After 1 $^1/_2$ miles, turn left (north) onto the unmarked minor road. Continue past Corlae and put in at the next bridge (661 992). The river is fished in season (mid February to end October) but not on Sundays.

Description At first the river is narrow and bushes can be a hazard, but it soon opens out onto a plain reminiscent of parts of the Upper Spey. It meanders through gravel rapids below remote hills of Galloway with wonderful names such as Alhang and Coranbae. The road bridge at (646 958) announces the start of the 1km long grade 3 section. After a bend this kicks off where bedrock breaks through the peaty banks creating a good stopper, best run river right. There is then a long section of rounded boulders which, at low water levels, create a maze with many blind endings. At high levels it's much more fun and no two paddlers will take the same route. After this the river reverts to a fast bouncy grade 2 but with remarkably few eddies when in spate.

Glorious Galloway countryside, with crags surmounted by hill forts and cairns, flashes by all too quickly. Fortunately the river slows down on the approach to the High Bridge of Ken and the take-out. Just above the bridge the river drops over a diagonal 1.5m ledge into a very large stopper before splitting into two slots under the bridge. The evil looking one on the left is surpassed by its neighbour on the right. The slots then develop into two narrow gorges before reuniting in a large pool 50m downstream - clearly a challenge for those with the ambition to run firsts, if not make a major contribution to the gene pool.

Contributor:
Douglas Wilcox

Other important points Don't miss the take-out!

Water of Deugh 217

Introduction The upper Water of Deugh is rarely paddled since it is in a remote, high valley far from the main road. It gives a good varied run, but it does need a lot of water as its headwaters are diverted for the Galloway hydro-electric scheme.

Grade	3
Length	15km
OS sheet	77

Water Level A typical Galloway spate burn, it needs to be very wet.

Gauge The water flowing under the bridge at the Green Well of Scotland (556 944) should cover all the rocks and the river should be mostly white water.

Access From the A713 Ayr to Castle Douglas road, just south of the watershed above Loch Doon, take the minor road signposted for Lamford at (517 997). Turn left where the road splits and drive to the bridge at (557 014). This is the put-in. For the take-out, return to the A713 and drive south to Carsphairn. Take the B729 and park on the verge where the river approaches the road (587 924). The river is fished in season (mid February to end October) but not on Sundays.

Description The river starts with some tight turns before developing into a series of standing waves (if the rocks are well covered) at a steady gradient through magnificent open scenery. The appearance of bedrock breaking through the peat banks announces several drops with small stoppers. The gradient eases and you enter still water behind a small dam which diverts the water westwards to the hydro-electric scheme. If enough water is

escaping down the river, re-enter the river by a sluice, river left, immediately below the dam. The banks become more wooded but there are still views of the distant conical hill of Craig Knockgray, beyond which is the take-out. On the left bank at Knockengorroch you will see some unusual wooden structures, some of which are frames for tepees. An alternative music festival is held here each May. A good but remote playwave follows at (563 960). The action picks up again as you approach the Green Well of Scotland. You can pass either side of its 'guardian', a rock with a large buffer wave in the middle of the river. After this you enter a short, twisty gorge section and will be impressed by flood debris up to 3m above you in the trees. Under the road bridge the gradient eases and the river meanders over a plain approaching the village of Carsphairn. Watch out for two river-wide fences, before the confluence with the Carsphairn Lane. If the hydro-electric scheme is generating, this can add a lot of volume to the river, returning its captured headwater and adding water pumped from Loch Doon. The gradient steepens again as you approach the road bridge south of the village. This gives a meaty grade 3 rapid and the section under the bridge is best taken river right. After this the river enters more gentle wooded countryside with rhododendron bushes. There is a delightful 1km long grade 2/3 section with a series of small ledges before the river slows down again at the take-out.

Contributor:
Douglas Wilcox

218 Girvan

Grade	3
Length	7km
OS sht.	77/70

Introduction This river first winds its way through farmland before entering an open wooded gorge. Here a series of sandstone ledges give entertaining drops of up to 3m in height and a few good playspots.

Water Level Wet. To be worth doing, it definitely needs heavy rain, although not a sustained downpour.

Gauge This is best judged at the take-out where there needs to be enough water to float without scraping. If the river looks high here then expect some substantial stoppers in the gorge.

Access From the Ayr bypass (A77) travel south through Minishant and take the B7045 for Straiton. At the edge of the village take the B741 west. After 100m it crosses the river; this is the put-in. The take-out is back down the B7045 to Aitkenhead. At the west end of the village take the minor road off to the left. There is a bridge a short distance down this way.

Description Initial easy water eventually leads to a man-made split in the river. If it's high enough, take the right fork as this bypasses Blairquhan Castle and avoids unnecessary disturbance. After another 1km the river enters the gorge and starts the action proper with a nice drop'n'slot. Next is Tranew Linn, a very wide ledge on a right bend. This is followed by a succession of enjoyable ledges and slabs with a few playspots.

Other important points The river flows through a sporting estate so watch out for shooting parties in the woods around the gorge. When the river is low it's hard to avoid the anglers and the lead in is far too tedious to be worth bothering with.

Contributor:
Max Twomey

Carrick Lane / Whitespout Lane 219

Introduction The Whitespout Lane flows from Loch Riecawr in the north of the Galloway Forest Park. It joins the Eglin Lane to become the Carrick Lane before flowing into Loch Doon. Its remote nature and wonderfully clean water gives the trip a genuine wilderness feel. The best of the white water is in the last kilometre, and can be accessed by walking up from the bottom. This gives a mostly bouldery grade 3 run that includes some granite mini-gorges and can be quite entertaining after heavy rain. The trip finishes with a spectacular set of falls, the height of which depend on the level of the loch.

Grade **2/3(4)**
Length **5km**
OS sheet **77**

Water Level Wet/Very wet. A typical Galloway spate burn, it needs to be very wet for the whole trip to be on. The large granite catchment area does however mean the level rises quickly, even after a dry spell, so it can provide a good paddle after a heavy summer downpour. The last 200m can be run with only a small amount of water.

Gauge The flow can be judged from the bridge at the take-out. If this looks to be only just full enough then it's probably not worth the effort, particularly if you intend to carry your boat up

to do the lower section. Alternatively, look over the bridge at (477 940). The large concrete block below the bridge should be completely covered. Water spilling over the top of the Riecawr dam (440 937) is also a good sign.

Access Drive south along the A713, through Dalmellington. After the town, take the second right signposted to Loch Doon. Drive past the dam (the put-in for the Ness Glen section of the Doon) and follow the road to a car park – there is no tarmac for the last half mile. From here Carrick Forest Drive (officially open from Easter until the end of October, but if you're lucky at other times too), leads to the upper put-in just below the dam. If the gate is locked, or you don't fancy the upper stretch, there are 2 lower put-ins. To reach the bridge at (453 933) and put on below Whitespout Linn, follow the Forest Drive for a little under 2km, then take the path on your left that leads down to the river. For a shorter walk that still gives the best of the action, portage up the forest drive then cut down to the river after about 1km, before the start of the forest.

Description   At first the river runs though a sort of walled channel through dense forest. Watch out for wind-blown trees, which might require a portage. It then drifts lazily for 2km through Loch Gower with only a few small drops until a horizon line announces Whitespout Linn (452 933). Unfortunately this 5m fall ends in a very shallow bed of rocks. At high water levels there is a small chicken-shoot, river right, which may be blocked by the tops of wind-fallen trees (bring a saw). After this the gradient steepens for the final 2km. After the confluence with the Eglin Lane the river increases substantially in volume. The forest soon opens up to moorland, and there is a powerful stopper, river left, called the Washing Machine. After increasingly good grade 3 water, the river bends left through the steep fast canyon section before coming to an interesting bedrock rapid, S-Bend, which in high water can be bypassed river left. Paddle under the bridge (where you left a car) and continue to the Carrick Falls by which the Lane plunges into Loch Doon. The height of these and the best line is dependent on the level of the loch and varies from 2 to 6m.

Contributors:
Max Twomey and
Douglas Wilcox

Water of Minnoch 220

Grade	**4/5**
Length	**15km**
OS sheet	**77**

Introduction Running through the Galloway Forest, the section above Palgowan Bridge is a moderately steep alpine type run that is challenging, but never desperate. This leads into the middle section, a committing bouldery run through a heavily wooded area, with several grade 5 rapids. The lower section is a gentler prospect, with fewer rocks and generally a more open aspect.

Water Level This river needs quite a bit of rain to bring it up. It doesn't hold its water, often rising and falling again in a matter of hours.

Gauge There is a gauge at Stroan Bridge, next to the Glen Trool Visitor Centre. The river is generally worthwhile if the level is above 4', but better if the gauge reads 5' or more. The exception is the middle, which can be run with slightly less water: it is not recommended below 3' and gets pushy above 5'.

Access To reach the put-in for the upper section, drive north from Palgowan Bridge on the minor road until a picnic site is reached. The take-out for the upper, and put-in for the middle is at Palgowan Bridge. The middle take-out is at Glen Trool Visitor Centre. A good place to check the gauge and peek at Dog Leg Falls (Gd 5). This is also the start for the lower section. The final egress point is at Borgan Bridge. Turn off the A714 just north of the confluence with the Cree.

Description From the picnic site, the river is flat and gentle for a while, until a definite horizon line warns of the first interesting fall (Gd 4+). After this the river is fairly continuous, but never exceeds grade 4. It eases off as it gets closer to Palgowan Bridge, and the upper take-out. Below the bridge, the river is gentle for a while. The grade picks up again at the point where the banks become wooded, with the first grade 5 about 1km further downstream. The next section is good grade 4, with the exception of the undercut Falls of Minnoch (Gd 5+) and the Black Linn (Gd 5). Take out at Stroon Bridge, or if you're having a good day check out Dog Leg Falls (Gd 5), just below the bridge. The final section below the falls starts gently. It picks up to give nice long grade 3/4 rapids. The last drop below Borgan Bridge is slightly more difficult (Gd 4+).

221 Cree

Grade **4(5)**
Length **9½km**
OS sheet **77**

Introduction The River Cree flows through Galloway, off the A714. A beautiful river running through remote farmland, the Cree can be run as a grade 4 trip with two portages.

Water Level Wet. This run needs water, but stays up after rain for longer than the Minnoch.

Gauge The Cree is best when the gauge at Stroan Bridge on the Minnoch is above 5.

Access Put in at the A714 road bridge, 17 miles east of Girvan. Take out where the A714 crosses the river upstream of the confluence with the Minnoch.

Description The river starts with a flat meandering section, with one grade 3/4 drop. However, things soon pick up giving a more continuous section of grade 4 white water. The first of the harder drops follows a long rapid and is immediately after a sharp left-hand bend. From here the grade eases briefly before a sharp right bend and a 3m waterfall in a box canyon (Gd 5). This is followed immediately by another good rapid. Several grade 4's later, you reach the lower gorge. This stretch can get tricky in spate conditions, and may be worth a quick look before you commit yourself when the river is high.

Contributors:
Neil Farmer and
Greg McColm

222 Pulhowan Burn (Larg Hill Burn)

Grade **5**
Length **250m**
OS sheet **77**

Introduction A tributary of the the River Cree, this steep ditch flows off Larg Hill, near Newton Stewart. The short section described runs in a steep twisting gorge from the base of a significant fall down to the road bridge, just before the confluence with the River Cree.

Water Level Local water levels need to be at around a medium level.

Gauge The long slide, which is the main event on this short section, is visible from the road - make up your own mind regarding water level. The section above the slide needs a bit more water, but not too much. The whole section can be inspected in a few minutes.

Access From Newton Stewart, follow the minor road that runs parallel to the A714, on the opposite bank of the River Cree. After around 4 miles near a picnic site on the left, you cross the Pulhowan Burn. Park at the picnic site and walk up to the base of a significant fall.

Description The run starts below the obviously large fall with a series of difficult confined drops, the severity of which are highly water level dependent. A very short flat section follows and leads to an impressive horizon line and a 10-12m steep slide. The first 2m of the slide are the steepest with the potential to pin or trip, the rest is downhill all the way. Watch out for a constriction at the base and keep your paddles pointing forwards.

Other important points This run is probably best treated as a stunt by those looking for some excitement. As one local paddler described it, a silly steep ditch for "dunderheeds".

Contributor:
Bob Evans

Big Water of Fleet 223

Introduction First run some 20 years ago, the Big Water of Fleet flows through a beautiful valley, has lovely clean water, and deserves to be paddled more often.

Grade **3/4+**
Length **6½km**
OS sheet **83**

Water Level This river has a large granite catchment area on the weather side of the Galloway Hills. This means the level rises quickly, even after a dry spell, and falls quickly. The Fleet is a typical Galloway spate burn and is only runnable if it's very wet.

Gauge All the boulders under the take-out bridge should be well covered. At the put-in the (narrow) river should be bank full.

Access From the A75 enter Gatehouse of Fleet and take the B796 north for Gatehouse Station. To reach the take-out, turn off to the right at Nether Rusko and park on the west side of the bridge (586 601). To reach the put-in, continue to Gatehouse Station and turn right for Dromore. Drive through the gate, continue on the dirt road and park under the Big Water of Fleet Viaduct (558 642). You can inspect the major fall (565 623) from the road at Rusko Cottage (559 622). The large pool below the falls is popular with local swimmers, but you won't see anyone there when it's running!

Description For the first 2km, the Fleet is a fast boulder dodge. It then steepens and becomes tight and twisty, with frequent small ledges but no significant playspots. At 2.7km the gradient eases and a significant horizon line appears, the S Triple Falls (Gd 4+). Take the right-hand channel for the first 2m drop, avoiding the attraction of the undercut wall on the right. The next 1.5m fall ends in a short pool before the final river-wide ledge drop of 1m, which ends in a large catching pool. In severe spate the falls become more serious as the flow pushes towards the undercut, but portaging is easy. The gradient remains steep for a further 2km through Lamagowan Gorge, where overhanging trees can be a problem, before the river flattens as the valley opens out again.

Other important points The salmon fishing season is 25 Feb-31 Oct.

Contributors:
Jonni Aiton and
Douglas Wilcox

Borders

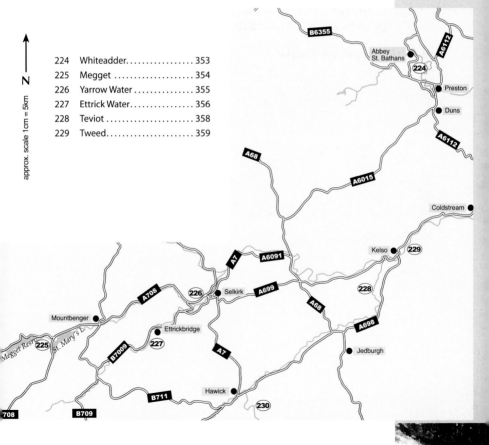

N
↑

approx. scale 1cm = 5km

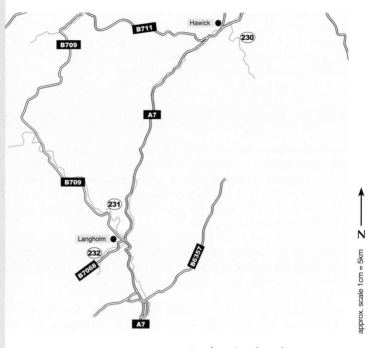

approx. scale 1cm = 5km

N

Borders Continued

Borders

If you're a free falling, adrenaline riding, rip-it-up kind of a dude, you might feel this chapter would be better titled 'The Bored-rs'! This area offers generally straightforward trips, often with easy road access. The exceptions to this are the Megget, Gameshope Burn and Slitrig, which are all steep spate runs. The other rivers featured are ideal for those who like more of a journey than a pure white-knuckle ride. Take care though when the rivers are high, as even the most benign section can quickly get out of hand when in flood.

Whiteadder 224

Grade	**3**
Length	**7km**
OS sheet	**67**

Introduction The Whiteadder is the most scenic river in the Borders offering something of interest to most types of paddlers. When large quantities of rain fall on the Lammermuirs, a gorge section from the attractive estate village of Abbey St Bathans provides some exciting white water. Further downstream, a more gentle paddle can be found.

Water Level Very wet over the Lammermuirs. This spate river runs low the majority of the time, and heavy rain is needed for an enjoyable paddle.

Gauge A gauge in feet from 1-6 is found at Abbey St Bathans ford. Below 1 and the river is low, 2 is at least medium and 2.5+ is high. Over 4, the river becomes much more serious.

Access The put-in is at Abbey St Bathans ford next to the 'River Café', (763 619). There is plenty of open space and access to the river is straightforward. Parking for the take-out can be found in a rough area of ground on the west side of a bridge crossing the Whitadder, 1½ miles west of Preston (774 577).

Description From Abbey St Bathans the Whiteadder flows gently. When you pass the Retreat House (a unique circular building tucked away on the left) the water becomes more challenging with a brief continuous grade 2/3 section. As the next rapid grows closer, watch out for a 2nd Century fort and broch, located high up on the hills to the right. Calm water leads to a couple of bigger drops, the second of which might be considered grade 4.

In low water, protruding rocks obstruct the main channel on the left. The river now relaxes until Elba. A footbridge and a right bend mark a 1m fall. From here the valley opens out, and straightforward, shallow rapids lead to a ford built over pipes, which should be portaged.

Other important points High water may result in fast flows and tree blockages. This run is generally shallow and pins are a potential danger. The scenic half-day trip from Dexter's Bridge on the Duns-Chirnside road to Canys also comes well recommended. This includes several small rapids, drops and caulds.

Contributors:
Gordon Ross
and Keith Hall

225 Megget

Grade	**4**
Length	**2km**
OS sheet	**73**

Introduction This short river, which flows into St Mary's Loch some 12 miles west of Selkirk, eventually finds its way to the Tweed. When enough water is pumping down this bouldery river bed you get a fast shallow and continuous spate trip, which is a joy.

Water Level Very wet. The dam at the end of the Megget Reservoir captures most of the water, giving a dry river bed, except in near flood conditions.

Gauge The river should look bank full and bursting.

Access Driving south-west from Selkirk to Moffat on the A708, turn right halfway along St Mary's Loch at Cappercleuch. This is the take-out. To reach the put-in, continue along the minor road towards Tweedsmuir until you get to the Megget Reservoir. Put in below the dam.

Description This is real read and run territory. Made up of steep continuous boulders, it splits round islands in several places. With no set lines, just continuous crashing water - it's 'take it as you find it', and everyone for themselves. This is a great run if you manage to catch it with water, but not one to undertake lightly. The river is too shallow to roll, and a swimmer would take a real beating.

Other important points If it is wet, but the Megget is not quite high enough, you might like to try the **Gameshope Burn**. This steep (Gd 5?) run is full of constricted drops and slides and will probably require a fair amount of portaging, as well as a good amount of water. To reach the put-in from the Megget, take the road past the Megget Reservoir heading to Talla Linnfoots. When the road drops down steeply and makes a sharp right-hand turn, park at the lay-by. The river is on the left running into Talla Resevoir. Carry up the track on river right.

Contributors:
Tom Prentice
and Mark Lyons

Yarrow Water 226

Grade	**2/3**
Length	**8km**
OS sheet	**73**

Introduction The Yarrow is part of the Tweed river system, joining the Ettrick Water near Selkirk. In the valley, areas of historic interest include the Yarrow Stone, Newark Castle and the country house of Bowhill. The Yarrow is a sheltered grade 2/3 trip with an attractive gorge midway down. Joining the Ettrick Water, the valley opens out, and the increased volume carries you to the take-out in Selkirk.

Water Level Wet/Very wet.

Gauge If the majority of rocks are covered at the put-in, and the river at this point looks easily navigable, then the trip shouldn't be too rocky. 0.8 on the SEPA gauge is recommended minimum for a pleasant run, although the gorge gives an OK paddle as low as 0.4 if you are prepared to scrape down the sections outside the gorge.

Access There are two put-in points for the Yarrow. The first is in Yarrowford, which is located around 6 miles up the Yarrow valley on the A708. There is a car park and phone box here. The second is around 4 miles further up the valley where a road from the Ettrick valley crosses over (355 278). There is space for around 4 cars here. Alternately in very high water, you could get on at St Mary's Loch but there is not much of interest on this section. You can take out either at the General's Bridge, which is the turn off to Bowhill Estates and over to the Ettrick valley, or continue down onto the Ettrick Water and get out at Selkirk swimming pool.

Description The section from the top put-in down is only worth running in high water levels and consists of more or less constant bouncy grade 2 all the way down to the lower put-in at Yarrowford. The next 2km, until the ruins of Newark Castle come into

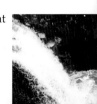

view on the right, is predominantly grade 1, with a few grade 2 rapids. The river then enters a gorge with small enjoyable rapids leading into a more continuous grade 2/3 section. The river narrows and disappears round a bend, warning of a slightly harder drop (Gd 3+). Below the fall, which may merit inspection, mid stream rocks catch the unwary, particularly at high flows when they could be partially hidden. This is the end of the gorge and after paddling under an old bridge the river banks drop to reveal the surrounding countryside. From here it is only a short stretch of calm water until the river joins the much larger Ettrick Water. This too is generally calm, other than the initial cauld, which is easily portaged, and some interesting waves which appear when the river is very high. The take-out at the swimming pool comes up about 300m below the main road bridge.

Contributors:
Gordon Ross and
Douglas Rae

Other important points Watch out for strainers! The banks are heavily wooded and fallen trees can become jammed in the gorge. Overhanging branches may also obstruct the flow and restrict access to the bank. There are currently ropes attached to the gorge walls, which cause a major hazard in high flows.

227 Ettrick Water

Grade	**2/3**
Length	**2km**
OS sheet	**73**

◯◯◯

Introduction The Ettrick Water is one of the main early feeders into the River Tweed. The most interesting section of the Ettrick Water is found some 8 miles south of Selkirk at Ettrickbridge. Here this normally gentle river picks up to provide a short attractive paddle.

Water Level Wet/Very wet. The Ettrick comes from the same source hills as the Border Esk, so if the Esk is up, the Ettrick will be too. The restricted nature of the gorge means that the river becomes much faster and more powerful as the level rises. The final continuous section of the gorge in particular can have some large waves. The gorge can still be paddled at more moderate flows, but the lower section needs plenty of water.

Gauge The river level can be gauged at Ettrickbridge. Alternatively, go down to Selkirk road bridge (near the swimming pool) and look upstream. If it looks like you can paddle down the flat section above the bridge then the river is runnable, but may be low.

Access Driving west from Selkirk on the B7009, pass through Ettrickbridge and continue for another 1½ miles until the road meets the river again. Just before the bridge to the Ettrickshaws Hotel, there is a lay-by on the right that will hold two cars. Please do not park on the verge or drive across the bridge - unless you plan to visit the hotel. It is possible to put in/take out after the gorge, at Helmburn Bridge. Drive back through Ettrickbridge and take the 2nd turn beyond the village by some houses, about 400m from the Welcome to Ettrickbridge sign. For a longer trip drive back towards Selkirk and take out at Colin's Bridge, a couple of miles further along the B7009 where a road turns off towards the Yarrow valley, or at Selkirk swimming pool.

Description This short trip starts slowly, then gradually picks up with a few grade 2 rapids. After about 1½km the river widens and a sharp right-hand bend marks the approach of Manse Falls (Gd 3+), a two-tier rapid and the hardest on the river. In higher water the current pushes onto a large rock wall and, if you wish to scout the drop, you may want to make an eddy well upstream. From Manse Falls, bouncy grade 2/3 takes you to Ettrickbridge, and the first take-out river left. After the gorge, the Ettrick settles down to some solid grade 2 paddling. In recent floods, part of the centre of Ettrick weir was washed away creating a mean towback in the centre. The weir is easily inspected and best shot on the far left. About 500m below this, there are a row of iron spikes in the river, which can be passed on river right.

Other important points The lack of parking means that this is a trip where it is advisable to have a shuttle driver, or someone keen enough to run/cycle the shuttle.
This is a Tweed tributary so be prepared to meet a few fishermen in and above the Selkirk section.
If the river is high then there is another rapid section further up the valley on a small Ettrick tributary that flows from Loch Tima.

Contributors:
Gordon Ross
Douglas Rae and
Malcolm Ross

228 Teviot

Grade **2(3-)**
Length **5km**
OS sheet **80**

Introduction The Teviot is a tributary of the River Tweed, joining the larger river in the historic town of Kelso. In its upper reaches, the river resembles something of an urban battleground, particularly during the fishing season, with overhanging trees and attendant shopping trolleys. Further downstream the river mellows, even if some of the anglers don't, and gradually meanders eastwards to join the Tweed. If you don't want to talk to the fishermen, consider paddling on Sundays or outwith the fishing season (which runs from April to November).The section described is a good run to take beginners on after they have a few trips under their belt - a good step up from the Tweed. The river provides challenges without being too difficult, but still has enough on it to keep more experienced paddlers from crying with boredom. In addition to the grade 3-, there are numerous bouncy grade 2 sections with some surfable waves as you go down.

Water Level Moderately wet/Very wet. The bigger the better. The river is runnable all year round although if there has been no rain for a while it is a bit scrapey especially when running the weir and on the section before the Slitrig joins the Teviot.

Access Put in at the side of Martin's Bridge, just near the A7 at the B711 turn off, about one mile south of Hawick. Just over the bridge is a small car park with room for about 4 cars - the car park is used by walkers so there may be others parked in it. The take-out is about 1½ miles below Hawick near the Riverside Caravan Park. There is a small slip road off to the left just before the caravan park where it is possible to park. The turn off is quite easy to miss - if you pass the caravan park you have gone too far. To reach the take-out, turn off on to the A698 at the roundabout in front of the Safeway's garage at the bottom end of Hawick High Street.

Description Straightforward water leads from the put-in to an island just above the rugby pitches. Stick to the right-hand side where there is more flow as the other routes have bushes and trees stuck in them. As you enter Hawick a short paddle on flat water leads to a long smooth weir, which has a salmon ladder in the middle. Running the ladder adds a bit of excitement for more experienced paddlers, or take a safer route down either side.

Next a shoot over a small weir is followed by a bend and you are presented with a lot of bushes growing in the river - stick with the main flow to the right. The river then turns another sharpish corner and you are into the Horn's Hole section (Gd 3-). Bouncy waves and a few stoppers with some rocks to dodge run on down to a small fall that disappears into a wave at higher levels. The take-out is just after this above the stone bridge. It's not the easiest take-out point in the world, but the current here is slow and it's shallow near the bank.

Other important points This trip can be combined with a run on the Slitrig if the rivers are high. It joins the Teviot in Hawick centre just after the first weir and creates some interesting currents.

Contributors:
Douglas Rae and
Keith Hall

Tweed 229

Grade **1 (2/3)**
Length   -
OS sht.**74/75**

Description Many stretches of the Tweed are regularly paddled, from Manor Bridge, just above Peebles, downwards. The main rapids are Fairnilee (Gd 2) near where the A708 forks off the A72, and Makerstoun (Gd 2/3) between Newton St Boswells and Kelso. From Kelso to Berwick provides a full day's trip that can be split into several shorter sections, and provides mainly grade 1 paddling with a few small rapids and weirs. The Tweed can be paddled in almost all conditions, although a flow of at least 1.2 on the SEPA gauge is recommended. In high spate the river can rise as much as 5m. It is a popular fishing destination.

Contributors:
Keith Hall and
Malcolm Ross

Slitrig 230

Grade **2/3 (4)**
Length **1 ½km**
OS sheet   **79**

Introduction The Slitrig is fast flowing and very narrow, providing a good but short trip if there is enough water. In spate conditions the river is a good grade 4+ run, but at more reasonable levels it is suitable for competent intermediate paddlers.

Water Level The Slitrig can only be run after heavy rainfall in the area.

Gauge As long as the main fall looks runnable the rest of the river should be OK.

Access From Hawick, take the B6399 towards Newcastleton. After about a mile, put in at the first bridge just past the scrap yard. Next to the bridge there is room to park one car at the entrance to a walking route. The best take-out in Hawick is on the opposite side of the river to the Leisure Centre (near Safeway) on the River Teviot. Here the bank is easily accessed from the road and there is room to park.

Description There are 2 notable features to be negotiated on the Slitrig. First is a broken weir (Gd 3+) which can be run straight down the centre and leads on into a short grade 3 section. The second and more difficult is the fall into a tunnel that runs under an old mill and Hawick High Street. This section is reminiscent of the run under the bridge on the Kinglas in Argyle. The tunnel is about 100m long and can be inspected before the trip is undertaken by going down an old flight of steps at the side of the old mill building. The fall becomes more difficult as the water level rises, ranging from grade 3 to 4+. There are also a couple of good stoppers after the confluence with the Teviot before the take-out.

Contributors:
Douglas Rae and
Mark Lyons

Other important points Watch out for strainers on the way down. Once on the river, it's very hard to get out, especially at higher flows. This trip can be combined with a run on down the Teviot (Gd 2/3).

231 Esk

Grade **1/2(3)**
Length   -
OS sheet   **79**

◯◯◯

◉◯◯

Introduction Flowing from Davington across the border and into the Solway Firth, this trip is a true cross-border raid. Surely Scotland's most southerly river! The Esk offers several different sections suitable for beginners.

Water Level Dry / Very wet.

Gauge The level can be checked from the road. 0.8 on the SEPA gauge is the minimum recommend level.

Access The river runs close to the road with several access and egress points either side of Langholm. For a grade 1 trip, drive north from Langholm on the B709 for approx 9 miles. There is good access and adequate parking where the river first crosses the road at Enzieholm Bridge. Alternatively, several minor roads provide access to the river, and for a shorter trip, turn right onto any one of these. There are possible access/egress points at Benpath Bridge, Burnfoot Bridge, Potholm Bridge and finally Langholm Bridge. Access at Langholm Bridge itself is good. Driving south along the A7, access to the river is possible at Skipper's Bridge (after approx 1 mile), or turn left to reach the river at Hollows or Canonbie.

Description Starting at Enzieholm Bridge the river is grade 1 as far as Langholm. The short stretch from Langholm to Skippers Bridge is also grade 1, with the exception of Skippers, a 300m grade 3 rapid near the end of the trip. In the event of a mishap, the pool below the bridge allows sufficient slack water for rescue. Egress to the B6318 can be made at this point. Dog Island is the site of the next major rapid (Gd 2/3). It is normally tackled on the right-hand side. However it is important to cross to the left before the final run into the pool, avoiding a nasty rock and ledge on the right. The next island just after Irvine House should be paddled on the right (Gd 2/3). In low water, watch out for a large rock half way down the rapid on the right-hand side. From here, the river is again grade 1, with the exception of Hollows Weir, just above the Hollows Bridge.

Contributors:
Gordon Ross and
Douglas Rae

Other important points The River Liddle, which is close at hand, has a nice grade 4 section on it at Penton Linn.

Wauchope Water 232

Introduction The Wauchope Water runs alongside the B7068 Langholm-Lockerbie road and joins the Esk in Langholm, at the top of the classic section.

Grade	3
Length	2½km
OS sheet	79

Water Level Wet/Very wet. This river comes up after a few hours of heavy rain. It was winter and the ground was already wet when I ran it.

Gauge Look over the road bridge as you come out of Langholm. If all the rocks are covered and you could float down it will go.

Access The river is visible on your left as you drive out of Langholm towards Lockerbie on the B7068. Go over a bridge and drive a couple of miles up the road. Put on where the river comes close to the road (335 825). Take out in Langholm or continue down the Esk (which will be high).

Description This is a good alternative start to the Border Esk if it's been raining. It starts with a few easy rapids and lots of tree dodging. After 1km there is a 1m drop with a powerful hole, followed by a smaller drop (Gd 3). You can see this from the road as you drive up. 30m below this there is a barbed wire fence (portage). A kilometre of easier water brings you to the road bridge (354 838), which is followed by a longer grade 3 rapid. There is a 1m sloping weir as you come into Langholm. 500m of easier water leads to the take-out in Langholm or you can continue on to join the Esk.

Contributor:
Tom Botterill

Appendices

SCA Hydro Campaign: www.scot-canoe.org/access/hydro.htm
SCA Water levels guide: www.scot-canoe.org/levels/
SCA Access homepage: www.scot-canoe.org/access/index.html
Online rivers guide: www.ukriversguidebook.co.uk
Douglas Wilcox's Photo Gallery: www.gla.ac.medicalgenetics/whitewater.htm

Corrections and Additions

If you come across anything covered by this guide that you feel needs updating we would be happy to hear from you.
Please send any relevant information, comments, and new rivers information for future editions to:

'Guidebook'
The Scottish Canoe Association,
Caledonia House,
South Gyle,
Edinburgh,
EH12 9DG.

guidebook@scot-canoe.org

Pronouncing Gaelic

You've found your way to the river and had a life affirming day's boating, but how are you going to be able to describe it all? To help you here are some phonetic spellings of the Gaelic used.

NB - Phonetic spellings such as (owlt a' choorun) and (ess a' cha-ay) should be pronounced **ch** as in lo**ch**, rather than as in **ch**urch.

abhainn (ahveen) river.

allt (owlt) burn — double l changes the vowel sound.

eas (ess) waterfall — plural easan (essan) but the diminutive is also easan, little fall.

dubh (doo) black — adjectives change to agree with the number, gender and case of nouns, so this appears in a variety of forms — easan dubha (black waterfalls).

Abhainn Chia-aig meaning unclear, but Arkaig is derived from it.

Abhainn Shlatach (ahveen latach) twiggy river — shlatach means abounding in rods or twigs. The h silences the s.

Abhainn sron Chreagain the river of the promontory (nose) of the outcrops.

A' chraos the big mouth, has connotations of gluttony — the Falls of Lora.

Allt Camgharaidh (owlt camagarry) possibly means burn of the bent wall/enclosure.

Allt Féith a Mhoraire (owlt fay uh vorair) burn of the lord's boggy rivulet.

Allt Mhuic (owlt voochk) This name is grammatically odd but almost certainly means pig burn.

An t-Súileag (an toolyek) the little eye — súileag (soolyek) is the diminutive form of súil an eye.

Comar confluence

Dubh Lighe (doo lee) lighe has two meanings, (1) fullness / flood (2) the stagnant part of a river.

Eas nan Long (ess nan long) waterfall of the ships.

Abhainn Eite the Etive.

Kiachnish is, like many, a derived name. Gaelic spelling does not use j, k, q ,v, w, x, y, or z.

Loy, Abhainn Laoigh, calf river.

Meall an t-Suidhe (myowl an too-ee) hill of the seat — suidhe (sooie) seat or sit.

Nevis, various translations have been offered for Ben Nevis — heavenly mountain and venomous mountain being the most popular.

Contributor:
Ron Cameron

Many river names are pre-Gaelic, being Pictish or Welsh. The Braan is a good example. It is Welsh and means Raven, often used as a name for dogs.

Acknowledgements

This guide wouldn't have been possible without the help of so many people from across the country. Paddlers have provided river descriptions, photos and stories, checked countless drafts, commented on grades, walked down empty rivers and paddled runs which had grown hazy in the midst of time to check upon that vital point. Others have provided Gaelic translations, technical advice and much appreciated help and support in all kinds of ways.

A big thank you to you all. This guide is both richer in character and more accurate for your efforts.

Adrian Disney
Al Collis
Alan Meikle
Alex Coon
Ali Martin
Amanda Mutton
Andrew Quick
Andy Blobby Burton
Andy Dytch
Andy England
Andy Jackson
Andy Sime
Andy Watt
Anna Gordon
Ben Hughes
Bill Kersel
Bob Evans
Brian Taggart
Bridget Thomas
Bruce Poll
Callum Anderson
Cam Allan
Charlie Leppard
Charlie Wood
Chris Dickinson
Chris Forrest
Chris Gould
Colin Aitken
Colin Matheson
Kris Waring
Dave Alldritt
Dave Craig
Dave Francis
Dave Kwant
Dave Lee
Dave Matthew
Dave Walsh
Dave Waugh
David Wilbraham

Douglas Rae
Douglas Wilcox
Drew Milroy
Duncan Fraser
Duncan Ostler
Eddie Palmer
Fran Pothecary
Garry Smith
Gordon Ross
Graeme Bruce
Graham at wickedwave
Greg Nicks
Gregor Muir
Greig McColm
Heather Smith
Iain Mckendry
Iain Murray
Ian Ross
Ian Thom
Jacob Ahlquist
James Brocklehurst
Janet Moxley
Jay Sigbrant
Jennifer Berry
Jim Gibson
Joan Smith
John Mason
John Ross
Johnny McLaren
Jonathan Goldthorp
Jonni Aiton
Keith Bremner
Keith Hall
Kenny Biggin
Kenny Mutton
Kingsley Ash
Mags Duncan Stirling
Malcolm Ross
Mark Lyons

Mark Rainsley
Mark Sherriff
Max Twomey
Mick Kelleher
'Muzza' Trail
Neil Farmer
Nigel Blandford
'Packman' Hughes
Paul Cromey
Paul Currant
Paul Jackson
Paul Stone
Pete Crane
Pete Gwatkin
Pete Kyriakoudis
Richard Rogers
Richard Salmond
Robert Craig
Robin Cole
Robin Lofthouse
Rod Webster
Roger Palin
Roland Bone
Ron Cameron
Rory Stewart
Ryan Clements
Stefan Janick
Steve MacDonald
Steve Mackinnon
Steve Rogers
Stew Rogers
Stuart Nyquist
Terry Storry
Tom Botterill
Tom Prentice
Yvonne Yost
Zosia Patterson

Thanks for their support

A word of thanks to the companies who have placed adverts. All the income from advertisements placed has gone directly into the access fund.

Bunkhouses and Accommodation:

Course Providers and Activities:

Boats and Paddling Kit:

Special thanks

For this second edition thanks again go to Andy and Bridget, whose house in Fort William once more became the 'nerve centre' of the guidebook operation. Andy Jackson has been working toward this ever since the first edition left the presses. However during the compilation he has also been heavily involved with the Access Code, the water levels website and the Hydro Campaign for paddlers. So it is a very special "thank you" to Bridget Thomas who has done the major part of the work/editing of this edition.

Thanks also to Andrew Quick who provided cartoons for the guide, to Mark Rainsley for allowing us to plagiarise his online guidebook, to Ron Cameron for his humour filled proof reading and Neil Farmer for his enthusiasm and sales work.

And lastly thanks to Franco Ferrero at Pesda Press whose patience and support have been steady throughout and to Pete Wood who once again worked with Franco on the artwork and design for the guide.